PRAISE FOR *ADVANCED MARKETING MANAGEMENT*

'A must-read for marketing professionals who want to create innovative and disruptive marketing interventions. This book addresses new trends – neuroscience, predictive skills, innovation and adaptability skills – all in a single title.' **Dominic Fernandes, Vice President, Head of Business Marketing, Emirates NBD**

'Change is something that modern businesses cannot escape, and more so marketing. New technologies, heightened competition and demanding customers have posed never-seen-before challenges for marketers who often try to respond with outdated models and incomplete solutions. This book offers a holistic approach to marketers, covering a wide range of topics, such as neuroscience, predictive analytics and creative problem solving. The authors argue convincingly for the need for a new marketer who will lead not only the marketing department but the company as a whole. Highly recommended.' **Max Hauser, Partner and Managing Director, The Boston Consulting Group, Russia and CIS**

'Marketing is long overdue for disruption. In *Advanced* authors brilliantly argue for the "Why?" and provide a "What?" The book is packed from cover to cover with cutting-edge array of tools to best equip aspiring dis for that much-needed overhaul.' **Anthony Tham, Executive Creative Publicis Worldwide Shanghai**

'A groundbreaking and innovative guide, full of contemporary marketing cases and examples for those who are passionate about marketing and want to extend their knowledge beyond the conventional marketing practices.' **Panayiota Alevizou, Lecturer in Marketing, Sheffield University Management School**

'There has never been a more exciting time to be in marketing. The modern marketer now has even greater influence over tangible brand success, but it's a position which is complex, ever-changing, and challenging. *Advanced Marketing*

Management acknowledges this complex landscape we work in and provides clear and compelling thought and insight to dismiss the chaos and embrace the tremendous opportunity.' **Graham Forsyth, Director of Marketing, Spredfast**

'The world of marketing has been constantly evolving. It is immensely important that marketers understand and appreciate the end of a current and the beginning of a new (marketing) era. This book is a perfect guide for coping with this transition, both offering a brilliant vision into how the evolution of marketing should progress and, most importantly, what the role of marketers is in it. It is omni-relevant from an industry perspective and will have ubiquitous influence on the marketing sentiment.' **Filip Luneski, Senior Category and Customer Marketing Manager, Molson Coors Europe**

'Scientifically grounded and backed up by contemporary real-life business examples, this is a CEO-must-read practical guide to how to avoid the Marketing Paradox, understand which half of marketing budget is being wasted and how to fix this. And the new Marketing Mix 4EPs concept is a phenomenally simple and powerful response to the many disruptions that every industry now faces.' **Mikhail Merkulov, CEO, Arricano Real Estate PLC**

'This book is a boot camp for modern marketers in the post-Trump, post-Brexit, post-Cambridge Analytica world, where the challenge is to find the most impactful insights from an Everest of data. It underlines the fact that what our sector is lacking is better questions, not more answers.' **Adrian Cockle, Principal Consultant, Hootsuite**

'If you are a curious learner and marketer who seeks to improve constantly, seek no more! The book in front of you explores relevant topics and skills in the new marketing era, such as neuroscience, predictability, innovation and adaptability, while providing a fresh outlook on the 4Ps as tools with a core in empathy, experiential, ever-presence and engagement. The authors' line of thought is impeccable: from setting the chapter objectives and specific marketing challenge, through a meaty core packed with practical examples, both successes and failures, the importance of ethics in controversial topics such as the origins of big data, to ending with last-thought boxes, resources to inspire and questions to ask yourself after reading. And although each chapter can be read as a standalone, the curious will find it hard to resist any of the book! With this fresh outlook, and customer-centric from cover to cover, *Advanced Marketing Management* is a must-have toolkit for modern marketers aspiring to become transformational leaders.' **Natasa Josic, Commercial Excellence Director, Coca-Cola HBC, Austria**

'If there's one thing we marketers like to do, it's talk about marketing. This book makes sure we're talking smart, relevant, science-y, data-y and, most importantly, like we still know what we're talking about. So we can all feel like experts again. This is the science behind the craft we've known we need, translated for the marketing mind.' **Stephanie Pickerill, Senior Marketing Manager, FTSE 100 bank**

'This book highlights many key marketing and neuromarketing concepts! It is a great read for any marketing and sales professional who needs to stay on top of new trends.' **Patrick Renvoise, Co-founder, SalesBrain, and co-author,** *Neuromarketing: Understanding the buy button in your customers' brain* **and** *The Persuasion Code*

'An eye-opening book for marketers and others about modern marketing as an art. The authors have gathered here everything we need to know to successfully deal with the complex and unpredictable world we live in today.' **Yuliya Melnyk, Deputy Director for Corporate Development, European Business Association, Ukraine**

'Rarely will the reader find a book on a "moving-sand" topic like the marketing domain today, which can work both as a fluid manual and, at the same time, not only inspire but also create a vivid reference platform for everyday comparison of one's professional encounters. Kudos to the authors.' **Marinos Vathis, Country Manager, National Bank of Greece, London branch**

'Success in business has become harder today than ever before. It is definitely time for a new, transformative marketer who needs to be vital before becoming viral. The methods of the past can only find shelter on bookshelves. *Advanced Marketing Management* is the solution for all those marketers in search of business success. It is also a marketing bible for students looking for a disruptive approach.' **Michael R Virardi, speaker, trainer, author**

'A refreshingly lucid and intelligible upgrade of traditional marketing fundamentals with a modern perspective that creates a meaningful whole.

Simply, *Advanced Marketing Management* is a holistic positioning of future marketing, scientifically documented, laced with wisdom, grand in its ambition and deeply humane.' **Monika Lapanja, Director, Centre of Business Excellence, Faculty of Economics, University of Ljubljana**

'The authors have their fingers on the pulse of marketing and the challenges marketers face today. *Advanced Marketing Management* is a terrific guide for students and practitioners of marketing that will help them become more transformational marketing leaders.' **Mick Doran, Head of Research, Planning and Brand, Sainsbury's Bank, and Chair, The Marketing Society, Scotland**

'What will the role of marketing be in the future and for what developments should a marketer be prepared? *Advanced Marketing Management* is full of vision and advice to help marketers answer these questions and to face the disruptive and uncertain world in which we live.' **Bert Jan Vukkink, Chief Marketing Officer, Lenta LLC, Russia**

'In a complex, uncertain and volatile global business context, where everyone is trying to find ways to thrive, the authors of this book present a thoughtful, comprehensive, focused and useful approach to marketing management. Providing a highly reliable combination of scientific evidence and current thinking on marketing management, *Advanced Marketing Management* presents a pragmatic pathway for understanding the dynamics of human behaviour for the creation and delivery of marketing strategies. Importantly, it differentiates itself from other books in the field by driving the reader to the pure essence of marketing logic by synthesizing input from neuroscience, behavioural science, social psychology, management science and of course marketing. This book is a must for aspiring marketing leaders and managers, as well as for students and scholars of marketing.' **Professor Alexandros Psychogios, Professor of International HRM, PhD Programme Director, Birmingham City University**

'This is an essential workout for the modern marketer who wants to be taken seriously and achieve the best results.' **Diane Earles, Chartered Marketer**

Advanced Marketing Management

Advanced Marketing Management

Principles, skills and tools

Nikolaos Dimitriadis
Neda Jovanovic Dimitriadis
Jillian Ney

KoganPage

Publisher's note

Every possible effort has been made to ensure that the information contained in this book is accurate at the time of going to press, and the publisher and authors cannot accept responsibility for any errors or omissions, however caused. No responsibility for loss or damage occasioned to any person acting, or refraining from action, as a result of the material in this publication can be accepted by the editor, the publisher or any of the authors.

First published in Great Britain and the United States in 2019 by Kogan Page Limited

2nd Floor, 45 Gee Street	c/o Martin P Hill Consulting	4737/23 Ansari Road
London EC1V 3RS	122 W 27th St, 10th Floor	Daryaganj
United Kingdom	New York NY 10001	New Delhi 110002
www.koganpage.com	USA	India

© Nikolaos Dimitriadis, Neda Jovanovic Dimitriadis and Jillian Ney, 2019

ISBN   978 0 7494 8037 0
E-ISBN   978 0 7494 8038 7

British Library Cataloguing-in-Publication Data

A CIP record for this book is available from the British Library.

Library of Congress Cataloging-in-Publication Data

Names: Dimitriadis, Nikolaos, author. | Dimitriadis, Neda Jovanovic, author.
   | Ney, Jillian, author.
Title: Advanced marketing management : principles, skills and tools /
   Nikolaos Dimitriadis, Neda Jovanovic Dimitriadis, Jillian Ney.
Description: 1 Edition. | New York, NY : Kogan Page, [2018] | Includes
   bibliographical references and index.
Identifiers: LCCN 2018039084 (print) | LCCN 2018041238 (ebook) | ISBN
   9780749480387 (ebook) | ISBN 9780749480370 (pbk.) | ISBN 9780749480387
   (eISBN)
Subjects: LCSH: Marketing–Psychological aspects. | Decision making.
Classification: LCC HF5415 (ebook) | LCC HF5415 .D48856 2018 (print) | DDC
   658.8–dc23

Typeset by Integra Software Services, Pondicherry
Print production managed by Jellyfish
Printed and bound by CPI Group (UK) Ltd, Croydon, CR0 4YY

To all the marketing enthusiasts, never stop learning!

CONTENTS

Online resources

To support teaching and learning, please find the following downloadable material at **www.koganpage.com/AMM**

- lecture slides;
- activity sheets;
- group work activities;
- lists of further resources including associations, websites, blogs, TedTalks, YouTube videos, publications etc.

LIST OF FIGURES

LIST OF TABLES

LIST OF COMPANIES AND BRANDS FEATURED IN THE BOOK

3M
Absolut Vodka
Accenture
Adobe
Affectiva
Airbnb
Alibaba
Altimeter Group
Amazon
AOL
Apple
Bank of America
BMW
The Boston Consulting Group
Brandwatch
British Petroleum
Cadbury
Cambridge Analytica
Citibank
CNN
Coca-Cola
Deciem
Deloitte
Disney
Facebook
Forbes
Ford
Forrester Research
Fortune

The Fournaise Marketing Group
Fyre Festival
Gartner
Google
Google Analytics
Hasbro
Hewlett-Packard
Honda
Iberia
IBM
IBM Watson
IDEO
IKEA
Interbrand
Ipsos
Kanye West
KPMG
LEGO
Lightwave
LinkedIn
Mad Men
The Marketer
Mastercard
McDonald's
McKinsey
Mentos
Mercedes-Benz
Microsoft
Monopoly

NASA
Netflix
Neural Sense
NeuroWine
Nielsen
Nokia
PepsiCo
Pixar
Play-Doh
PricewaterhouseCoopers
Procter & Gamble
Publicis
Radio Shack
Revlon
Royal Dutch Shell
SalesBrain
SAP
SAS

Sony
SoulCycle
Southwest Airlines
SpaceX
Target
Tesla
Toyota
Twitter
Uber
Unilever
United Airlines
Vodafone UK
Whole Foods
World Economic Forum
WPP
Zafu
Zappos
Zest

ABOUT THE AUTHORS

Dr Nikolaos Dimitriadis is an award-winning communications professional, educator and consultant. He is the co-author of the book *Neuroscience for Leaders: A brain adaptive leadership approach* (Kogan Page). He spoke at TEDx University of Strathclyde for the urgent need for brain-based communication, he is a certified neuromarketer and he contributed to the Neuromarketing Manager Programme at Hamburg Media School. As a lecturer at the Sheffield University Management School in the UK he was selected by MBA students as best lecturer on the programme. He has worked with international brands such as IKEA, IBM, Nestlé, Johnson&Johnson, Pierre Fabre, Coca-Cola, Siemens, Banca Intesa Sanpaolo, Raiffeisen Bank, Emirates NBD, JTI, Rauch, Unicredit, Teekanne, USAID, AstraZeneca and others. His opinions are often featured in business and mainstream media, most notably in INC.COM. He is the CEO of Trizma Neuro, a cutting-edge neuromarketing and NeuroHR company, and Regional Director of the University of Sheffield International Faculty, City College, for the Western Balkans. He has received his PhD and his MBA from the University of Sheffield. Dr Nikolaos Dimitriadis is a strong advocate of brain-based solutions to business challenges.

Dr Neda Jovanovic Dimitriadis is a diverse and passionate marketing professional, with both academic and practical experience. She obtained her bachelor degree in business studies with specialization in marketing from the University of Sheffield. During her undergraduate studies she received multiple awards such as the Paul Marshall Award for Outstanding Performance. She finished her MA in advertising and marketing at the University of Leeds. Her interest in media and branding research started with her master's thesis, ultimately leading her to conduct a cutting-edge doctoral study in this area. She was awarded her PhD at the Economics Faculty of the University of Belgrade, investigating the influence of media vehicles on perception and evaluation of advertised brands, by conducting forward-thinking behavioural experiments. Dr Jovanovic Dimitriadis is a member of The Chartered Institute of Marketing (CIM), where she obtained a postgraduate diploma in marketing, and a Chartered Marketer since 2007. Besides academic research she has gained considerable practical experience working in the industry both at the agency and client sides. Dr Jovanovic Dimitriadis has given guest lectures on marketing topics and presented her work in major marketing conferences including those organized by the European Marketing Academy and the Academy of Marketing, UK.

Dr Jillian Ney specializes in the behavioural analysis of data to understand how people make decisions. She is a consultant and corporate trainer to large organizations, helping them to understand how their customers make decisions and how this can lead to opportunities to optimize marketing, product development and innovation initiatives. She has worked with international organizations including PwC, Huawei, Manchester City Football Club, Quantcast, the Edrington Group, and Vanquis Bank. In 2018, Dr Ney founded the Social Intelligence Lab, where people managing social listening programmes for big brands come to connect, share best practice and receive specialist social data analysis training and support. Her opinions on the behavioural analysis of social data are often featured in media, including the BBC, Forbes and MyCustomer.com. She has presented at TEDx, Social Media Week, NATO and the Market Research Society. She received her undergraduate degree and PhD from the University of Strathclyde. Dr Jillian Ney believes that the missing piece of the data analysis puzzle is the focus on behavioural insights.

PREFACE

Marketers in turmoil

It is often said nowadays that marketing is in a mess. It definitely looks that way: new technologies, disruptive business models, changing consumer habits and increased market unpredictability are putting unprecedented pressure on marketing to deliver results. It is more accurate, though, to say that marketers are the ones in a mess. Not marketing. Marketing, as a core business philosophy and practice, is probably doing better than ever; not least, judging by various chief executive officers (CEOs) behaving like marketing personnel themselves. Elon Musk, the CEO of Tesla cars, is famous for having the habit of communicating directly to customers through social media, offering real solutions to real customer problems (Korosec, 2017).

But how is it possible that there is such a discrepancy between the status of marketers and the status of marketing? Aren't those two closely interrelated, if not the same thing? We wrote this book to address major paradoxes that marketers are facing today – and there are many paradoxes indeed.

Take, for example, the seemingly unstoppable power of digital media and tools in modern marketing. There is hardly any discussion, article, blogpost or event about marketing that does not include, sometimes exclusively, digital marketing. At a first glance, this seems appropriate taking into account that 2016 was the year when, for the first time ever, overall marketing spending on digital channels surpassed that on TV (Slefo, 2017) – undoubtedly a clear milestone for digital marketing. But then, how is it possible that, albeit the voices proclaiming the death of TV as a major marketing channel, TV commercials during the 2018 Super Bowl in the United States cost more (almost double!) than they did 10 years ago (Fry, 2018)? As it turns out, it is not as straightforward and clear-cut for marketing decision makers today as many would like it to be – and things will only get tougher.

Consider what Vollmer, Bennin and Bothum (2016) identify as the marketer's dilemma: today's marketer has more options to reach his or her target audience. Yet it has never been more difficult to earn the attention of that user. They make a valid point. Never before in the history of marketing and business have there been so many tools, methods, media, solutions and ideas available on how to understand, approach and serve customers. Never before was there so much marketing information, shared online and offline, and so many marketing, sales, communications and customer experience-related events as today. However, few outside the consulting and the marketing ecosystem can claim, without doubt, that marketers are doing better than ever before in their core responsibilities. On the contrary, as explained in detail in Chapter 1, marketers face today the toughest criticism and their biggest uphill battles, in the boardroom and beyond.

Purpose of the book

This book comes as an acknowledgement of those struggles and, we hope, as a convincing answer to the greatest marketing challenges of our day. We also wrote this book because of a simple but profound educational need. Although more and more is asked from marketers in the complex and hyper-dynamic business environment we live in, many books offered to them for preparing themselves do not cover adequately all major challenges. In our observation, there are three main categories of marketing books available:

- **Basic textbooks:** these include, usually sizeable, books that try to explain all aspects and history of the marketing function. They aim at creating skilful and knowledgeable marketing professionals, offering the widest view possible of the marketing universe.

- **Specialized books:** the exact opposite to the above, these books usually offer a deeper view in very specialized, or narrow, marketing topics. They aim at shedding light on modern and very specific marketing problems.

- **Big idea books:** these marketing books often try to offer a new and completely different marketing viewpoint from the past ones. They usually talk about paradigm shifts and aim, in an epiphany-like way, at changing the way marketers perceive marketing.

This book resembles more a combination of all the above rather than a new category in itself. This is not done accidentally. We strongly believe that this is the best way to provide a solution for the chaotic and far-reaching problems facing marketers today. As you will see throughout the book, marketers now need a wide variety of skills and methods not traditionally associated with their core profession. From neuroscience to data science and from adaptable decision making to extreme innovative thinking, marketers cannot afford any more to stay only within their restrictive marketing mental box. On the contrary, they need to go far and wide and use any idea that can help them, without caring from which department, science or part of the world it comes.

Marketing is too important to be left to the marketing department, David Packard, co-founder of Hewlett-Packard, famously said (Forbes, 2013) – but it would be more accurate here to say that *marketers are just too important to be left only within the borders of their marketing departments*!

Who is it for?

This book is particularly useful for: **senior-year students, students on post-graduate courses, executive students** and **practitioners**. It aims at adding a solid layer of advanced expertise, so necessary for marketers today, by tapping into a vast range of sources, sciences and practices typically not found in marketing textbooks. This is marketing *beyond* traditional marketing; it is marketing for the 21st century.

On a more personal note, we wrote the book that we could not find in the market for using in our classes and seminars when teaching contemporary marketing. Our audiences, such as students, corporate trainees and entrepreneurs alike, were constantly asking us for a comprehensive book that encapsulates what marketing today is all about, without repeating clichés and basic marketing literature. After years of putting together and testing in class the relevant materials, cases and models for modern marketers from a wide variety of sources, we decided to write the book ourselves. *If it is not there... go create it!* Simply put, the book is for anyone deeply interested in the current challenges and future state of marketing and the marketing profession.

The book's main premise

Marketers will survive and thrive only if they upgrade their game decisively and urgently, and address modern challenges with advanced management solutions, regardless of where these solutions come from. Sometimes they might come from the traditional marketing universe, but more often than not they will come from somewhere else.

The time is ripe for marketers to reach their full potential and produce real, measurable results. In becoming trustworthy business partners to their CEOs and to their other colleagues, marketers will be finally able to go beyond managing their own micro-worlds, their departments, and help actively in leading their organizations into a better future.

This is what *Advanced Marketing Management* is about: creating a new generation of advanced marketers who will spearhead customer innovation, industry-wide collaboration and brand leadership for years to come!

How to read the book

The book consists of nine chapters. Most of them are written in such a way that they can be read as standalone material dedicated to a specific subject, so you can read any chapter you desire based on your interests and needs. Chapters 6 and 7 work better together since they explain the updated marketing mix model.

We do suggest, however, that before you proceed to any specific chapter you first read Chapter 1 in order to understand the overall context and our main thesis to which each chapter then independently contributes.

We would like here to highlight the following learning elements that chapters contain:

- Advanced practice box. Every chapter starts with an 'Advanced practice' box, which includes cutting-edge case studies and/or global influencers' opinions about the state of marketing in relation to the chapter's topic. By reading this box you will develop the right frame of mind for the whole chapter. Chapters 6 and 7 share one such box at the beginning of Chapter 6, since both chapters refer to the same concept: the updated marketing mix model.

- The marketing challenge. Every chapter, apart from the concluding Chapter 9, continues after the advanced practice box with the 'marketing challenge' part, which explains the significance and the details of the chapter topic for marketing and marketers. Key marketing theory, old and new, is usually presented in this part of each chapter. Chapters 6 and 7 share the same marketing challenge, presented in Chapter 6.

- Last thought box: each chapter ends with a 'Last thought' box where we highlight the main conclusion of each chapter.

- Additional learning materials. All chapters include: a summary checklist with all key points of the chapter; a list of resources to inspire you, with links to online videos and articles to explore beyond the chapter; and revision questions that help make sure you will engage in an enhanced learning manner with the chapter's concepts, cases and managerial tools.

- Online supporting materials. The book is accompanied by immersive materials that can be accessed online. These include activity sheets, group work activities and links to associations, websites, blogs and other relevant sources. Lecture slides per chapter are also provided for teaching staff. Please see **www.koganpage.com/AMM**

Explore, question, search further, practise... but most importantly, help us elevate marketers to the organizational and business level they deserve to be. Let's advance the marketing profession together. Enjoy the book!

References

Forbes (2013) [accessed 18 June 2018] 22 Best Marketing Quotes to Drive Your Marketing Strategy, *ForbesBrandVoice* [Online] https://www.forbes.com/sites/sap/2013/01/16/22-best-marketing-quotes-to-drive-your-marketing-strategy/#416adc5d7e06

Fry, E (2018) [accessed 18 June 2018] Super Bowl Ads Can't Save TV, *Fortune*, 2 (February), pp 3–4

Korosec, K (2017) [accessed 18 June 2018] Elon Musk's Angry Customer Twitter Thread is a Gold Mine of Customer Service Advice, *Fortune* [Online] http://fortune.com/2017/09/18/elon-musk-customer-service-twitter/

Slefo, G (2017) [accessed 18 June 2018] Desktop and Mobile Ad Revenue Surpasses TV for the First Time, *Adage* [Online] http://adage.com/article/digital/digital-ad-revenue-surpasses-tv-desktop-iab/308808/

Vollmer, C, Bennin, C and Bothum, D (2016) The marketer's dilemma, *strategy+business*, 85 (Winter), pp 27–31

ACKNOWLEDGEMENTS

Writing this book has proven to be an inspiring, engaging and, at times, cathartic journey. It was also a path full of challenges. We would like to thank the following people who provided their assistance:

- Patrick Renvoise and Dr Christophe Morin at SalesBrain
- Brian Hopkins and Boris Evelson at Forrester
- Dave Chaffey at Smart Insights
- Susan Etlinger at Altimeter
- Steven Naert at Ipsos
- Matteo Venerucci at Trizma Neuro
- Professor Alexandros Psychogios at Birmingham City University

Special thanks goes to the wonderful, professional and enthusiastic team at Kogan Page: Chris Cudmore, Jenny Volich, Charlotte Owen, Philippa Fiszzon, Amanda Dackombe, Natasha Tulett, Rebecca Bush, Lachean Humphreys and everyone else at Kogan Page.

We would also like to thank our clients, students and business partners who constantly enrich our work through sharing their challenges, experiences and learnings with us.

Finally, we would like to thank our families and friends for their love, patience and support.

The need for the new marketer 01

CHAPTER LEARNING OBJECTIVES

After studying this chapter, you will be able to:

- Acknowledge the changing role of marketing over time and various factors that have influenced this change.
- Understand the challenges facing the marketing profession today and the occurrence of The Marketing Paradox.
- Understand the importance of focusing on customers in the new business era and appreciate the modern CEO's adoption of a complete customer-centric philosophy.
- Recognize the peculiarities of the marketing profession associated with the absence of reliability and predictability.
- Get familiar with the model of the new marketer suggested in this book, including the new set of skills, the updated marketing mix model and the empowered leadership role.

Advanced practice

It's official: marketing is changing!

Don Draper, the main character in the hit series *Mad Men*, has embodied the quintessential marketing persona for many people around the world. His direct, self-confident and no-nonsense approach in creating strategy, messages, campaigns and activities for brands has made him look like, albeit fictional, a *role model* of the inner workings of advertising agencies and the marketing mind. But are all marketing people, in advertising and elsewhere, like Draper? Who could be, in real life, the proper representative of the marketing mind in the business world?

This person can arguably be Sir Martin Sorrell, the CEO of WPP group of agencies, and what he says about the current state and future of marketing is both revealing and exciting. WPP is a global-reaching titan with almost 200,000 employees in 3,000 offices spread across 112 countries. WPP is the parent company of numerous advertising agencies, PR agencies, data analytics agencies, media agencies, digital agencies and other marketing-related services (Bothun and Gross, 2016). Famous agencies such as J Walter Thompson, Ogilvy & Mather, Grey, Young & Rubicam, Mindshare, Millward Brown and TNS belong to WPP, shaping the fates of many brands worldwide. When it comes to a spokesperson for the whole marketing and marketing services field, it is safe to say that Sir Martin Sorrell is the one to listen to. Does he believe that marketing is changing? What should the marketer of today look like?

At an International Advertising Association event in 2009, Sorrell 'implied that his company's competitive profile should focus more firmly beyond traditional media and creative advertising solutions on to offering the best strategic and consumer insight', leading to the significant assertion that *insight* is the necessary precursor of any marketing activity, creative solutions included (Campaign, 2009). Marketing services vendors, though, have not been fast enough in moving towards this direction. As *Campaign* reported: 'agencies have been slow to grasp the possibilities of scientific advancements such as brain mapping and neuromarketing… but to enhance and prove the value of their work, such techniques need to become a more prevalent part' in the overall marketing discipline (Campaign, 2009). In short, strategy and science must be urgently injected into marketing to make sure higher return on investment (ROI) and happier brands are achieved. Contemporary marketing value comes from, first and foremost, insightful strategy, and marketers need be able to generate and utilize powerful insights from everywhere… even from neuroscience. But are marketers educated to use neuroscience for building brands and creating loyal customers?

At the 2013 Data Summit of the American Association of Advertising Agencies, Sir Martin Sorrell revealed that 75 per cent of WPP's US $18 billion in revenues came not from traditional services but from digital advertising and data investment management. He did not hold back on the significance of data for the modern marketer: global-leading data management companies such as Nielsen, Facebook and Google are now WPP's major competitors, he said, together with the more traditional advertising networks (Taube, 2013). He even went so far as to say that WPP is no longer an advertising company (Marshall, 2013). It is more about the data than ever before. In distancing himself from Don Draper of *Mad Men*, he claimed that the word *advertising* did not represent what his group of companies was all about and that the days of *Mad Men* are long over. He stated that the word *advertising* 'suggests the legacy approach of media and art, not science. We want to be as aggressive in the science part of the business as we can possibly be' (Marshall, 2013).

Actionable insights, strategy, data, digital, ROI, science (and neuroscience) are key elements of today's marketing canvas in an ever-changing business landscape. The question then is not if marketing is changing but rather how marketers can advance their practice to match those developments when nothing can be taken for granted. Nothing. Even digital, that has become such a favourite for marketers globally. As Sorrell highlighted in an interview with the magazine *Marketing Week*, as of late, brands have started re-examining their involvement with digital since there are hints suggesting overinvestment in the field (Vizard, 2016). So, it is not about fads, buzz and industry hot-talk but about creating real brand value. Marketers are brand value creators not cultural shifters as they are portrayed in popular media.

More recently, in September 2016, at an event in Shanghai Sorrell presented his 10 top trends for marketing. These included (Marcomm, 2016): shift to new markets; overcapacity and shortage of human capital; the constant rise of the web; historic growth of retail and now e-power; importance of internal communications; global and local structures; relative power of finance and procurement; growth of government; acceptance of social responsibility and purpose; and industry consolidation and convergence. Although Sorrell left WPP in April 2018 after three decades at the company's top position, because of controversial usage of company assets (Coffee, 2018), his modern approach to marketing still challenges traditional misconceptions about marketers. Are today's marketers ready for this new, advanced world of marketing? What are the concepts, skills and tools that new marketers need to obtain in order to answer effectively to modern market challenges? Old marketing management and Don Drapers do not fit. Welcome to *Advanced Marketing Management*!

The marketing challenge

What do marketers do? Although this seems to be an unnecessary question for many traditional professions such as doctors, lawyers and designers, when it comes to marketing the answer is more elusive than expected. As revered Marketing Professor at Harvard Business School, John Quelch, and marketing consultant Katherine Jocz point out, marketing cannot be considered either a profession or a science. In their words (Quelch and Jocz, 2008):

'Perhaps marketers would be more self-confident about their contributions if marketing were a science with clear dos and don'ts. But marketing is as much art as science, as much right brain as left brain.'

These are some very strong words indeed. Quelch and Jocz do highlight the fact that this ambiguity of the marketing profession creates appropriate flexibility for innovation and diverse ideas to emerge. But at the same time, their assertion of the profession's vagueness exposes one of its key challenges. If we cannot pinpoint with confidence what marketers actually do, can we ever follow the profession's evolution? More importantly: how can we prepare the new marketer if we cannot define the profession accurately?

This ambiguity goes back a long way. It started in the early 1950s when Neil Borden, Professor of Advertising at Harvard, first coined the term *marketing mix* to describe the different tasks, 12 in total, performed by marketers at their everyday job. It was then solidified in the 1960s when Edmund Jerome McCarthy, an American Marketing Professor, created the now famous marketing mix concept of the 4Ps: Product, Price, Place and Promotion (Dominic, 2009). In his attempt to both capture marketing decision making as observed in practice and also to give marketing a modern flavour, McCarthy highlighted the managerial dimension of the profession as opposed to the older strictly functional one (McCarthy, 1960; Constantinides, 2006). Marketers are responsible for a list of professional activities within companies that require managerial decision making in order to deliver business value. These activities, according to McCarthy, could be better categorized and described in the 4Ps.

This model has shown extreme resilience. After half a century, it is still alive and well in marketing literature and marketing classrooms around the world – and this is without its fair share of criticisms. In the seminal paper 'Quo Vadis, marketing? Toward a relationship marketing paradigm', Cristian Grönroos (1994), a Finnish marketing academic, famously asked '*Marketing where are you going?*' by attacking the marketing mix model of the 4Ps and by suggesting a new future for marketing, which is more relationships-centred than ever before. In understanding marketing, for Grönroos, the marketing mix model is highly problematic both in the academic/theoretical domain and for practical usage. The increasing complexity that the world was experiencing in the 1990s, because of globalization and rapid technological advancements, was pushing marketing to adopt a different role than the one implied in the classic marketing mix model. For Grönroos, marketing and marketers should escape the profession's and function's innate isolation, which resulted by overrelying on the 4Ps concept, and help their companies more holistically and strategically. It is very interesting that, almost 20 years before Grönroos, two other academics, but from Australia this time, raised a similar argument in a paper titled in a very similar manner. Ray O'Leary and Ian Iredale (1976) from the University of New South Wales, titled their paper 'The marketing concept: Quo Vadis?'. O'Leary and Iredale, although approaching the issue from a distinct perspective, not only asked the same question as Grönroos but also had a very similar overall observation, which was that marketing needed to escape its narrow application only in consumer companies and enter more diverse organizations and institutions, like political parties. For them, marketing is not about the traditional 4Ps model or just about business markets. Both the 1970s and the 1990s Quo Vadis papers proved prophetic. The former, since marketing is now widely applied in all types of industries, organizations and settings, and the latter since relationships did become the focal point in marketing, especially due to the advent of social media.

Marketing is a far-reaching, varied profession that has the potential to achieve remarkable results spanning departments, industries, socio-economic and political domains, and business eras. The question though, '*Marketing where are you going?*' is more topical today than ever. Not least because marketing seems to be in a constant state of mid-life crisis during the last two decades.

Marketing's mid-life crisis

Studies have already pinpointed that happiness and life satisfaction tend to drop during middle age, which is roughly between 40 and 59 years of age (Ulloa, Møller and Sousa-Poza, 2013). This phenomenon, which is usually associated with loss of confidence and has other symptoms such as remorse, humiliation, longing and disconnect, is also characterized by an enhanced sense of confusion (Stern *et al*, 2016). We find that *confusion* is the most accurate word to describe the marketing profession nowadays. As we saw in the 'Advanced practice' box above – It's official: marketing is changing – marketing is undergoing tectonic shifts with data sciences, digital technologies and even neuroscience changing fundamentally the marketing profession. In such a volatile vortex of complexity there is little clarity or focus. Marketers are lost and marketing is experiencing its mid-life crisis. It is not accidental, then, that one of the most fundamental, influential and also debated marketing papers of all time was actually published in 1975 (Bagozzi, 1975). In a way, this puts marketing today in the right age group, 40+ years of age, for a proper mid-life crisis.

Marketing's mid-life crisis is not new, however, and it is not momentary – it is rather prolonged. Back in 1993, Brady and Davis, in their paper titled 'Marketing's mid-life crisis' in the *McKinsey Quarterly*, called marketing 'a function without a cause', criticizing marketers for not being able to deal fast and effectively with new market realities in retail (Brady and Davis, 1993). According to them, if marketing is to be appreciated more within companies, marketers need to think 'broader' and 'deeper'. Also, if marketers are to escape their mid-life crisis, marketing would have to 'take the lead in engineering its own future'. Did this happen? Can it ever happen if marketing is not a well-defined science and profession with clear dos and don'ts?

Regardless of the exact age of marketing, its mid-life crisis does not seem to go away. On the contrary, because of the increased complexity of the marketing landscape and profession, it only gets worse.

Chief marketing officers: more losing than winning?

As the world became more complex and unpredictable, as markets became more globalized and competitive, and as technology became more prominent and multipurpose, the marketer's role within companies got a boost. In the late 1990s and early 2000s, in an effort to respond to increasing challenges, brands upgraded marketers to the C-suite. The chief marketing officer, or CMO, became a reality and Fortune 500 companies appointed CMOs in order to get strategically more out of their marketing function (McGovern and Quelch, 2004). However, only a few companies were found to be happy with the new, upgraded role of marketers as CMOs, something that could be seen in the high turnover of people in that role.

As McGovern and Quelch (2004) reported, commenting on the low average tenure of CMOs in companies: 'the Starbucks Corporation staffed and restaffed its head of marketing five times in seven years; Coca-Cola Company changed its CMO four times in six years; and Kinko's staffed the position three times in five years'. The same authors found that the

CMO role was not clearly and consistently defined, with companies assigning CMOs en masse without taking the appropriate time to define the scope and nature of work for them to focus on. They concluded that: 'our research, supported by that of others, suggests this is a recipe for failure' (McGovern and Quelch, 2004).

A few years later in 2007, a similar picture was painted by David Court in his article 'The evolving role of the CMO' in the *McKinsey Quarterly* (Court, 2007). Although it would have been expected that companies learnt from previous mistakes and created better conditions for CMOs to succeed in their demanding new role, as well as that CMOs themselves did better in their new role, drastic improvements seemed not to have happened. Court found that the role of the CMO needed to change fast if CMOs were to contribute vitally into their companies' market success. As he emphasized at the beginning of his article: 'Many chief marketers still have narrowly defined roles that emphasize advertising, brand management, and market research. They will have to spread their wings.' So, here is the interesting position that CMOs found themselves in during the noughties. On the one hand, they were rushed into a more strategic role without much preparation, and on the other, the high pace of change required them to constantly redefine and adapt their role to new conditions and challenges. In comparison with other, better defined and more stable C-level positions, such as the chief financial officer (CFO), CMOs looked to be facing an uphill battle from the start.

The unfavourable position of CMOs within companies' C-suite can also be observed when considering the average tenure of marketers in leading US brands. In 2016, the average time CMOs spent at the same position was 42 months (Vranica, 2017). At the same time, CEO average tenure in the S&P 500 companies was a bit more than seven years and CFO average tenure in 2016 was 5.7 years in Fortune 500 companies (Vranica, 2017). As the article reports, this was the second year in a row that CMO tenure declined. The difference is remarkable. Why do CMOs stay for an average of 3.5 years in the same position while CFOs and CEOs stay for much longer at their positions? Is it an occupational hazard intrinsic to the marketing profession or can it be somehow addressed? The more one looks into the problems facing marketers today, the more the answer to this question appears negative for the profession.

Insights from Forrester Research and the Business Marketing Association study on if and how well marketers are prepared for modern business challenges are revealing (Johnson, 2016):

- 21 per cent claim that skills for which they were hired are already obsolete;
- 97 per cent see a drastic increase in the variety of skills needed for marketing;
- 97 per cent are doing completely new things;
- 45 per cent struggle to find candidates with the appropriate marketing skills.

In striving to find answers for the CMO tenure decline and the overall extremely challenging position of marketers today, Johnson (2016) cites a study by EffectiveBrands and the Association of National Advertisers involving interviews with 350 CEOs, CMOs and agency directors, and a survey of more than 10,000 marketers in 92 countries. In her own words, the solution to the marketing problem is that: 'We need marketing organizations that reflect our current business environment, rather than those designed in the 1980s.' It is not only that marketing theory is finding it hard to come up with convincing models of what marketers are doing, but marketing practice is failing to reflect business challenges in real time as well.

The tight spot that CMOs are finding themselves in has a simple but devastating effect. CEOs do not trust them. A 2012 study by the Fournaise Marketing Group, interviewing 1,200 CEOs in the United States, Europe, Asia and Australia, found that 80 per cent of these CEOs did not trust marketers nor were impressed by marketers' accomplishments (The Fournaise, 2012). At the same time, 90 per cent of them trusted and valued their CFOs and CIOs opinions. The study identified that the main problem in the CEO and marketer relationship is that marketers are too disconnected with the financial reality of their companies, and too vague on results and net contribution. Marketers need to become genuine business partners to the CEO and to their other colleagues by using appropriate data 'for the right purpose and the right decision making, with no fluff around' (The Fournaise, 2012). Thomas Barta (2015), a former McKinsey partner and current researcher in marketing leadership, has confirmed in an article on Adobe's CMO.COM the absence of trust in marketing leadership, explaining that marketers cannot provide convincing explanations for past performance and it takes more time for them to build trust with the CEO than other C-suite professionals. Barta, in line with previous data mentioned above, also observes a skills crisis and control crisis in the marketing profession, alongside the evident trust crisis.

The boardroom war and its marketing casualties

Al Ries, who is best known for introducing (together with Jack Trout) the very popular marketing concept of 'positioning' (Ries and Trout, 1980), published with his business partner and daughter Laura Ries in 2009 a book called *War in the Boardroom: Why left-brain management and right-brain marketing don't see eye-to-eye – and what to do about it* (Ries and Ries, 2009). The title of the book is quite self-explanatory. Ries and Ries believe that there is a 'velvet veil' between the left-brain (analytical, verbal, certainty-driven) management of the company, represented by CEOs and CFOs, and the right-brain (holistic, visual, creativity-driven) marketers. Using average tenure data available at that time, which showed that CMOs stayed indeed less time in companies than CEOs, CFOs and CIOs (26, 44, 39 and 36 months respectively), they highlighted the fact that the top marketing job is, as was emphatically proclaimed in *Businessweek* back then, *radioactive* (Ries and Ries, 2009). According to them, great companies are the ones that bring peace in the boardroom by allowing marketers to do their job properly and build strong brands in the long run. Until that happens though – if it ever happens completely – criticism against marketers from the outside and the inside of marketing suggest that casualties of the boardroom war are single-sided: marketers are losing more than they are winning.

With so much criticism, such a tough, undefinable job at hand and a troublesome past, what is the future of the marketer? In order to shed some light on the future of marketers we first need to look into an intriguing phenomenon. While marketing is becoming more important than ever, marketers themselves are not so highly perceived. This is what we call The Marketing Paradox.

The Marketing Paradox

The global economic meltdown at the end of the 2000s posed certain obstacles for marketing. As with previous economic crises, the first issue was the following: could all those overgenerous budgets going into questionable brand campaigns survive the tight financial conditions? The answer was simply no. But the problem was not only the decrease in marketing budgets. The main problem was if this latest crisis would uncover systemic weaknesses of the marketing profession that were hidden under easier corporate capital and self-absorbing marketing jargon. In an interview in *Businessweek* with revered leadership coach and author Marshall Goldsmith, the academic global authority on marketing, Professor Philip Kotler gave a simple but profound answer to Goldsmith's direct question, if it was a wise move to cut the marketing budget first because of the crisis. Kotler said (Goldsmith, 2009): 'Yes, if the marketers cannot provide performance metrics for their expenditures. Marketers have had it easy in the past.' There is a clear theme in the criticism of marketers' work: their inability to speak business on an equal level with their corporate colleagues, explain reliably the past and predict with a degree of confidence the future (thus, justify investments in advance). Such criticism can be very sharp, again coming from within the field. Professor of Marketing Jean-Claude Larréché had this to say just before the crisis about marketers: 'Unfortunately, many marketing people are much more attracted by fashion than they are by professionalism... If you go to marketing departments you will see how often they are very far from professional' (The Marketer, 2007).

The 2008 economic crisis indeed put enormous pressure on companies to cut their marketing budgets and especially concerning marketing communications (Forbes, 2008). But the crisis had the opposite effect on CEOs' appreciation of marketing and its contribution in business performance. It seems that market turbulence and decreased customers' expenditure brought about the realization that what companies should be looking at is a deeper understanding of their main source of income, their customers, and addressing better their needs on an everyday basis. Before crisis, with abundant capital and market opportunities globally, many companies focused on rapid expansion and on the internal organization of resources to make this expansion happen. In the process, they forgot the customer and the significance of marketing for the long-term ROI and even for business survival. This can be clearly seen in the following statements.

Paul Polman the then CEO of Unilever, one of the largest fast-moving consumer goods (FMCG) companies in the world, said while addressing shareholders in February 2009 (Unilever, 2009):

> So now, with the majority of the restructuring programme behind us we need to increasingly focus our energy externally versus internally. It requires us to put the consumer and customer firmly back at the heart of all we do.

During the same period, and talking as well about the effects of the crisis, the then CEO of Unilever's main competitor, Procter & Gamble (P&G), said something very similar with Paul Polman (Consumergoods.com, 2008):

> Organizationally, P&G was trying to do too much too fast, which was disruptive internally and affecting how we were doing in the marketplace. Organizational changes became internally focused, and we lost touch with our consumers.

This is remarkable. The CEOs of two of the globally leading FMCG companies had the same take on the crisis at the same time: in order to deal with it effectively and survive in the long run, they needed to change their approach and prioritize customers over internal processes. Someone would expect that FMCGs, of all companies, would have imprinted in their very DNA a certain organizational obsession with customers. This was not the case though. Customer attention was left to marketing, and to its own shortcomings, while the rest of the structure was engulfed in restructuring projects, complex and chaotic mergers and acquisitions, and multidimensional affairs of a predominantly internal nature. The crisis worked as a kind of wake-up call for re-establishing corporate priorities: from internal to external, from company to consumers, from operations to marketing.

David Packard, of Hewlett-Packard, on marketing

The co-founder of Hewlett-Packard, the US multinational information technology company, is accredited with one of the most insightful sayings about marketing: 'marketing is too important to be left to the marketing department' (Forbes, 2013). Many could interpret this statement to entail the essence of The Marketing Paradox, as it is going to be explained below. In a nutshell: CEOs love marketing… but they do not extend the same positive feeling for their marketers.

The CEO's love affair with marketing did not restrain itself exclusively in the crisis years (or in some instances even earlier as portrayed by the David Packard statement). It continued well into the noughties. Here is a selection of how CEOs of global brands have expressed their commitment to marketing:

- Indra Nooyi, the CEO of PepsiCo, admitted in a presentation to investors in 2012 that Pepsi's marketing efforts were seriously underfunded and that they have not been very effective (Colvin, 2012). By committing bigger budgets to marketing, she declared that she is taking major steps in improving it. According to Fortune's editor-at-large, Geoff Colvin, her main challenge at that time was that while she was not deviating from Pepsi's core strategy, 'she hasn't forgotten how Pepsi makes money' (Colvin, 2012). It is marketing that makes money and money is the foundation of a CEO's success.

- Nick Jeffrey, the CEO of Vodafone UK, said in 2017: 'Our ambition is to give our customers the best experience possible, providing an outstanding level of service and support' (Bunker, 2017). The company has dedicated to improve their customer service by employing more than 2,000 new customer service reps (Bunker, 2017). Customer experience is a central theme in modern marketing and CEOs have taken notice.

- Bill McDermott, the CEO of SAP, the German software multinational, said in an interview in 2014: 'I see everything through the eyes of the customer and, fortunately, I've encouraged 67,000 of my colleagues and 2.1 million people in our ecosystem to do the same. In the end, the customer must win' (Colvin, 2014). Since this was his response to the question of how he can run a tech company not being a 'techie' himself, customer orientation seems to be the fundamental ingredient for a CEO to run successfully a modern corporation, regardless the product, the industry or the market.

The contrast with the past is noteworthy. As Al Ries explains in his introductory YouTube video about his *War in the Boardroom* book, Jack Welsh, one of the most celebrated CEOs in the world, had almost nothing to say about marketing in his best-selling and highly influential book *Winning* (Ries, 2009). How did we go from CEOs considering marketing as peripheral to core business to CEOs incorporating typical marketing terminology, like customer orientation and customer experience, into their standard rhetoric? *The Age of the Customer*, a new business cycle that is about decoding and serving powerful customers (Shackell, 2014) and about companies that are literally obsessed with their customers (Forrester, 2014) has begun, according to Forrester Research. This new business era is characterized by technology, data, enhanced marketing responsibilities and a complete customer orientation. CEOs have been quick to join, and even take the lead, in this new era and this is highly evident when listening to CEOs of internet-related brands:

- **Airbnb** CEO, Brian Chesky: 'Love is the biggest priority for our company because we are in the business of delivering amazing experiences for our customers – that is the most important thing we need to do' (Harrison, 2012).

- **LinkedIn** CEO, Jeff Weiner: 'At LinkedIn, one of the values is simply stated as: Members First… If it benefits members, it will ultimately benefit the company' (Meister, 2012).

- **Amazon** CEO, Jeff Bezos: 'We've had three big ideas at Amazon that we've stuck with for 18 years, and they are the reason we're successful: Put the customer first. Invent. And be patient' (Farhi, 2013).

- **Alibaba** Executive Chairman, Jack Ma: 'It's customers number one, employees, two, and shareholders, three. It's the customer who pays us the money, it's the employees who drive the vision, and it's the shareholders who, when the crisis comes, these people ran away' (Meadows, 2015).

It is not only that modern CEOs have placed the customer at the very heart of what they say. They have also placed customers at the heart of what they do. Jeff Bezos is famous for leaving a chair free in strategic meetings to remind his colleagues that the customer, being the most important person in the room, should have a say in all significant corporate decisions (Thomson, 2016). Elon Musk, the CEO of Tesla cars and SpaceX, went even a step further doing something that traditionally CEOs would rarely do. When a Tesla driver complained on Twitter about other Tesla drivers parking their electric cars in spots designated for recharging them, and thus obstructing others of recharging their own cars, Musk replied personally and decisively:

Tesla customer tweet: @elonmusk *the San Mateo supercharger is always full with idiots who leave their tesla for hours even if already charged.* (11 Dec 2016)

Tesla CEO Elon Musk's response: @loic *You're right, this is becoming an issue. Supercharger spots are meant for charging, not parking. Will take action.* (11 Dec 2016)

Most remarkably, in only six days Tesla introduced a new policy that charged a fee to people who extended their stay in electrical recharging stations (Bariso, 2017). Elon Musk, a globally renowned CEO, listened to the customer directly (marketing research), replied to the complaint (communications) and provided a long-term solution (service improvement) in less than a week's time. CEOs nowadays do not only love marketing. They also perform marketing themselves with no involvement or interference of the marketing department, and they are ready to get into very public debates with each other over who is more customer-centric.

Another example is the online exchange between Apple CEO Tim Cook and Facebook CEO Mark Zuckerberg, about which company really cares about its customers. It started with Tim Cook commenting on online platforms by stating that: 'If [companies are] making money mainly by collecting gobs of personal data, I think you have a right to be worried... And companies I think should be very transparent about it' (Moss, 2014). Zuckerberg replied, in an interview with *Time* magazine, that business models should not be automatically confused with customer alignment. In his own words: 'What, you think because you're paying Apple that you're somehow in alignment with them? If you were in alignment with them, then they'd make their products a lot cheaper!' (Grossman, 2014).

This is the new normal. CEOs of high-profile global brands debate in the public arena their approach to customers. The race is on between famous CEOs to prove that they have the strongest commitment to their customers' wellbeing.

The CMO on top: not yet

If contemporary CEOs love marketing, and if the CEO position is becoming more marketing-related than ever, are CMOs given important positions in corporate boardrooms? Although there have been few high-profile cases of C-suite marketing professionals becoming CEOs – such as in McDonald's, Mercedes-Benz USA, Radio Shack and Royal Dutch Shell (Overby, 2015) – the overall influence of CMOs in corporate policy is not convincing yet. A study of boards in the Fortune 1000 companies showed that out of 9,800 board seats in those companies, only 38 were filled by CMOs (Welch, 2013). This is really a tiny fraction. Marketing is increasing its influence drastically and very fast... but marketers do not follow suit.

The Marketing Paradox is the following: if customer orientation is more important than ever, and if CEOs become increasingly obsessed with predominantly marketing concepts such as customer needs, customer care, experience, satisfaction and loyalty, then why are marketers not trusted nor respected as they should be within companies? As Regis McKenna, the pioneering technology marketer, emphatically put it: 'Marketing is doing very well... it's just not being done well by the marketing people' (The Marketer, 2007). The Marketing Paradox is not a secret. It is simply the marketers' main challenge.

The problem with the marketing profession

Criticism around the marketing profession within corporations, from a purely business perspective, has focused on reliability and predictability. Marketers cannot easily compare to other professionals in terms of how they can comprehensively explain their past performance and forecast their future one. Think of procurement, for example. Procurement managers can scan the market for alternative vendors of, let's say, office materials. Then they can shortlist them based on well-defined criteria such as price, quality and availability. When they make a decision and place the order they can be quite sure of what to expect. Their professional success can be assured by vendors delivering the order and by people in the company using the office materials they need. Can marketers do the same?

At an operational level, marketers can order products or services from vendors, such as promotional materials and advertising space, and they too can be sure that they will receive what was ordered. But when is their success defined? In a strategic level a marketer is judged by results in the market, not by operational deliveries. Did the promotional materials and advertising space change hearts, minds and behaviours? Did more customers visit the brand's stores and website? Did more people recommend the brand? Did more clients become loyal? Have sales increased? Such market effects are not dependent only on internal factors such as operational excellence, but on external ones that cannot be controlled by marketers such as competition, general economic conditions, social trends and technological advancements. Complexity is not the same for all professionals within companies, and marketers get the short end of the stick. Although we will discuss this topic in more detail in Chapter 5, it is worth highlighting here the extent of the problem.

One of the most impressive achievements in modern marketing history, and one that is least known, is that of Swedish powerhouse spirit brand Absolut Vodka (Peterson, 2001). The Absolut brand's rise to fame forms a compelling business case study that every marketer would love to experience and, even better, achieve. Results are staggering: a rather generic vodka brand at the beginning of the 1990s, which was selling at that time only about 100,000 cases globally per annum, turned into the third biggest spirits brand, selling more than 10 million cases per annum almost 15 years later (Johansson, 2012). This is game-changing success in all business levels. The marketer behind the brand's transformation and the spirit's takeover of the world is Michel Roux. When Roux and his team became responsible for Absolut the current attitude in the company was that the brand was about to die and that no one should deal with it seriously. Roux changed everything, from the bottle to the brand positioning and communications, to create a luxury brand that set high standards for the whole spirits industry globally. The most fascinating aspect of this ground-breaking success is this: it was not repeated. When asked about his recipe for success in taking an irrelevant brand and making it a world leader, redefining the entire product category in the process, Roux simply replied that 'if I knew *that*, I would do it again and again' (Johansson, 2012). Although Roux continued his career, helping spirits develop their brands globally, he did not repeat the market disruption he achieved with Absolut. Although he could easily offer an explanatory rhetoric for this success, using buzzwords and praising his unique approach and proprietary methodology – as many marketers and marketing consultants do – he was transparent enough to admit that disruptive success in marketing defies explanations and rational justifications. *Ex post*, or after the event, it is very convenient to look back and assign comfortable causes to an effect. *Ex ante*, or before the event though, this is almost impossible.

As we will see in Chapter 2, the high rate of failures in marketing activities, like introducing new products and delivering marketing messages effectively, prove that marketers do not have a reliable and predictable method for achieving noticeable objectives in the marketplace. This is the real problem with the marketing function within companies. For trend-defying, game-changing, disrupting, industry-bending results marketers have no recipe. For middle-of-the-road, lukewarm, trend-related, forgettable results marketers do seem to have the methods to achieve. These though are not the results CEOs are looking for in today's turbulent and challenging business environment.

But is it any different nowadays with a much more advanced business ecosystem? Do the huge amounts of data we can collect, even in real time today, and the substantial academic and market research that marketing has experienced over the last two decades, help to improve predictability and make marketing professionals more credible? The Absolut success is already a 20-year-old story, so definitely, marketers must have improved their sense of predictability and reliability. Or… have they?

Millennials, the demographic segment consisting of individuals born from the 1980s to the beginning of the noughties, has been a very prominent buzzword in marketing for over a decade. Evidently, it is such an overused concept that Joel Windels (2016), VP of Inbound Marketing at the UK online analytics firm Brandwatch, states: 'As a marketer, it is a term I see every single day. In fact, I started to get so sick of it.' The hype about millennials is largely based on the fact that an older demographic, that of the baby boomers, has been instrumental for marketing in the United States in previous decades, and also because millennials arrived together with new and exciting technologies for marketers such as the internet and mobile phones. Millennials and social media have become two almost interchangeable terms in marketing jargon – not always without good reason. Traditional brands find it increasingly difficult to connect to new demographics that have different expectations from brands than traditional segments, such as baby boomers.

Such a case was that of BMW, the world-famous German automobile manufacturer. Finding it challenging to appear as relevant and exciting to millennials as it did to older generations, BMW decided to use social media to reach new audiences (Fitzgerald, 2014). The Epic Driftmob video was produced featuring professional drivers in five M235i BMW cars performing *drifting* stunts, which are done by driving fast and then instantly turning and breaking in order to spin the car. The whole video was designed to resemble a flash mob, which is typically a surprising public performance made to look as a spontaneous act. The video was an instant success and went viral. Results recorded by YouGov's BrandIndex Meter showed increased word-of-mouth online discussions about BMW, and most importantly, enhanced possibility of millennials buying a BMW car (Fitzgerald, 2014). However, Florian Resinger from the team in BMW behind the Epic Driftmob is very clear when it comes to social media success. Additionally to the fact that he always has to warn his colleagues not to have high expectations on virability of branded content, since audiences can deem it irrelevant very easily and unpredictably, he stressed that: 'If I knew how to do this on a daily basis, I would not be sitting here. I'd be a number one chartbreaker doing it for every brand' (Fitzgerald, 2014).

When marketers are honest, as Absolut's Michel Roux and BMW's Florian Resinger, they admit marketing's problem: there are no proven methodologies and universally accepted professional tools to repeat great success on demand. This might very well be the reason why marketers stay for less time in the CMO position of a specific company than other C-level professionals. They try, they do their best, they might have a success or two, and then they move on to other companies to try their luck under different conditions. Luck is the keyword here, instead of leadership and/or professionalism.

Gorilla marketing at its best

One of the most effective examples that unpredictability, reliability and even luck are hardwired in traditional marketing, and one that we have been using in the classroom for almost a decade, is that of Cadbury's Gorilla Dairy Milk advert. Dairy Milk is the flagship product of the British confectionery company Cadbury, representing, at times, 50 per cent of the company's total sales (D&AD, 2008). In 2007 the company decided to air an advertisement that looked very different to anything that the industry had seen before. The ad featured a man in a gorilla suit playing the drums to the Phil Collins tune 'In the Air Tonight'. There were no kids, no chocolates, no milk, no gift-wrapped products, no eating chocolate with indulgence… nothing resembling a typical chocolate ad. This bold move – that even the company CEO said he did not comprehend when he viewed the ad for the first time – was deemed necessary because of the challenges Cadbury was facing: a salmonella-contamination scandal, higher production costs due to the rising price of cocoa, product recall and a campaign accusing the company of being racist (Jones, 2008). The ad aired for the first time in the UK on 31 August 2007 and it simply made history. It quickly accumulated 2 million views on YouTube, when brands rarely experienced such success on that platform, and all major core brand values measured by the company saw substantial growth with the ad (Jones, 2008); more than 300 spoof videos were uploaded on YouTube, showcasing extremely high engagement with the ad (D&AD, 2008); it won many awards, including the top award in the most important advertising festival in the world, Cannes Lion; and it increased sales of the brand by almost 9 per cent (Caird, 2016). This last achievement is the holy grail: tangible business results and real, business-sound return on investment. Success in business always breeds the desire for more success and the Cadbury marketing team together with their external partners tried to repeat the Gorilla success with two subsequent ads: Airport Trucks and Eyebrow Dance. Although both of them had some noticeable impact on social media, brand measurement variable and PR, the disruptive achievement of the Gorilla ad was not

> observed again. The strategy was there, the team was there, the experience was there but the same results were not. Marketers can produce acceptable numbers on demand… but for extraordinary, incomparable, brand-transforming results replicable methods have been elusive.

The absence of reliability and predictability that accompanies the marketing profession, on the one hand, and the strategic importance of marketing for company success in the turbulent times we live in, on the other, have created The Marketing Paradox: CEO's love of customer-centricity, which has always been the central marketing theme, and their simultaneous scepticism and distrust of marketers and the marketing department. In order for marketers to reclaim (or create for the first time?) their credibility and drive company growth in the long run, they need to change. They need to develop new skills, adopt new methods and take a new leadership role within the whole organization. This is what we call Advanced Marketing Management.

The 21st-century marketer

Customer-centricity, as *the* fundamental business imperative, is here to stay. Entrepreneurs, CEOs, shareholders and professionals from all business functions and organizations are getting to terms with the basic business truth that customers are the ones who drive survival and growth. Simply put: no customers, no business. This is a great opportunity for marketers. It is the time for them to shine. Unfortunately, The Marketing Paradox demonstrates that this is still not happening. Although marketers should be at the forefront of the customer-orientation awakening in companies over the world, they have not yet managed to play the central role expected of them. What is expected from them is a more enhanced, empowering and strategically significant role than they ever had before.

According to Bruce Rogers, Chief Insights Officer at Forbes, contemporary marketers 'are not only able to leverage data successfully but they have the ability [opportunity] to serve as the chief inspiration officer'. As he further points out: 'They need to drive efforts to train and educate the organization. They don't just have the responsibility but the obligation' (Whitler, 2015).

The current – and main – problem for marketers to embrace this historical obligation though, and the key reason for The Marketing Paradox, is that 'these transformational CMOs are in short supply' (Whitler, 2015). This book is the direct response to the call for increasing the supply of transformational marketers. But transformational marketers, or advanced marketers as they are called in this book, need to go through a different curriculum than the one typically offered today. Figure 1.1 shows the model of Advanced Marketing Management described and justified in this book.

The new set of skills for modern marketers proposed here is varied and demanding. It covers the complete spectrum of modern business, going far beyond the traditional and typical skills of marketing from the past. If marketers are to lead business transformation well into the 21st century, they need to seriously revamp the whole profession. Times have changed and it is time for marketers to change as well.

Neuroscience applied in understanding and influencing customer behaviour is a reality. As explained in depth in Chapter 2, marketers cannot apply any more common-sense marketing. They need to understand how the human brain works and how neurons and our bodies as a whole react to marketing stimuli, as this is a much better predictor of actual customer behaviour than surveys and focus groups. The extent to which neuroscience and cutting-edge brain and behavioural research alters traditional marketing decision making can be staggering.

Consider the intriguing findings of a study by Psychology Professor Ana Vivas and her associates. They found out that when something distracts us from a task, and we want to ignore it or forget it in order to perform the task effectively, we subconsciously assign negative value to the distractor (Vivas *et al*, 2016). This means that we create negative memories in things that pull our attention away from points we want to focus on. Next time we encounter the distractor, the negative memory has the potential of nudging our behaviour away from it. Think of online advertisements such as banners. While you are trying to pay a bill on your mobile banking platform the bank might be trying to sell you a new loan or a credit card by displaying relevant banners. Since your brain is in a task-oriented mode, the ad can be perceived by your brain as a distractor and thus form a negative memory in your subconscious. This is definitely something that the marketing department does NOT intend to do with the banner ad.

Figure 1.1   The Advanced Marketing Management model

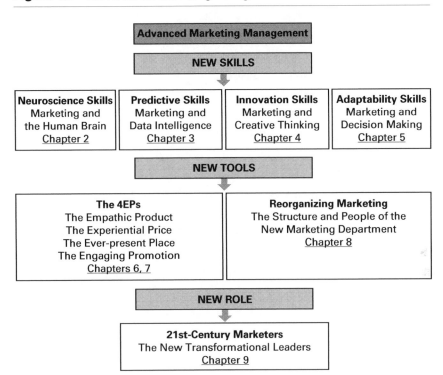

The adblocking phenomenon

The extreme annoyance of invading ads while we consume online content has not remained only at the subconscious level. The astounding increase of people using adblocking software online has taken the marketing industry by storm. According to some estimates, more than 200 million people in the world are using such software to free their online content from interrupting ads (Mysore, 2016), which more often than not are deemed irrelevant and irritating, and this number is set to double by 2020 (Business Insider, 2016). Contemporary brain and behavioural research methods can reveal such problems before they become reality in the marketplace, making marketers look unprofessional… and again as if they are 'caught by surprise' by customers' negative responses.

Half-baked models of the past need to be replaced by new scientific approaches that require a holistic understanding of what makes us human and what influences our behaviour. Marketers need to become fluent in brain science and to stop being *brain blind* in their profession. At the same time they need to become more fluent in data.

This is a well-publicized development, as already mentioned in this chapter. Data is all around us and will be even more so in the future. The term for the amount of data today is the *zettabyte*, or 1 billion terabytes. The world is new to zettabytes, since in 2006 the world total data storage did not exceed 0.16 of a zettabyte, while in 2013 that number went dramatically up to 4.4 zettabytes (Johnston, 2015). As Johnston (2015) emphasized: 'After thousands of years of civilization, within a few short years our world has produced over 90 per cent of the data that the planet has ever known.' Digital literacy, analytics and technology are now top-rated skills for marketers. A survey by The Economist Intelligence Unit showed that the top skills rated by marketers themselves are (Angulo, 2016):

- digital engagement (39 per cent);
- technology (39 per cent);
- strategy and planning (38 per cent);
- data analysis (32 per cent);
- customer acquisition (32 per cent);
- customer experience (27 per cent);
- advertising and branding (26 per cent);
- creative and graphics (16 per cent).

This is not a recent phenomenon. Back in 2007, Regis McKenna proclaimed that marketing is becoming increasingly technology-driven and that marketers are losing the battle to more tech-savvy colleagues outside of marketing (The Marketer, 2007). The trend is only getting stronger, and today marketing has become almost synonymous to data, technology and the digital world. But more data does not necessarily mean better marketing and this is why marketers need to understand better the available methods, possibilities and challenges of data to deliver more meaningful solutions to their clients.

Another word highly associated with data, technology and digital in the world of business is *innovation*. Innovation is at the very heart of business today, since it is the only way to stay in touch with an ever-changing reality.

For companies around the world, innovation is intrinsically customer-centric. Innovations that do not attract customers by solving new or existing problems practically and convincingly become obsolete very fast.

In the award-winning book *Customer Innovation: Customer-centric strategy for enduring growth*, Marketing Professor Marion Debruyne (2014) emphasizes the fact that, when it comes to innovation: 'The sole and unique focus is on customer needs. Innovations are crafted to formulate a response to an unmet customer need.' Peter Diamandis, renowned entrepreneur and co-founder of the Singularity University, usually pinpoints the fact that if a company or start-up wants to grow it needs to make sure that it influences positively the lives of 1 billion people within 10 years (Winfrey, 2014). Real innovation is about solving unsolved problems, impacting positively and decisively the lives of people. In order for innovation to work nowadays, traditional research and development (R&D) models, where marketers were typically educated to perform formal marketing research and help companies launch successful products and services, do not help any more. In fact, PricewaterhouseCoopers's (PwC) longitudinal and ongoing study on innovation and R&D shows that there is no relation between the two and that the top 10 innovative companies are rarely the top 10 investors in R&D as well (Viki, 2016). Companies, and especially marketers, need to become more creative in everyday problem solving in order to constantly develop innovations that customers will want to buy. Creative thinking, as a necessary ingredient of market innovation, should not be confined to marketing agencies. Long gone is the era where creativity was a monopoly of advertising people and marketing communications professionals. Although effective creativity is needed in advertising more than ever, for addressing the adblocking phenomenon for example, creative problem solving has a wider and more strategic role to play. Creative thinking is now included in all major lists of key general skills for the world's population for the 21st century (ie World Economic Forum, 2016) and marketers have some catching up to do.

The last, but not least, new skill set for advanced marketers recommended in this book is about complex decision making and adaptability. The world has become a chaotic place. So much so that it has become commonplace to recite the adage: change itself has changed. The popularity among business people of complexity-related ideas such as those of Nassim Nicholas Taleb, author of the best-selling books *The Black Swan: The impact of the highly improbable* (2007) and *Antifragile: Things that gain from disorder* (2013), as well as of the surprising and entertaining correlations in Steve Levitt's and Stephen Dubner's book series on what they call *Freakonomics* (2006, 2010), showcase that a new type of decision making and overall perception of reality in business is needed. This new decision-making model has to be more flexible, collaborative, adaptive and open. Traditionally, marketers have been focusing on learning the specifics of their trade and less universal decision-making models and techniques. They were more sectoral experts than holistic business influencers. To turn themselves into the requested transformational leaders though, marketers need to change their mindset and adopt new analytical, decision and forecasting techniques. Even better, they should play the Chief Inspirational Officer role mentioned earlier and infuse those mindsets and techniques into the whole organization.

New skills are necessary but new tools are necessary too. Alongside, the numerous methods and techniques offered in the skills chapters (Chapters 2, 3, 4 and 5), this book proposes an update to the all-powerful 4Ps model. By resisting the general trend of marketing authors to reject the 4Ps and suggest their own, new and improved marketing mix model, the Advanced Marketing Management approach capitalizes on the longevity of the most successful marketing mix model of all times and brings it to the 21st century. The 4EPs, with the addition of an 'E' in front of every 'P' are explained analytically in Chapters 6 and 7. A snapshot can be found in Figure 1.2.

New skills and an updated marketing mix model, from 4Ps to 4EPs, are absolutely necessary conditions for developing the 21st-century transformational marketer but they are not sufficient. What is also needed is a more comprehensive and holistic approach to marketers as organizational leaders. As mentioned before, marketers were traditionally sectoral experts rather than integrated business influencers, and this can change by marketing professionals upgrading their understanding and impact on significant topics such as company structure, employee engagement and external network management. First, marketers cannot continue behaving as if the company's entire future is in someone else's hands, and second, they also cannot continue behaving as if people engagement in their team, in other teams in the company and even in partnering external teams, is not a central part of their job. The role 'Chief Inspiring Officer' says it all. Globally leading brands are moving towards new and innovative structures and roles to address external and internal needs for change at the top.

Figure 1.2   The 4EPs for 21st-century marketing

Advanced Marketing Management

The New 4EPs

The Empathic Product
Product, the first element of the traditional mix, is not as it used to be. A key change is the move from a company-oriented perspective to a full-customer one. Empathy is emerging as a major new tool for marketers in helping them develop products, services and experiences.

The Experiential Price
Price is the marketing mix element least trusted to marketers. This is unacceptable if they want to become true business leaders. Price is an important decision influencer and the way customers experience price and react behaviourally to pricing techniques is paramount to success.

The Ever-present Place
Brands need to know where their customers are and how to approach them. Place has been transformed from few traditional touchpoints, like retail, wholesale and websites, to practically everything and everywhere. Smart devices keep us connected on the go, and every space can become an innovative touchpoint.

The Engaging Promotion
Customer engagement is at the heart of modern marketing. Moving from the traditional one-way approach, delivered through mass media, to a two-way or multi-way conversation, facilitated mainly through new media, marketers aim at enhancing customer engagement and achieving advocacy and loyalty.

Most notably, the Coca-Cola Company announced in 2017 the following changes in key positions (Coca-Cola, 2017):

- A new Chief Growth Officer is assigned leading the, now combined, functions of global marketing, customer and commercial leadership, and strategy.

- A new Chief Innovation Officer is assigned to elevate global R&D into an independent innovation-focused function, which will be reporting to the CEO directly.

- The information technology (IT) function is now directly reporting to the CEO, showcasing the importance of digitization as a key enabler for business growth.

Chief Growth Officer? Chief Innovation Officer? IT as a direct report to the CEO at an FMCG company? The world is changing fast and companies are too. They have to if they want to remain relevant and compete in a complex, dynamic and unpredictable business environment. In an era where CMOs will be spending more time on IT than the typical Chief Information Officer, and where almost 85 per cent of businesspeople believe that customer engagement will surpass productivity as main growth driver, marketers have a central organizational role to play, inside or outside the traditional CMO job title (Sklar, 2014). They have the historic obligation to get out of their comfort zone and the habits of the past, and lead brands into an unknown but exciting future. Regardless if their role is that of the CMO, the Chief Growth Officer, the Chief Innovation Officer, the Chief Customer Officer, the Chief Customer Experience or Customer Engagement Officer, the Chief Insights Officer, the Chief Brand Officer or, hopefully in the near future, the Chief Executive Officer, they need to deliver. Predictably, reliably, scientifically, strategically, convincingly and, above all, decisively. This book is written to help them do exactly that. Are you ready for the advanced marketing manager?

... And still, things go horribly wrong

The first half of 2017 was not promising for marketers. The three high-profile brand blunders set out below indicate that there is still a long way to go until corporations embrace fully customer-centricity. Marketers' input towards this direction was both unavoidable and paramount.

Case 1: United Airlines

On 9 April 2017, a United Airlines flight was about to depart from Chicago's international airport, when an announcement was made for four passengers to debark the flight. This apparently happened because United needed to fly four of their own crew members outside Chicago and the flight was fully booked. United is said to have offered US $800 as compensation, plus accommodation and a next-day flight, but one passenger refused to debark, claiming professional obligations at the destination. Law enforcement was called and appeared to violently remove the passenger, who was seen injured and bleeding while being in distress. This was reported via a mobile-phone camera and public outrage broke out soon after. This escalated when United CEO Oscar Munoz issued a statement that was perceived as insensitive, talking about reaccommodating the passenger as opposed to causing distress. He scored zero on empathy. Later on, Munoz apologized in the media many times, saying: 'That first response was insensitive beyond belief. It did not represent how I felt... I messed up, plain and simple' (Boston Globe, 2017). Apart from the immense PR and online backlash, the incident and the way it was handled prompted a congress inquiry, in which Munoz faced 'grilling from lawmakers' (Fortune, 2017). It also prompted the company to cancel its plan to name Munoz the company's next chairman in 2018, as originally planned (Shugerman, 2017). If all reports are true, this case shows customer-centricity, care and experience at their worst.

Case 2: Pepsi

At the beginning of April 2017, Pepsi aired a TV advertisement in the United States, starring Kendall Jenner, of the celebrity family the Kardashians. The ad story was about protesters of different professional backgrounds and races joining forces on the street at a civil-rights-style demonstration. Jenner sees the demonstration while she is posing as a model for a fashion photoshoot and decides to join them. When the demonstrators reach a police line on the street, Jenner approaches a young police officer and offers him a can of Pepsi as a token of peace. He accepts it, smiling. Result? Pepsi was forced to withdraw the ad almost immediately, issuing a public apology. In this apology, the company said: 'Pepsi was trying to project a global message of unity, peace and understanding. Clearly we missed the mark, and we apologize. We did not intend to make light of any serious issue' (Tobak, 2017). When brands try to capitalize on important social issues and appear relevant, the exact opposite can happen. Marketing, and especially brand communications, are not easy nor straightforward. They can seriously backfire if marketers are not sensitive to social sentiments and do not understand adequately wider forces that shape public opinion and people's behaviour.

Case 3: Fyre Festival

At the end of April 2017, the Fyre music festival was planned to take place on an exotic and remote Bahamas island. Promoted as a once-in-a-life opportunity to experience a luxurious event with VIPs, and priced from US $450 to $250,000, Fyre set out to create a unique festival, in a unique location, for unique people. The event was cancelled after its first day, with everything going wrong: the accommodation proved to be aid-relief tents, the food proved to consist of low-quality sandwiches, and the sewage infrastructure broke early in the first day (Vincent, 2017). The organizers issued fast a statement claiming that: 'Fyre Festival set out to provide a once-in-a-lifetime musical experience on the islands of Exuma. Due to circumstances beyond our control, we must postpone this experience' (Vincent, 2017). An employee of the event, giving her own version of what happened with the event in her article titled 'I worked at Fyre Festival. It was always going to be a disaster' for *NYMag*, claimed that the organizers had serious concerns as to whether they would be able to deliver and were considering postponing the whole event (Gordon, 2017). She says that: 'The best idea, they said, would be to roll everyone's tickets over to 2018 and start planning for the next year immediately. They had a meeting with the Fyre execs to deliver the news. A guy from the marketing team said, "Let's just do it and be legends, man"' (Gordon, 2017).

Marketers need to embrace customer-centricity fully and integrate it in all marketing operations as well as wider corporate behaviours. Currently, marketing seems to suffer, to a degree, from marketers who fail to fulfil successfully their higher business purpose. If marketing is to actively improve brands, companies and, ultimately, society, this has to change.

Last thought

Marketing is doing better than ever. CEOs, and other business executives, are rushing to claim leadership over traditional marketing territory. Customer insights, customer care and overall customer-orientation are not exclusively kept within the marketing department any more. There is strong evidence suggesting that companies worldwide are becoming more marketing-aware and customer-obsessed, which is great. However, marketers are not necessarily participating in this marketing renaissance as much as expected, nor do they appear to be leading such efforts. If marketers are to increase their contribution to companies' success and their influence in the strategic development of businesses, they need to step up. Traditional marketing can only bring them up to the level they are today; to go further and to go higher, marketers need advanced marketing.

SUMMARY CHECKLIST

- Get comfortable with the fact that the marketing profession has changed drastically from the past and that it keeps changing.
- Always have in mind that criticism to the marketing profession coming from marketers themselves, academics and practitioners, focuses mainly on issues of predictability, reliability, seriousness and professionalism.

- Use the fact that CEOs recognize the increased importance of marketing to your advantage by being a role model for the new transformational marketer.
- Solve marketing's mid-life crisis and The Marketing Paradox by adopting the model of Advanced Marketing Management suggested in this book.
- Work hard on developing the new skills, using the new tools and adopting the new role required for being a successful marketer in the 21st century.
- Search for marketing blunders to learn fast from others' mistakes and to remain humble about what marketers are able to do or not do in today's landscape.
- Be part of the marketing profession's renaissance by being a true marketing leader.

Resources to inspire you

- War in the boardroom, introduction video: https://www.youtube.com/watch?v=MDgf0NOXu9A
- Cadbury's Dairy Milk chocolate advertisements:
  - Gorilla: https://www.youtube.com/watch?v=SP8E6ouSiC0
  - Airport trucks: https://www.youtube.com/watch?v=BGYMMsPg_ME
  - Eyebrow dance: https://www.youtube.com/watch?v=t0SchmcLXMQ
- The Epic Driftmob feat, BMW M235i viral video: https://www.youtube.com/watch?v=vz2rAgXjkCA
- CNN report – United takes a beating on social media: https://www.youtube.com/watch?v=E-IZ2blJsDU

Revision questions

1 How is the marketing profession today different than in the past? What factors have influenced this change?

2 Can you explain what is meant by The Marketing Paradox nowadays?

3 In what ways are modern CEOs embracing *The Age of the Customer*? Use examples to support your answer.

4 Explain the Advanced Marketing Management model. What new skills and tools do marketers need to adopt in order to become successful in the 21st century?

References

Angulo, N (2016) [accessed 18 June 2018] Digital Marketing Skills are in Demand – Here's What Recruiters are Looking For, *Marketing Dive* [Online] http://www.marketingdive.com/news/digital-marketing-skills-in-demand-recruiters/417884/

Bagozzi, R P (1975) Marketing as exchange, *The Journal of Marketing*, 39 (4), pp 32–39

Bariso, J (2017) [accessed 18 June 2018] Elon Musk Takes Customer Complaint on Twitter From Idea to Execution in 6 Days, *INC.COM* [Online] https://www.inc.com/justin-bariso/elon-musk-takes-customer-complaint-on-twitter-from-idea-to-execution-in-6-days.html?cid=sf01002&sr_share=facebook

Barta, T (2015) [accessed 18 June 2018] Why Leading Marketing is Hard, *CMO.COM* [Online] http://www.cmo.com/features/articles/2015/6/26/why-leading-marketing-is-hard.html#gs.mNlbitQ

Boston Globe (2017) [accessed 18 June 2018] United CEO Says He 'Messed Up' With Initial Response To Seating Incident, *Boston Globe* [Online] https://www.bostonglobe.com/business/2017/04/27/united-ceo-says-messed-with-initial-response-seating-incident/tF6Lfj0X4Jt5piiq9J8SZJ/story.html

Bothun, D and Gross, D (2016) [accessed 18 June 2018] Sir Martin Sorrell of WPP on Coming Together, *Strategy+Business* [Online] https://www.strategy-business.com/article/Sir-Martin-Sorrell-of-WPP-on-Coming-Together?gko=e906a

Brady, J and Davis, I (1993) Marketing's mid-life crisis, *McKinsey Quarterly*, 2, pp 17–29

Bunker, A (2017) [accessed 18 June 2018] 2,100 Ways We're Planning To Make Your Customer Service Experience Better, *Vodafone Blog* [Online] https://blog.vodafone.co.uk/2017/03/13/2100-ways-planning-make-customer-service-experience-better/

Business Insider (2016) [accessed 18 June 2018] US Ad Block Usage Expected To More Than Double By 2020, *Businessinsider.com* [Online] http://www.businessinsider.com/us-ad-block-usage-expected-to-more-than-double-by-2020-2016-5

Caird, J (2016) [accessed 18 June 2018] 'I was basically told: you are never showing this' – How We Made Cadbury's Gorilla Ad, *The Guardian* [Online] https://www.theguardian.com/media-network/2016/jan/07/how-we-made-cadburys-gorilla-ad

Campaign (2009) [accessed 18 June 2018] Close-Up: Is insight More Crucial Than Creative?, *Campaign US* [Online] http://www.campaignlive.com/article/close-up-insight-crucial-creative/877554

Coca-Cola (2017) [accessed 18 June 2018] The Coca-Cola Company Announces Senior Leadership Appointments, *The Coca-Cola Company Press Release* [Online] http://www.coca-colacompany.com/press-center/press-releases/the-coca-cola-company-announces-senior-leadership-appointments

Coffee, P (2018) [accessed 18 June 2018] Martin Sorrell Plans His Return to the Ad Industry Via Little-Known Shell Company, *AdWeek* [Online] https://www.adweek.com/agencies/martin-sorrell-plans-his-return-to-the-ad-industry-via-little-known-shell-company/

Colvin, G (2012) [accessed 18 June 2018] Pepsi's CEO Faces Her Biggest Challenge, *Fortune* [Online] http://fortune.com/2012/02/13/pepsis-ceo-faces-her-biggest-challenge/

Colvin, G (2014) [accessed 18 June 2018] SAP's Bill McDermott Provides a CEO's Plan To Defy Disruption, *Fortune* [Online] http://fortune.com/2014/10/30/sap-bill-mcdermott-ceo-plan-to-defy-disruption/

Constantinides, E (2006) The marketing mix revisited: towards the 21st century marketing, *Journal of Marketing Management,* **22**, pp 407–38

Consumergoods.com (2008) [accessed 18 June 2018] Taking the Lead June 2008 [Online] https://consumergoods.com/taking-lead-june-2008

Court, D (2007) The evolving role of the CMO, *McKinsey Quarterly*, **3**, p 28

D&AD (2008) [accessed 18 June 2018] Case Study: Cadbury Gorilla, *D&AD* [Online] https://www.dandad.org/en/d-ad-cadbury-gorilla-case-study-insights/

Debruyne, M (2014) *Customer Innovation: Customer-centric strategy for enduring growth*, Kogan Page, London

Dominic, G (2009) From marketing mix to e-marketing mix: a literature review, *International Journal of Business and Management*, **9** (4), pp 17–24

Farhi, P (2013) [accessed 18 June 2018] Jeffrey Bezos, Washington Post's Next Owner, Aims For a New 'Golden Era' at the Newspaper, *Washington Post* [Online] https://www.washingtonpost.com/lifestyle/style/jeffrey-bezos-washington-posts-next-owner-aims-for-a-new-golden-era-at-the-newspaper/2013/09/02/30c00b60-13f6-11e3-b182-1b3bb2eb474c_story.html

Fitzgerald, M (2014) [accessed 18 June 2018] The Man Who Convinced BMW To Rethink Social Media, *Fast Company* [Online] https://www.fastcompany.com/3038405/the-man-who-convinced-bmw-to-rethink-social-media

Forbes (2008) [accessed 18 June 2018] Don't Skimp On Ad Budgets, *Forbes* [Online] https://www.forbes.com/2008/12/01/advertising-recession-wharton-ent-sales-cx_1201whartonadvertising.html

Forbes (2013) [accessed 18 June 2018] 22 Best Marketing Quotes To Drive Your Marketing Strategy, *ForbesBrandVoice* [Online] https://www.forbes.com/sites/sap/2013/01/16/22-best-marketing-quotes-to-drive-your-marketing-strategy/#416adc5d7e06

Forrester (2014) [accessed 18 June 2018] The Evolved CMO in 2014, *Forrester: Heidrick & Struggles* [Online] https://cequityknowledge.files.wordpress.com/2014/03/the-evolved-cmo-in-2014.pdf

Fortune (2017) [accessed 18 June 2018] United CEO Oscar Munoz Faces Grilling From Lawmakers Over Dragging Incident, *Fortune* [Online] http://fortune.com/2017/05/02/united-ceo-munoz-congress/

Goldsmith, M (2009) [accessed 18 June 2018] Marketing in the Age of Turbulence, *Marshall Goldsmith* [Online] http://www.marshallgoldsmith.com/articles/marketing-in-the-age-of-turbulence/

Gordon, C (2017) [accessed 18 June 2018] I Worked at Fyre Festival. It Was Always Going to Be a Disaster, *NYMag.com* [Online] http://nymag.com/thecut/2017/04/fyre-festival-exumas-bahamas-disaster.html?mid=twitter_cut

Grönroos, C (1994) Quo Vadis, marketing? Toward a relationship marketing paradigm, *Journal of Marketing Management*, **10** (5), pp 347–60

Grossman, L (2014) [accessed 18 June 2018] Inside Facebook's Plan to Wire the World, *Time* [Online] http://time.com/facebook-world-plan/

Harrison, L (2012) [accessed 18 June 2018] Airbnb CEO Brian Chesky On Weighing Your Priorities, *Fast Company* [Online] https://www.fastcompany.com/3003085/airbnb-ceo-brian-chesky-weighing-your-priorities

Johansson, F (2012) *The Click Moment: Seizing opportunity in an unpredictable world*, Portfolio Penguin, London

Johnson, C (2016) [accessed 18 June 2018] From Great to Good: What's Causing CMO Tenure Decline?, *TypeA Communications* [Online] http://typeacommunications.com/great-good-whats-causing-cmo-tenure-decline/

Johnston, N (2015) *Adaptive Marketing: Leveraging real-time data to become a more competitive and successful company*, Palgrave Macmillan, New York

Jones, H (2008) Gorilla Tactics, *The Marketer*, June, pp 24–27

Levitt, S and Dubner, S (2006) *Freakonomics: A rouge economist explores the hidden side of everything*, Penguin, London

Levitt, S and Dubner, S (2010) *Superfreakonomics: Global cooling, patriotic prostitutes and why suicide bombers should buy insurance*, Penguin, London

Marcomm (2016) [accessed 18 June 2018] WPP CEO Sir Martin Sorrell on Global Trends in Advertising and Marketing Services, *Marcomm* [Online] http://www.marcomm.news/wpp-ceo-sir-martin-sorrell-on-global-trends-in-advertising-and-marketing-services/

Marshall, J (2013) [accessed 18 June 2018] Martin Sorrell: WPP Isn't an Advertising Company, *Digiday UK* [Online] http://digiday.com/marketing/martin-sorrell-wpp-isnt-an-advertising-company/

McCarthy, E J (1960) *Basic Marketing: A managerial approach*, Richard D Irwin, Homewood, IL

McGovern, G and Quelch, J A (2004) The fall and rise of the CMO, *strategy+business*, 37, pp 45–51

Meadows, M (2015) [accessed 18 June 2018] 10 Times Jack Ma Said He Doesn't Care About Alibaba Shareholders, *Benzinga* [Online] https://www.benzinga.

com/news/earnings/15/01/5190735/10-times-jack-ma-said-he-doesnt-care-about-alibaba-shareholders

Meister, J (2012) [accessed 18 June 2018] 10 Leadership Lessons From Jeff Weiner, CEO of LinkedIn, *Forbes* [Online] https://www.forbes.com/sites/jeannemeister/2012/09/10/10-leadership-lessons-from-jeff-weiner-ceo-of-linkedin/#89ec53539a4d

Moss, C (2014) [accessed 18 June 2018] Mark Zuckerberg Slams Tim Cook: You're Not In Alignment With Your Customers, *Businessinsider* [Online] http://www.businessinsider.com/mark-zuckerberg-slams-tim-cook-2014-12

Mysore, V K (2016) [accessed 18 June 2018] Why the Advertising Industry Needs To Embrace AdBlock, *TechCrunch.com* [Online] https://techcrunch.com/2016/09/05/why-the-advertising-industry-needs-to-embrace-adblock/

O'Leary, R and Iredale, I (1976) The marketing concept: Quo Vadis?, *European Journal of Marketing*, **10** (3), pp 146–57

Overby, S (2015) [accessed 18 June 2018] CMOs Are Beginning To Fill CEO Seats, *CMO.COM* [Online] http://www.cmo.com/features/articles/2015/3/17/cmo_to_ceos_.html#gs.FuAUDNA

Peterson, T (2001) [accessed 18 June 2018] Absolut Michel Roux, *Bloomberg* [Online] https://www.bloomberg.com/news/articles/2001-12-03/absolut-michel-roux

Quelch, J and Jocz, K (2008) Branded For Good, *The American*, November–December, **2** (6), pp 72–77

Ries, A (2009) War in the Boardroom: Introduction, YouTube video [Online] https://www.youtube.com/watch?v=MDgf0NOXu9A&t=6s

Ries, A and Ries, L (2009) *War in the Boardroom: Why left-brain management and right-brain marketing don't see eye-to-eye – and what to do about it*, Harper Business, New York

Ries, A and Trout, J (1980) [accessed 18 June 2018] *Positioning: The battle for your mind*, McGrawHill, New York

Shackell, S (2014) [accessed 18 June 2018] Is the CMO Ready For Today's Boardroom?, *The Guardian* [Online] https://www.theguardian.com/media-network/media-network-blog/2014/apr/16/cmo-ready-boardroom-evolving-role

Shugerman, E (2017) [accessed 18 June 2018] United Airlines Reverses Plans To Make CEO Oscar Munoz Chairman After Passenger Dragging Scandal, *Independent* [Online] http://www.independent.co.uk/news/world/americas/united-airlines-david-dao-ceo-oscar-munoz-not-promoted-dragging-scandal-a7696266.html

Sklar, C (2014) [accessed 18 June 2018] The Traditional CMO Role Is Dead: Long Live the Chief Customer Officer, *The Guardian* [Online] https://www.theguardian.com/media-network/media-network-blog/2014/feb/19/cmo-role-dead-customer-officer-engagement

Stern, T A, Fava, M, Wilens, T E and Rosenbaum, J F (2016) *Massachusetts General Hospital Comprehensive Clinical Psychiatry*, Elsevier Health Sciences, London

Taleb, N N (2007) *The Black Swan: The impact of the highly improbable*, Penguin, London

Taleb, N N (2013) *Antifragile: Things that gain from disorder*, Penguin, London

Taube, A (2013) [accessed 18 June 2018] WPP's Sorrell Says Publicis-Omnicom Group Doesn't Stand a Chance Against Facebook, *Business Insider* [Online] http://www.businessinsider.com/sorrell-pog-cant-compete-with-facebook-2013-10

The Fournaise (2012) [accessed 18 June 2018] 80% of CEOs Do Not Really Trust Marketers (Except If They Are 'ROI Marketers®', *The Fournaise Marketing Group* [Online] https://www.fournaisegroup.com/ceos-do-not-trust-marketers/

The Marketer (2007) Marketing masters: tips from the top, *The Marketer*, 35, May, pp 30–31

Thomson, B (2016) [accessed 18 June 2018] Take a Tip from Bezos: Customers Always Need a Seat at the Table, *Entrepreneur* [Online] https://www.entrepreneur.com/article/234254

Tobak, S (2017) [accessed 18 June 2018] 3 Lessons From Pepsi's Controversial Kendall Jenner Protest Ad, *Entrepreneur* [Online] https://www.entrepreneur.com/article/292538

Ulloa, B F L, Møller, V and Sousa-Poza, A (2013) How does subjective well-being evolve with age? A literature review, *Journal of Population Ageing*, 6, pp 227–46

Unilever (2009) [accessed 18 June 2018] Unilever 2008 Full Year and Q4 Results, *Unilever* [Online] https://www.unilever.com/Images/ir-q4-2008-ir-speech-final_tcm244-421358_en.pdf

Viki, T (2016) [accessed 18 June 2018] Why R&D Spending is Not a Measure of Innovation, *Forbes* [Online] https://www.forbes.com/sites/tendayiviki/2016/08/21/why-rd-spending-is-not-a-measure-of-innovation/#109b746ec77d

Vincent, A (2017) [accessed 18 June 2018] Fyre Festival: How the Disaster Unfolded and Why Bahamas Officials Have the Site on Lockdown, *The Telegraph* [Online] http://www.telegraph.co.uk/music/news/fyre-festival-disaster-unfolded-bahamas-officials-have-site/

Vivas, A B, Marful, A, Panagiotidou, D and Bajo, T (2016) Instruction to forget lead to emotional devaluation, *Cognition*, 150, pp 85–91

Vizard, S (2016) [accessed 18 June 2018] Sir Martin Sorrell: 'Brands Are Starting To Question If They Have Overinvested in Digital', *Marketing Week* [Online] https://www.marketingweek.com/2016/08/24/sir-martin-sorrell-brands-are-starting-to-question-if-they-have-over-invested-in-digital/

Vranica, S (2017) [accessed 18 June 2018] Average Tenure of CMO Continues To Decline, *Wall Street Journal* [Online] https://www.wsj.com/articles/average-tenure-of-cmo-continues-to-decline-1489777765

Welch, G (2013) [accessed 18 June 2018] Serving on a Corporate Board?, *Adage* [Online] http://adage.com/article/cmo-strategy/marketers-positions-a-corporate-board/244763/

Whitler, K A (2015) [accessed 18 June 2018] Are Today's Marketers Tomorrow's CEOs?, *Forbes* [Online] https://www.forbes.com/sites/kimberlywhitler/2015/02/05/why-todays-marketers-are-tomorrows-ceos/2/#55dfc2aa259a

Windels, J (2016) [accessed 18 June 2018] Millennials and Marketing: Why Brands are Getting it So, So Wrong, *Social Media Week* [Online] https://socialmediaweek.org/blog/2016/03/millennials-marketing-why-brands-are-getting-it-so-so-wrong/

Winfrey, G (2014) [accessed 18 June 2018] Peter Diamandis: Want to Be a Billionaire? Solve a Billion-Person Problem, *INC.COM* [Online] https://www.inc.com/graham-winfrey/peter-diamandis-billion-dollar-problems.html

World Economic Forum (2016) [accessed 18 June 2018] What Are the 21st-Century Skills Every Student Needs?, *World Economic Forum* [Online] https://www.weforum.org/agenda/2016/03/21st-century-skills-future-jobs-students/

Neuroscience skills

Marketing and the human brain

CHAPTER LEARNING OBJECTIVES

After studying this chapter, you will be able to:

- Understand the shortcomings of the traditional marketing research methods involving self-reporting.
- Appreciate the importance of brain science for understanding consumer behaviour.
- Recognize the significance of emotions in decision making.
- Identify the main neuromarketing tools available to advanced marketing managers, as well as their advantages and disadvantages.
- Realize the proven effectiveness of brain-based marketing.
- Acknowledge the challenges and controversy associated with neuromarketing today.
- Understand the ethical concerns of applying neuroscience to marketing research.

Advanced practice

It's time for... NeuroWine!

How do winemakers decide on the best blend of grape varieties for a new wine? Traditionally, this was a straightforward process. The winemaker, sometimes with the help of winemaking experts, tried several varieties and combinations, and decided on the new blend based on experience, knowledge and intentions. This process, while logical, is highly flawed. This is because our ability as human beings to report reliably on what we think, feel and do is very limited. To get the right answers we need to go deeper – and going deeper gave birth to the world's first NeuroWine!

Pieter H Walser, a winemaker from South Africa mostly known for the BLANKBottle label, partnered with neuromarketing consulting Neural Sense to create a new blend. In the process, they tested 21 different white wines and 20 red wines from across the country. To identify the best combination of varieties and unlock the optimal new taste, the wine producer together with the marketing consultant applied methods that are normally associated with the health sector rather than with product research. Electroencephalogram (EEG), emotional facial recognition and eye tracking are methods sounding too alien for business – for the simple reason that they originate in very different scientific fields. However, their value for marketing research is increasing drastically, allowing even winemakers to test their new wines.

Through EEG, which records the brain's electrical activity on the top of the skull, and other techniques, Walser and his partners determined which blend of varieties, which bottle and label design made the brain happier. Happier brain equals happier customer and thus one red wine and one white of NeuroWine were born. The main problem of the traditional approach, Walser admitted, was the biases he carried with him when trying the wines himself. His extensive experience and already-formed opinions of both varieties and vineyards could interfere and alter the test results. To avoid that he went directly to the brain.

'Our job as neuroscientists and neuromarketers is to build an understanding of how people experience things… Using neuromarketing techniques and technologies, we are able to explore the subconscious and the underlying emotional drivers that drive decision making', explained Mark Dummond from Neural Sense.

Asking people to evaluate marketing stimuli (for example an online ad, a promotional price or new packaging) based on their opinion is not reliable any more. There is too much at risk for marketers to take important decisions just by trusting people's ability to reflect accurately on their experiences. So, who is to tell if a new wine tastes great? Wine producers, experienced sommeliers or the final customer? What is the best way to harvest the right opinions from the right people? Until recently, the answer would be quantitative and qualitative marketing research. Today, the correct answer is neuroscience.

SOURCE Neural Sense (2016)

The marketing challenge

The most powerful notion in marketing is that everything should start from and end with the customer. The fundamental idea that everything that a company offers should be seen from the eyes of the customer is what makes marketing so different, concrete and important. Customer-centricity, apart from being at the heart of marketing philosophy for decades, has recently become very popular in companies around the world. Having a customer-centricity value is a necessary condition in many 'corporate values' exercises in modern corporations. Being customer-centric, though, requires businesses to understand extensively how customers take decisions and behave in the marketplace. Without this deep understanding, marketing actions will be perpetually misguided and will ultimately misfire.

Exploring customers' needs and wants, attitudes and opinions, satisfaction and intentions is the main job of marketing research. In typically five steps, marketers were trained to go from defining the decision-making challenge to delivering the cutting-edge insights for their brands. These steps are (Malhotra and Birks, 2003):

1 problem definition;

2 research design developed;

3 data collection;

4 data analysis;

5 report presentation.

In the all-important third step, data collection, the main options for marketers were quantitative and qualitative research. Briefly, the former is about collecting numbers; the second is about collecting text. In both cases, though, the source of data is people responding consciously on the tasks they are asked to perform. Here is the challenge: can we trust people's self-reflection?

Traditional marketing research examples

Quantitative question on a 5-point scale – survey

Overall, how satisfied are you with doing business with [company]?

1 Very Dissatisfied

2 Somewhat Dissatisfied

3 Average/Neither

4 Somewhat Satisfied

5 Very Satisfied

Qualitative interview question – individual or focus group

Can you please describe what doing business with [company] feels like? Please use examples to illustrate your points whenever possible.

In both cases, regardless of the method to produce numbers or text as data, results represent the respondent's conscious, or self-reflective, opinion. In order to use those results to produce insights and inform brand decisions, we need to trust that the respondents gave an answer that depicts accurately what happens in their brain. This assumption – that people are the right representatives of their own brain – underlined most, if not all, marketing research efforts to help marketers make good decisions. If people said so (ticking a box or talking about it) then it must be how it is.

This challenge is not just faced by marketers. Psychologists are also questioning the value of self-reflection when building their models of human cognition and behaviour. The most extreme, and maybe brutally realistic, view is that of Robert Trivers, the prominent US evolutionary biologist and sociobiologist, Professor of Anthropology and Biological Sciences at Rutgers University. His aversion to self-reflection techniques and thus for most of model development in psychology can be clearly seen in the following statement in an interview with the magazine *Psychology Today*:

Robert Trivers on self-reflection in psychology

'You cannot build up a science based on a whole series of correlations between how people answer questionnaires. By definition it cannot work, if only because we don't know most of what is causing us to do things, and second, we don't necessarily tell the truth.'

SOURCE Hutson (2016)

Regardless of how controversial this statement is for many psychologists, it engulfs the key concern with using people's conscious responses to our questions for building models of human inner existence and behaviour.

But today, with the advancements in neuroscience and other behavioural sciences, we don't have to rely solely on self-reporting to get the answers we need. In Advanced Marketing Management, the customer's self-reflective opinions are accompanied, or even replaced, with reading directly the brain or the involuntary (non-controlled) physical reactions to marketing stimuli. For advanced marketing managers, the source of data for informing brand decisions is not customers but their brains!

The significance of this point for marketers is explicitly pointed out by applied neuromarketer Patrick Renvoise in his famous TEDxBend speech on neuromarketing titled, 'Is there a buy button inside the brain?'

Patrick Renvoise on self-reflection in marketing

'Neuromarketing started because marketing does not work. Why?… In traditional marketing we take consumers and ask them what they want… Do you know what is the problem with their response? Guess what! They don't know what they want! Instead, in neuromarketing, what we are going to do is this: we are going to ask them what they want but we are not going to trust their answer because we know they don't know. Instead, we are going to look at various physiological changes that happen in their body when we ask them this.'

SOURCE Renvoise (2013). Reproduced with permission from SalesBrain LLC. Copyright SalesBrain 2002–17

The motivation behind trying new and better ways to understand customers, and thus fulfil better the key marketing requirement of customer-centricity, is simpler than it looks. As Renvoise highlights, it is the failure of traditional approaches that pushes marketers to constantly search for more effective methods and techniques. In addition to marketing peculiarities mentioned in Chapter 1, consider the rate of failure in new products. Although the often mentioned 80 per cent failure rate has been found to be an urban myth, the rate is still approximately one failed new product out of two (Castellion and Markham, 2013). This rate, though, accounts only for the products that failed completely and were discontinued. What about those that failed to achieve the intended goals and had to change or 'pivot'? Counting them in increases the rate drastically. Furthermore, different industries experience different rates. For example, in the high-volatile start-up arena the failure rate is found by Harvard Business School's Shikhar Ghosh to be 75 per cent (Black, 2013). So, three out of four start-ups fail in the marketplace! The same failure rate was reported by the Fournaise Marketing Group when surveying marketing executives in 2014 in the UK: 75 per cent of marketing strategies and ad campaigns underperformed and failed to meet management expectations on sales, market share, conversion rate etc (Fournaise Group, 2015).

When something is broken it needs to be fixed – and fixing marketing starts from diving deeper into the customer brain.

The brain über alles

The fact is that people are not aware of what is actually happening inside their brain and they unintentionally report a completely different reality than the one in their inner world when asked about it. This fact is really what makes neuroscience inevitable for marketers. If people are actually unaware of the inner working of their brain and body, and if these inner workings are better predictors of behaviour, then how can marketing continue without brain science?

The proof

Back in the 1970s, psychologists Dutton and Aaron published what is now known as the Capilano Suspension Bridge Experiment (Dutton and Aaron, 1974). The researchers exposed a group of young men to an attractive female researcher conducting a survey (the survey itself was irrelevant/neutral to the main focus of the study). They wanted to investigate how many would call the female researcher back after the experiment, since the female researcher provided them with her personal phone number (for any potential questions after the experiment). One group met the female researcher in the middle of an unstable suspension bridge and the other on stable ground. Results? Those on the suspension bridge called the female researcher more than those on the ground. The group on the unstable bridge misinterpreted their feelings of arousal and excitement to attractiveness towards the female researcher rather than their fear of falling. The emotion was fear but their response was attraction.

There is a disconnection between brain reactions and conscious understanding and self-reflection. The Capilano Suspension Bridge Experiment gave very strong indications about the gap between real emotions and perception of emotions. In other words, it was the foundation for differentiating concrete emotions, as altered states in affective neural networks in our brain, and their subjective interpretation by the individual, which we call feelings. With neuroscience, marketers can bypass a customer's biased interpretation and see directly the 'raw data' from the brain. In essence, customer neuroscience is an attempt to become more objective in marketing research by avoiding subjective interferences by the respondent. The closer we get to the source (ie the brain) the closer we can get to reality!

Our own experience early on in our involvement with brain sciences confirmed this in the most impressive way, when one of us was involved in a research initiative by a bank in south-east Europe. The bank wanted to introduce a new credit card to clients of competing banks and ordered a large-scale qualitative research project in the region. Numerous focus groups were conducted to reveal the main insight for the bank's marketing team: what information potential clients would like to receive in order to take a new card from a new bank. All focus group participants were heavy credit-card users. The bank was confident it had developed an irresistible offer that heavy card users would find it difficult to refuse once it hit the market.

Seemingly, there is nothing more natural, sincere and transparent than asking adults with healthy brains what they would like to know when approached with a new offer. 'What would you like to know if a bank you do not do business with approached you with a new credit card offer?' was the key question in the focus groups. The marketing team expected to get the decision-making criteria by which clients choose between offers and then use this insight to formulate their offer in the best possible way to achieve maximum attention. People replied, openly and directly. The vast majority of them said *interest rates* followed by other financial information such as fees, grace period, other costs etc. Logical? Yes. Real? No! Being aware of the hidden forces that actually shape customer behaviour we added one more question to the discussion: 'What was the interest rate last month on the credit card you are using the most?' No one knew. Probed for explanation, the conversation almost miraculously shifted away from numbers into habits and trust.

The risk for the new credit card to fail if the marketing team based the campaign launch on interest rates and other numbers, because of what was first said in the focus groups, was huge. How could customers ever compare reliably the new and shiny interest rate if they did not know the one they pay for their current card? Would they dismiss the information altogether or would they refer to some outdated or fictitious interest rate that their brain used as an anchor price? In both cases the risk was too high. By digging deeper, we went beyond the obvious knee-jerk response (which focused on numbers) and uncovered that what looked like a rational decision was actually an emotional and/or behavioural one.

Customers will always try to respond to a question with what comes into their minds. The issue, though, is if what comes into their minds is what physically happens in their brains. Trusting the brain more than the individual is the main imperative of neuromarketing.

Emotions versus rationality?

Acceptance of a more emotionally driven decision-making process in the human brain is becoming mainstream. The old dilemma of emotion versus rationality is becoming obsolete. This is because our brain is always emotionally on, and this is for a good reason: to be able to take a decision. 'Scientists used to assume that emotion and rationality were opposed to each other, but Antonio Damasio, now Professor of Neuroscience at the University of Southern California, has found that people who lose the ability to perceive or experience emotions as the result of a brain injury find it hard or impossible to make any decisions at all. They can't shop' (The Economist, 2008). The old perception of an emotional decision as an a priori bad decision is now replaced with the more scientifically accurate perception of no emotion, no decision. So simple... and so profound.

Above all, studying the human brain in a marketing context comes to solve a long-lasting embarrassing confession by earlier marketers about marketing's inability to grasp the depths of human experience: the so-called customers' 'Black Box' (Kotler and Armstrong, 2012). Consumer behaviour literature was unapologetically admitting that, as marketers, there are some things we can do to affect buying behaviour (marketing stimuli such as products, prices, places and promotions) and some things we cannot do or control ourselves (environmental stimuli such as politics, tech trends, the economy, legislation, social factors and our competitors). All these controlled and uncontrolled factors are the inputs to customers to take decisions. At the same time, as marketers, we can observe the output of the process – the actual customer decisions and behaviours concerning what they buy, when they buy, how they buy, from where they buy, how much they buy, in what prices they buy and what they do next. Between the inputs and the outputs we could only observe generic decision steps, possible roles and customer characteristics BUT not the 'magic moment' of the actual decision and how it was really taken. These big unknowns constituted the core of the Black Box that marketers could influence (Table 2.1); they could observe its outputs but could not pick into it and comprehend it in depth.

Table 2.1 The customer's Black Box process

Input	Inner Workings	Ouput
Marketing stimuli	Decision-making process	Customer decisions
Environmental stimuli	Customer roles and characteristics	Customer behaviours

Well, neuroscience is opening the Black Box for the first time in marketing history, allowing marketers to look inside and make better decisions about their brands and activities. They do not have to take decisions in the dark any more!

The inability to look into the Black Box of human behaviour brought the inevitable urge to decode humans theoretically and not empirically. This meant that various philosophers, economists and psychologists adopted an artificial view of why and how humans behave, based on their own biases and wishes. The model dominating the world since the 18th century is this of the so-called *Homo economicus*. This theoretical, even dogmatic, approach to human nature focuses solely on personal interests rather on communities or the multidimensional relations within societies. *Homo economicus* is an ultra-individualistic view of humanity, dismissive of any emotional or social dimensions, which considers as natural law the ultimate self-interest of one person, leading to an ultra-egocentric model of decision making (Pesch, 2002). The model takes for granted that individuals have a 'knowing mind' and that they can freely access (Uhl-Bien, 2006) and control (Dachler and Hosking, 1995) the contents of their mind. Deriving from neoclassical economics and characterized by an extreme obsession for rational decision making (always aiming to maximize results and minimize costs), the *Homo economicus* is finally subsiding: *Homo reciprocans*, *Homo sociologicus* and *Homo socioeconomicus* are new models replacing *Homo economicus* by trying to understand better the complex inner workings of our brain that actually shape our decisions and behaviours (O'Boyle, 2007).

Dethroning *Homo economicus*

The Black Box and *Homo economicus* were just different sides of the same coin. Ignorance of brain functionality leads to dogmatic and unrealistic views on what drives human behaviour. Opening the Black Box unescapably dethrones *Homo economicus* as the working model of human understanding.

Table 2.2 offers a curated list of interesting, useful and relevant brain facts for advanced marketing managers:

Table 2.2　Brain facts for advanced marketers

Brain Fact	Advanced Marketing Management Insight
The brain is the most energy-devouring organ we have. It represents only 2% of our total body mass but consumes 20% of our total body energy.	Easy does it! Don't be demanding on how much energy your customers' brains need to spend for doing what you want them to do. Their brains will reject you or hate you – unless they are utterly passionate about your brand.
From all brain activity, 90% (at least) goes for processes that run in the **unconscious.** People are dimly aware of what drives their behaviour. Most of our explanations are post-justifications or post-rationalizations.	Although people will explain in detail why and how they do things, what they want and how they feel about your brand, most of it cannot be trusted or used. To understand people, you need to go deeper.
All decisions are **emotional.** Emotions form the bedrock of all decision making in healthy human brains. Rationality is added later to check if the already-taken decision is socially appropriate.	Always consider the emotional background in which your customers take decisions, behave and interact with you. Every decision is rooted in the mood that precedes it.

(continued)

Table 2.2 (*Continued*)

Brain Fact	Advanced Marketing Management Insight
There are no good and bad emotions. All emotions have evolved to play important roles. Both negative and positive emotions are great **motivators** – negative emotions even more than positive ones.	Do not fall into the trap of the eternal sunshine of the happy brand. Negative emotions are great motivators and should be used strategically to drive the customer towards your brand as the ultimate solution to their problems. Positive emotions are always the goal; the road, though, can include negative emotions too.
Memories and emotions are deeply connected. The more emotional the moment the more it is engraved in memory. Actually, this is how the brain assigns value to memories; through emotions.	The era of fake and one-size-fits-all emotions is over. Brands need to get closer to their customers and create meaningful memories through solid and true emotions. Connecting with them through generic photos from databases is just not good enough any more.
Tangible always beats abstract. The brain has evolved through millennia by interacting with the physical world around us. 'What you see is what you get' is its tagline.	Never underestimate – just because of digital living – the power of influence that the physical world has over your customers' brains. Also, prove your claim directly, transparently and with concrete evidence. Not with blah-blah and wishful thinking.
Trust is a chemical in the brain and it is called oxytocin. Oxytocin regulates social behaviour and relationships through trust and morality.	Loyalty is NOT about loyalty programmes. It is about making sure a lot of oxytocin is produced in your customers' brains in every brand touchpoint. Erasing elements that cause concern, disbelief and even aggression in your customers' brains allows for more oxytocin and thus for more trust and loyalty.
Habits are the bread and butter of the brain's functionality since they save precious energy and create stronger neural connections. They are difficult to break because the brain loves them!	If you are a challenger brand, trying to break habits, you need to be bold and to follow closely all the insights mentioned above. If you are a leading brand, trying to retain habits, make sure you do not break the trust by doing something arrogant or threatening to your customers.
Our brain is a **social** organ. It has developed to exist within groups, tribes and societies. The latest approaches to consciousness suggest that we are conscious not for decision making (since decisions are taken deeper in the brain) but making sure our actions fit our social needs and goals.	Being social is bigger than just being present on social media. Are you a brand that people would love to socialize with? Do your customers' brains consider your brand as capable of forming social relations or are you categorized as just another profit-seeking business? How does your brand help your customers meet their social needs and goals?

SOURCE Adapted from Dimitriadis and Psychogios (2016)

The way of the brain

'Our brains underlie everything we do – from waking up in the morning to navigating the physical, social and emotional shoals of the day, to falling asleep, perchance to dream. Collectively, our brains organize enterprises and societies. But the fact that the brain is extraordinarily complicated does not imply that it is forever incomprehensible' (Kosslyn and Miller, 2013). All your customers' thoughts, emotions and behaviours are rooted in their brains. All their choices, frustrations, loyalties and habits live there. No modern marketer can afford to ignore what the brain says!

Why do we have a brain? This is one of our favourite questions when we address audiences in class and in the boardroom alike. Interestingly and predictably enough, the most popular answer is: to think! This could not be further from the truth. Our brain is there to help us survive and thrive. Thinking is just one of the tools it has to achieve its goals. Neuroscientifically speaking, it is not the most important one! The quicker that marketers realize this the better. However, this realization makes our work as marketers much more complex, dynamic and exciting than ever before. Do not let your thinking brain degrade our emotional and habitual processes as 'easy' – as they are highly intelligent and are difficult to address in an effective way.

The methods

The brain's importance in customer behaviour is not debatable any more. What is still very debatable though is the ways, in terms of technologies and methods, by which marketers listen to the brain. Is there a secure and agreed-by-all method to observe the brain and the human body in order to take the best brand decisions possible?

The battle of the two Ranas

In the fast-paced world of start-ups, two attracted a lot of attention concerning capturing brain and body reactions from customers. By a fantastic coincidence both of them are run by females bearing the same name: Rana! The first is Rana June, a former professional DJ and founder of Lightwave (www.lightwave.io), a company that utilizes biometric data taken in real time from people wearing a special wristband with sensors in events such as sports games, corporate-sponsored parties and even at the cinema. Their customers include Pepsi, Google and Jaguar. The second is Rana el Kaliouby, the co-founder of Affectiva (www.affectiva.com), a company specializing in emotional facial recognition, with clients such as Coca-Cola, MARS and CBS. Affectiva mentions on its official website that it has scanned more than 4 million faces by the end of January 2017. Both companies operate in what has been labelled as the 'emotion economy'. This is the emerging and fast-developing industry of technology helping us to decode the emotional and mental states of our customers.

Regardless of which Rana will finally win the race of better emotional understanding, marketing has already won! The era of corporate emotional blindness is over and the future of the field seems to be very exciting indeed!

SOURCE Foster (2016)

As illustrated in the battle of the two Ranas, there is a feverish and global race of who will develop the best technology to peer into customers', voters' and citizens' brains faster and more effectively. Developments in this field are astounding. As announced by BBC News in May 2015, there was an impressive 'surge in US "brain-reading" patents' (BBC News, 2015). The trend is unmistakable. In 2014, 1,600 patents concerning brain-reading technology were filed in the United States alone. In comparison, less than 400 such patents had been filed per year between 2000 and 2009. Since 2010, though, applications have doubled. The two companies with the most applications in 2014 were Nielsen and Microsoft.

This is the golden era of neurotechnology. Apart from patents the trend can also be seen in science and technology festivals around the world. As reported by online science website PHYS.ORG: 'the next frontier for the tech sector is the human brain... A number of the innovations were on display at the Consumer Electronics Show in Las Vegas, where computer scientists and biomedical experts showcased ways to tap into and use brain signals' (PHYS.ORG, 2016). As reported in the *Wall Street Journal*, major venture capital companies such as Y Combinator, Andreessen Horowitz and Peter Thiel's Founders Fund have taken notice and invested heavily into ventures focusing in understanding and altering the human brain (Dwoskin, 2016). Technology, industry and funding come together to engage in what can be characterized as a unique moment in human history: putting the brain in focus and creating new ways of getting the, until recently, hidden information from inside our heads.

Regardless of whether they are called neuromarketing, consumer neurosciences, neurofeedback or biometrics methods, the technologies described below form the main toolbox of advanced marketers for non-self-reporting research. Each method is briefly explained, accompanied by key advantages and disadvantages for helping advanced marketers decide when and how to use them. This section is mainly based on a more detailed explanation of the technologies provided in Gorgiev and Dimitriadis (2015) and Bridger (2015), as well as on our practical experience with the tools.

EEG (electroencephalography) Measures the electrical activity of the brain through electrodes placed on the scalp of the subjects in the form of a cap. The signals from the electrodes pass through an electric amplifier into the computer for recording and analysing. This tool allows us to identify attention, emotional engagement, emotional valence and intensity, consumer motivation for product/brand and cognitive load.

Table 2.3 Advantages and disadvantages of EEG

Advantages	Disadvantages
– Ability to monitor emotional reactions to marketing stimuli in real time – Ability to combine with other technologies such as eye tracking – Wireless EEG devices can be used in real retail and other business environments – Reasonable cost – Variety of measurements	– Poor spatial resolution; it can only identify activity occurring close to the scalp and not deeper in the brain – Possible interference of other sources of electrical activity – Possible interference of irrelevant muscle activity that result in electrical activity in the brain (eg blinking)

fMRI (functional magnetic resonance imaging) Measures the change in the blood flow in the brain, which indicates the activity taking place in certain areas of the brain. This tool can help gain insight into memory, perception, preference, decision-making, propensity to action, sensory processing, language processing, emotion processing.

Table 2.4 Advantages and disadvantages of fMRI

Advantages	Disadvantages
– Excellent spatial resolution; very specific activities can be recorded, even in the deep areas of the brain – High acceptance by the scientific community worldwide	– Very expensive – Restricted accessibility to fMRI machines for most marketers – Poor time resolution; each picture of the brain is taken over the course of four to six seconds, thus the brief activities in the brain might pass unidentified – Unpleasant user experience; subjects are placed in a chamber, which can feel claustrophobic, and have to be very still during measurement

Eye tracking This technology allows us to measure eye activity such as eye fixation, pattern of eye movement, blinking rate and pupil dilations. The most popular measures with eye tracking are fixation points, time to first fixation, total time of fixation, order of fixation points. These measures can indicate focus, interest and attentional patterns. Researchers typically deliver results in the form of heat maps and gaze plots. Eye-tracking technology can be in the form of a fixed infrared camera placed in front of a screen, eyeglasses that participants can wear in real environments, and even a webcam.

Table 2.5 Advantages and disadvantages of eye tracking

Advantages	Disadvantages
– Comparably cheap – Comfortable for participants – With glasses, research can take place in real environments – With webcam, very large samples can be reached – Results can be quickly generated and easily understood	– It does not easily reveal the emotions behind certain eye movements (eg it can show where someone's gaze is focused, but not why) – Webcam is currently less accurate than the other two eye-tracking technologies (glasses and bar camera)

Emotional facial recognition Facial expressions representing six core emotions (happiness, surprise, sadness, fear, disgust, anger) are found to be universal across cultures. Therefore, based on interpretation of involuntary and voluntary facial muscle movement, different emotions can be observed as a reaction to marketing stimuli. This interpretation is nowadays typically performed by sophisticated computer software.

Table 2.6   Advantages and disadvantages of emotional facial recognition

Advantages	Disadvantages
– No special hardware required – It can be performed using HD camera from any possible device (laptop, mobile, tablets, TVs, even ATMs) – Results can be quickly generated and easily understood – Large samples can be reached – Comparatively cost effective	– Limited range of results, usually basic emotions and engagement – There is a chance that consumers can fake certain expressions and hide their real feelings – Facial features such as a beard or glasses can alter results – Generates probabilistic results (the possibility that an emotion is present)

Emotion voice recognition This technology is looking for changes in people's uttered speech when they talk about a marketing activity or element. It detects vocal micro-frequencies, prosodic cues (rhythm, loudness, pitch, pause and others), actual words spoken and intensity of speech to reveal emotions and attitudes.

Table 2.7   Advantages and disadvantages of emotion voice recognition

Advantages	Disadvantages
– Can be done remotely (online or by phone) – Big samples can be utilized simultaneously – No need for equipment purchase (licensed software) – Variety of results (exact emotions, moods, decision-making cues) – Cost effective	– Not all emotions are always detected with the same accuracy – Results can contradict other methods such as EEG – Some of the variables can carry cultural biases – Some tools offer analysis per few seconds, not per milliseconds, so if more than one person is speaking it is challenging to allocate results to one individual.

Biometrics These include measures of the nonconscious responses of the body such as heart rate, respiratory rate and skin conductance, which can indicate intensity of reaction to marketing stimuli (arousal) as well as primal emotional reactions such as: transfixion, fight or flight responses, fear, nervousness, stress and relief.

Table 2.8 Advantages and disadvantages of biometrics

Advantages	Disadvantages
– Comparatively cheap	– Not appropriate for measuring specific emotions
– Results can be quickly generated and easily understood	– Low diversity of results
– Can be easily combined with other measures	– Cannot easily reveal by themselves the reasons or sources of the response
– Wireless devices can trace biometrics in real situations and environments	– Humidity and other environmental conditions can affect results of skin conductance
– Wide acceptance by the public due to popularity of commercially available wearables providing fitness and bio data	– Responses can delay, so matching stimuli with the right reading is crucial

Implicit response tests These are typically computer tests that provide measures of unconscious impact of a marketing output (eg ad, brand). The more the participants have been primed for a certain concept, the faster they will react to something they implicitly associate with that concept when they are exposed to it on a screen.

Table 2.9 Advantages and disadvantages of implicit response tests

Advantages	Disadvantages
– Very fast and cost effective	– Potential difficulties when comparing results across cultures, since words used can have different meanings
– Can run remotely (online)	
– Big samples can be obtained	– Age affects speed of response
– Very suitable for brand associations studies	– Some participants can consciously alter their responses
	– The order of shown associations can influence results

Results and controversy

Marketers are not short of options when it comes to tools for reading the customer's brain and understanding better cognition, emotions and behaviour. As with almost everything in business, though, results will determine the ultimate usefulness and success of those tools with marketers. Does it work?

Traditional versus neuro... or New Coke revisited

One of the most famous cases in marketing – and in business in general – is the introduction of New Coke by the Coca-Cola Company back in 1985. As Coke explains in its own take on the case, the pressure from a slowing demand for 15 years, together with a decrease in customer preference and in awareness of the brand, led the company to decide to change the original Coca-Cola recipe, name and design, introducing New Coke. Before doing that, they conducted extensive consumer research involving 200,000 people, testing the new formula (Coca-Cola Company, 2012). Those tests were focusing on taste, downgrading the impact of the brand: consumers were to try Cola drinks while being blindfolded. Based on taste results alone Coke decided to introduce New Coke by retrieving 'old Coke' from the market. The hostile reaction by both consumers and channel partners pushed Coke to reintroduce the original Cola after just 79 days. Could Coke have taken a different decision if neurofeedback methods were available then?

Neuroscientist Samuel McClure and his colleagues conducted a, now classic, study published in 2004 trying to answer the question above (McClure *et al*, 2004). They gave to 67 individuals Coke and Pepsi, labelled and unlabelled, while measuring brain activity within an fMRI machine. While they found no significant difference on how people's brain responded while drinking Pepsi with or without viewing first a Pepsi image, the difference with Coke was substantial. Results indicated that there are different brain areas involved when people drink Coke in an 'anonymous' setting or while viewing the brand. In the first case, the ventromedial prefrontal cortex (VMPFC) was highly activated. This part of the brain, according to the authors of the paper, 'is strongly implicated in signalling basic appetitive aspects of reward'. This means taste rules when not viewing labels. In the second case, great brain activity was shown in the dorsolateral prefrontal context (DLPFC), the hippocampus and the midbrain. The first two are strongly associated with 'modifying behaviour based on emotion and affect' and 'the DLPFC is commonly implicated in aspects of cognitive control, including working memory'. This means that logos and brand names carry cultural value within our brains, but not all an equal one. Activating different brain regions will lead to different customer decisions and behaviour.

By conducting neuro or bio feedback studies, marketers can decrease the risk of taking a wrong decision, or strengthen their confidence when a decision is found to be robust.

The neuromarketing industry is fast in promoting impressive results through official company websites, case studies, presentations in industry conventions, blogs etc. One of the most impressive claims to date was made by Nielsen Consumer Neuroscience in June 2016: 77 per cent of in-market purchase behaviour was explained by using a combination of neuromarketing tools (Nielsen, 2016). This is a breakthrough in consumer behaviour – and in marketing in general – since it means that 77 per cent of the Black Box is now a transparent box... at least for the experimental setting of this study. Nielsen used a complex methodology, including neuromarketing methods, such as EEG, biometrics and emotional facial recognition, ad exposure and actual sales. In a five-month study Nielsen Consumer Neuroscience and Nielsen Catalina Solutions unit used 60 video advertisements from a variety of packaged consumer goods in order to examine which neuromarketing methods would explain more accurately the actual sales in the market after the ads were aired. The sample was expansive: more than 4 million cable set-top-box households and retail purchase behaviour from more than 90 million households. Separate consumer neuroscience methods did from poorly (9 per cent emotional facial recognition alone) to fairly well (62 per cent EEG alone). But when combined, the results sky-rocketed to 77 per cent.

Nielsen on neuromarketing effectiveness

As highlighted by Dr Carl Marci, Chief Neuroscientist at Nielsen Consumer Neuroscience: We believe this is the holy grail for marketers: confidence in knowing creative's potential impact on the bottom line – before it ever enters the market. However, not all neuroscience measures are created equal. We've learnt that only a few key combinations have the predictive power for in-market sales' (Nielsen, 2016).

An academic study, which is now classic, showcasing the high predictability of consumer choice when applying neuroscientific methods is the one by Paul Glimcher, who is considered a founder of the field of neuroeconomics (de Ternay and Devlin, 2016), and his associates. Glimcher and his team asked people who were placed in an fMRI scan to look at 20 consumer items such as DVDs, CDs, posters and others without expressing any opinion or making any choice (Levy *et al*, 2011). As step two, outside the fMRI the same people had to express their preference when they viewed the same items sorted into pairs. By looking at the automatic/unconscious/unprompted valuation in people's brains while in the fMRI scan, the team could predict up to 83 per cent of the choices people made in step two when those items were sorted in pairs consisting of two items with high valuation difference. The areas of interest in the brain during the test were the medial prefrontal cortex (MPFC) and the striatum. The MPFC is involved in memory consolidation and decision making while the striatum, or striate nucleus, is associated with rewards, motivation and reinforcement. Just looking at something, without having to perform a task, can automatically trigger the brain's valuation system for that item. The fact that the smaller the scanned differences in valuation the lower the predictability, means that brands need to ensure high perceived differentiation through the right positioning strategies if they want their customers' brain to spring into positive action by simply being exposed to the brand.

Another study that demonstrates the value of neuromarketing methods versus self-reporting is the one by the world's leading authority in oxytocin research, Dr Paul Zak and associates. The study was published in 2013 and involved people watching advertisements calling for donation, or public service announcements as they are called (Lin *et al*, 2013). In the first experiment in this study, researchers discovered that people who received oxytocin donated 56 per cent more money after watching the ads than those who received a placebo. This in itself is a very significant finding since it draws a strong link between brain chemical changes and behavioural responses to advertising messages. In the second experiment, researchers found that, in a separate sample of participants who did not receive any external chemical, people donating more were the ones with the highest endogenous spike of the adrenocorticotropin hormone and of oxytocin in their blood after watching the ads. This suggests that in order for an advertisement to induce a behavioural change, people's brain physiology has to change. Interestingly enough, the study found that in the self-reporting phase of the second experiment there were no conclusive connections found. The researchers concluded that (Lin *et al*, 2013): 'The AIDA model is typically tested using self-reports and the findings here suggest this may be inappropriate because the brain mechanisms producing attention and action... occur largely outside of one's conscious awareness. Indeed, people often are unable and inconsistent in articulating why they are doing what they are doing.'

Such numbers cannot be ignored: 77 per cent predictability of ads on retail purchasing behaviour, 83 per cent predictability of consumer choice based on the brain's automatic valuation system, 57 per cent increase in donation because of externally received oxytocin, and a notable difference between self-reporting and bio-feedback measures in explaining generosity-related behaviour – and these are only a few selected studies on the topic. In our own experience with using such tools, results can be even more impressive. There is a clear indication of the urgent need for adopting new research methods that are available, tested and proven. Everything else is an excuse.

Traditional marketing backfires!

Not using neuromarketing tools to understand better the customer brain can lead to wrong decision making and, most importantly, to producing opposite results than those expected. The following examples showcase the high risk of using old marketing thinking and ignoring neuroscience:

Study 1: in an fMRI study, conducted in 2006, on the impact that anti-smoking messages – printed on packaging – have on smokers' brains, marketing guru Martin Lindstrom found that such messages had the opposite effect. *Smoking Kills* messages, instead of stimulating the amygdala (our fear centre) in smokers' brains, 'stimulated the nucleus accumbens, sometimes called the "craving spot", which lights up on fMRI whenever a person craves something, whether it is alcohol, drugs, tobacco or gambling… they appear to work mainly as a marketing tool to keep smokers smoking' (Lindstrom, 2008).

Study 2: another public service campaign that seems to backfire is Drug Abuse Restriction Education (DARE) in the United States. DARE was created by the Los Angeles Police Department in 1983 and involved police officers in uniform visiting schools to convince students not to use illegal drugs and other harmful substances. As a report in *Scientific American* claimed, DARE might backfire. A 2002 review found 'a slight tendency for teens who went through DARE to be more likely to drink and smoke than adolescents not exposed to the programme. Small negative effects for DARE-like programmes on drinking and smoking were also reported in a 2009 study (Lilienfeld and Arkowitz, 2014).

Study 3: a third study, this time by persuasion guru Robert B Cialdini and associates, found out a similar backfiring effect of specific messaging on people's behaviour, but this time a much more drastic one. Trying to convince people not to steal pieces from a petrified forest in Arizona, researchers tested different types of messages. Their findings suggest that, apart from the fact that some messages work better than others, some messages can seriously backfire: 'Compared with a no-sign controlled condition, in which 2.92 per cent of the pieces were stolen, the negative social proof message resulted in *more* theft (7.92 per cent). In essence, it almost tripled theft. This was not a crime prevention strategy; it was a *crime promotion strategy*' (Goldstein, Martin and Cialdini, 2008).

These, and other similar studies with such findings, indicate strongly that the traditional process by which marketers decided on marketing initiatives and messages cannot proceed as before. Not applying the latest scientific methods for revealing which parts of the brain are active under which conditions will lead to more mistakes and backfires! Don't use neuro to improve, use it to stop harming your brand!

Such a profound change in marketing thinking and doing could not come about without a certain degree of controversy.

One of the most publicized attacks on neuromarketing was various neuroscientists' negative commentary to Martin Lindstrom's article in the *New York Times*. The article, published online in September 2011, was titled 'You Love Your iPhone. Literally.' – and described a study of 16 people, using an fMRI machine to detect which brain regions were activated when people were exposed, separately, to video and audio of a ringing and vibrating iPhone (Lindstrom, 2011). The first interesting result was that both the audio and the video stimuli, regardless of the fact that they were presented to participants separately, prompted response in both the auditory and visual regions of the brain simultaneously. When you hear your iPhone, you 'see' it with your mind's eye too, and when you see it vibrating, you 'hear' it with your mind's ear as well. The controversial claim, though, was that since those stimuli activated the insular cortex area of the brain, then, Lindstrom stated, you must be loving your phone. This is because, as again he claimed in the article, the insular is associated with the feelings of love and compassion. Neuroscientists were fast in the response to point out that the insular is also associated with negative emotions so no such claim was possible. For example, Russ Poldrack, a neuroscientist at University of Texas, as early as 1 October that year responded online with the emphatic title, 'NYT Op-Ed + fMRI = Complete Crap' (Poldrack, 2011). Poldrack explained that many studies on love recorded no activity in the insular and that in as many as one-third of all neuroimaging studies the insular is found to be firing up.

The insular cortex has been traditionally a great mystery for neuroscience until recently (Blakeslee, 2007). This brain part has emerged as a very interesting and important brain structure that is associated with many fundamental brain functions. The most significant claim is that of Damasio, who suggested that the insular cortex plays a very important role in the formation of feelings and subsequent motivation to act (Damasio, Damasio and Tranel, 2013). Although not even basic feelings can be experienced without its help, the insular is crucial for the higher process of feelings and ultimate decision making. This central role of the insular cortex in sensing what is happening in us and translating this to action is amplified by neuroscientist Arthur D Craig who suggested that the insular cortex is a vital part of our consciousness, since it connects the inside with the outside, controlling functions such as bowel distension, orgasm, cigarette craving, maternal love, decision making, sudden insight and others (Craig, 2009).

Lindstrom seems to have committed the ultimate sin in neuroscience, which is to attribute a specific function to a brain area without considering what this area has also, or even mainly, been associated with, or without submitting a rigorous methodology to convince that his claims are scientifically valid. Although this public debate on neuromarketing and the use of neuroimaging methods in business is healthy and should continue, the lesson learnt for marketers is something else. See box below.

The verdict on 'love' for iPhones?

Our take on the controversy is that we should be very careful with general claims when it comes to relating specific brain regions to functionality, especially when science points otherwise or when we do not have our own robust study to prove it. At the same time though, both neuromarketing enthusiasts and neuromarketing attackers might be missing the point by ignoring the context of the discussion. In this case, the fact that the insular cortex fired when exposed to video and images of iPhones actually creates a series of interesting questions: since the insula is central to forming our subjective feelings and our response decisions it means that the iPhone has a considerable effect on us; an effect that requires response based on an inflow of feelings. It sparks our awareness to life and asks for reaction. Is this based on love, social pressure, pain or disgust? Future research should shed more light on this. However, advanced marketers should take notice that exposure to iPhone stimuli by users does not go unnoticed easily!

Another study that created a buzz about neuromarketing was published in 2015 in the *Journal of Marketing Research*. In that study, led by Vinod Venkatraman of Temple University, researchers examined results from a variety of neurophysiological methods, such as eye tracking, biometrics, EEG and fMRI, and compared them with traditional methods of self-reporting, when respondents were exposed to three-second advertisements (Venkatraman *et al*, 2015). The aim was to see which methods explained better actual demand of products in the market after advertisements aired. The team found out that it was only fMRI measure that did better than traditional self-reporting methods, prompting both positive and negative reactions from the industry. Most notably, prominent neuromarketing blogger Roger Dooley, in a *Forbes* article titled 'Neuromarketing: pseudoscience no more', claimed that because of that study neuromarketers have concrete evidence that, at least, one method works (Dooley, 2015). But what about the others? Does this study disqualify all other methods used in neuromarketing? First, as Dooley himself highlighted, this was indeed good news for consumer neuroscience. Attacks on its trustworthiness should stop due to the fact that it was academically found to work. Furthermore, as we have seen earlier in this chapter, Nielsen found 77 per cent predictability by using a combination of other methods, excluding fMRI, which creates an interesting dynamic for marketers. Since using fMRI can be both time consuming and cost demanding, other methods that are more accessible to marketers can be employed to increase predictability and help testing marketing initiatives. One thing is for sure: the more studies, both academic and from the industry, the better for marketers. Encouraging results are already in.

A very interesting study published in 2015 in the *Journal of Advertising Research* was that of Varan and associates, who tried to find how much different vendors of neuromarketing services agreed on concepts and methods (Varan *et al*, 2015). Results strongly indicated that various neuro vendors explained different concepts, such as attention and emotional engagement, in a different way. At the same time, the methods applied to measure those variables also differed, resulting in different insights when used on the same advertisements. This means that there are significant issues around reliability and validity between different neuroservices vendors. If different neuromarketing agencies understand and measure variables differently how can marketers be sure they get the results they pay for?

The answer, although not easy, lies with advanced practice: marketers should be very thorough when choosing neuroservices vendors, focusing on proven methods, professional background checks, references and testimonials, and on their own educated understanding of the field. Most importantly, differences in measures suggest that marketers should build relationships with neuroservices providers based on results and on long-term collaboration. Changing neuroproviders often will inevitably lead to serious problems with comparison of results since methods used are not identical. Until the neuromarketing industry reaches a level where methods are comparable, then switching costs will be lower for marketers. Currently, the best strategy is for advanced marketers to search relentlessly, choose carefully and stick to their choice in order to utilize methods of a single vendor to the maximum.

Ethics and neuromarketing

The single most popular concern expressed in our neuromarketing speeches and project pitches is ethics. Commonly, people ask: 'Is it right to manipulate people's brains to buy our products?'

Although this particular question reveals more the widespread ignorance of what neuromarketing research is all about, it does reveal a deep worry about applying neuroscientific methods to read people's brains and about how much influence marketers can ultimately have in inducing people's consumer behaviour. In the direction of addressing such issues, the Neuromarketing Science and Business Association (NMSBA) has published a code of conduct on its website for all involved in neuromarketing research to follow. This code consists of 12 articles, briefly summarized below (the whole code can be found at the following link: http://www.nmsba.com/ethics):

Article 1. Core principles: this article refers to applying country-specific research standards, protecting neuromarketing's reputation and delivering exaggeration-free reports and claims to neuroservices clients.

Article 2. Integrity: this article is about not stressing-out, harming, deceiving or selling anything to neuroresearch participants. It also instructs neuromarketers to be clear about their skills and experience.

Article 3. Credibility: this is about sharing with NMSBA concerns or criticism of neuroprojects and also about having specific protocols when using fMRI in the case of incidental findings (health-related findings not intended by the scope of the neuromarketing study).

Article 4. Transparency: this article concerns the voluntary nature of all neuromarketing studies, the clear description of services, credentials and addresses by the vendor, and the complete and utter freedom of the client to audit the process and all related materials of neuroservices in order to ensure applicability and relevance to their challenges.

Article 5. Consent: this is about participants' ability to access information about, and understand the protocol, tools and objectives of the neuro-study, as well as the ability to withdraw their data after the end of the study.

Article 6. Privacy: this crucial article concerns information about privacy and accessibility to data collected with neuromarketing methods, any additional consent needed by participants, duration of storing the data, and utilization of data only for the purpose of the specific study.

Article 7. Participant rights: this article is about making sure that participants are fully aware of their right to confirm their participation to the study, to ask for modification or withdrawal of their data after the study has finished, to receive guarantees that data will not be transferred or used by others. If data travels beyond borders of one country, this article makes sure that the whole code will be applied in the destination country as well.

Article 8. Children and young people: as with usual research practice, if participants are below 18 years old they can take part only with informed consent by their parents.

Article 9. Subcontracting: any involvement of outside consultants or other agencies should be disclosed before the study starts. It also prevents neuro-marketers from getting their name associated with studies that they were not personally involved in and that they cannot defend in public.

Article 10. Publication: this article asks neuromarketers to present their data by separating the data-interpretation part from the data-analysis part (key findings).

Article 11. Commitment: this article asks for full commitment in applying this code, otherwise membership to the association will be terminated.

Article 12. Implementation: this last article asks members to publish the code on their website as an indication of their acceptance of the code, and also it asks both vendors and clients to express their knowledge of the code and any additional regulatory framework in their respective countries.

These 12 articles capture most of the points made earlier by Murphy and associates when recommending their own neuroethics framework for neuromarketers in a paper published in the *Journal of Consumer Behaviour* (Murphy, Illes and Reiner, 2008). This model consists broadly of three elements: protection of participants; transparent disclosure and representation from the side of neuromarketing agencies; and dissemination of validity issues. The first two are fully covered by the NMSBA code. The third element, though, needs further exploration, especially as it also coincides with the problems indicated by the Varan and associates study discussed earlier in this chapter. So, what about consumers? What do they think about neuromarketing? Interestingly enough, a study published in 2014 revealed that consumers favoured the use of neuromarketing by non-profit organizations (NPOs) while they did not favour for-profit companies for doing so (Flores *et al*, 2014). Researchers concluded that consumers trusted NPOs more and thus wanted them to use neuromarketing to achieve their good-for-society goals, while they did not trust as much for-profits and thus did not want them to use neuromarketing to achieve their 'selfish' goals. This is another strong indication of the need for companies to establish mutual trust between their brands and consumers. Since trust is an oxytocin-induced state of mind, neuroresearch should be used to help brands identify how to increase trust in the marketplace!

Last thought

The validity point is the biggest challenge, and most significant opportunity, for neuromarketing in the near future. The human brain is indeed marketing's last frontier, and neuromarketing has the ultimate set of tools for finally opening up the customer's Black Box. To deliver reliably on all its promises, though, the neuromarketing industry needs to strive towards agreed definitions and methods. Until then, advanced marketers around the world will have to find their own way with preferred vendors and methods. With the help of this book they are one step closer in becoming effective brain-based communicators.

SUMMARY CHECKLIST

- Abandon the exclusive use of self-reflection, self-reporting marketing research methods.

- Replace the outdated and scientifically discredited *Homo economicus* mindset with a more modern one that takes humans for what they are: emotional, relational, dynamic and difficult to comprehend.

- Combine a variety of neuromarketing methods for optimum results.

- Avoid making broad claims about brain areas and brain functionality. Instead dig deeper into neurorelated research and discover the extraordinary depth and richness of our brain's inner workings.

- Choose carefully the neuromarketing vendor(s) to work with but invest in the relationship to ensure long-term results.

- Use the NMSBA ethical code in conjunction with any applicable market research national code.

Resources to inspire you

- Dr Nikolaos Dimitriadis TEDx talk on brain-based communications: https://www.youtube.com/watch?v=GvXPuQGPLB8&t=1s

- Patrick Renvoise TEDx talk on neuromarketing: https://www.youtube.com/watch?v=_rKceOe-Jr0&t=5s

- Daniel Amen TEDx talk on brain scanning: https://www.youtube.com/watch?v=esPRsT-Imw8&t=6s

- Jenni Cross TEDx talk on behavioural change: https://www.youtube.com/watch?v=I5d8GW6GdR0&t=7s

- Ray Burke TEDx talk on tracking shopping behaviour: https://www.youtube.com/watch?v=jeQ7C4JLpug&t=13s

- Rana El Kaliouby TEDx talk on emotional facial recognition: https://www.youtube.com/watch?v=o3VwYIazybI&t=559s

- Dan Emodi TEDx talk on emotional voice recognition: https://www.youtube.com/watch?v=mD_MXOCvVYo

Revision questions

1 What are the limitations of traditional marketing research methods? How can neuroscience help in overcoming these limitations?

2 What are the problems associated with the *Homo economicus* model of human nature?

3 Which key brain facts are important for marketing and how can marketers use them to their brands' advantage?

4 Name the main neuromarketing tools and discuss their advantages and disadvantages.

5 Discuss the ethical considerations concerning neuromarketing research today.

References

BBC News (2015) [accessed 18 June 2018] Surge in US 'Brain-Reading' Patents, *BBC* [Online] http://www.bbc.com/news/technology-32623063

Black, S (2013) Why the lean start-up changes everything, *Harvard Business Review*, **91** (5), pp 63–72

Blakeslee, S (2007) [accessed 18 June 2018] A Small Part of the Brain, and Its Profound Effects, *The New York Times* [Online] http://www.nytimes.com/2007/02/06/health/psychology/06brain.html

Bridger, D (2015) *Decoding the Irrational Consumer: How to commission, run and generate insights from neuromarketing research*, Kogan Page, London

Castellion, G and Markham, S K (2013) Perspective: new product failure rates: influence of argumentum ad populum and self-interest, *Journal of Product Innovation Management*, **30** (5), pp 976–79

Coca-Cola Company (2012) [accessed 18 June 2018] The Real Story of New Coke, *Coca-Cola* [Online] http://www.coca-colacompany.com/stories/coke-lore-new-coke

Craig, A D (2009) How do you feel – now? The anterior insula and human awareness, *Nature Reviews Neuroscience*, **10**, pp 59–70

Dachler, H P and Hosking, D M (1995) The primacy of relations in socially constructing organizational realities, in *Management and Organization: Relational alternatives to individualism*, ed D M Hosking, H P Dachler and K J Gergen, pp 1–29, Avebury, Aldershot

Damasio A, Damasio H and Tranel D (2013) Persistence of feelings and sentience after bilateral damage of the insula, *Cerebral Cortex*, **23** (4), pp 833–46

de Ternay, G and Devlin, J (2016) [accessed 18 June 2018] Can Neuromarketing Really Offer You Useful Customer Insights?, *London Entrepreneurship Review* [Online] http://www.londonentrepreneurshipreview.com/article/can-neuromarketing-really-offer-you-useful-customer-insights

Dimitriadis, N and Psychogios, A (2016) Neuroscience for Leaders: A brain adaptive leadership approach, Kogan Page, London

Dooley, R (2015) [accessed 18 June 2018] Neuromarketing: Pseudoscience No More, *Forbes* [Online] http://www.forbes.com/sites/rogerdooley/2015/02/24/neuromarketing-temple/#357ca9fa259a

Dutton, D G and Aaron, A P (1974) Some evidence for heightened sexual attraction under conditions of high anxiety, *Journal of Personality and Social Psychology*, **30**, pp 510–17

Dwoskin, E (2016) [accessed 18 June 2018] Putting a Computer in Your Brain is No Longer Science Fiction, *The Washington Post* [Online] https://www.washingtonpost.com/news/the-switch/wp/2016/08/15/putting-a-computer-in-your-brain-is-no-longer-science-fiction/?utm_term=.9f9af3bcde84

Flores, J, Baruca, A and Saldivar, R (2014), Is neuromarketing ethical? Consumers say yes. Consumers say no, *Journal of Legal, Ethical and Regulatory Issues*, **17** (2), pp 77–91

Foster, T (2016) [accessed 18 June 2018] Ready or Not, Companies Will Soon Be Tracking Your Emotions, *INC.COM* [Online] http://www.inc.com/magazine/201607/tom-foster/lightwave-monitor-customer-emotions.html

Fournaise Group (2015) [accessed 18 June 2018] Marketers Made 3 Effectiveness Mistakes in 2014 [Online] https://www.fournaisegroup.com/marketers-made-3-effectiveness-mistakes-in-2014/

Goldstein, N J, Martin, S J and Cialdini, R (2008) *Yes!: 50 scientifically proven ways to be persuasive*, Simon and Schuster, New York

Gorgiev, A and Dimitriadis, N (2015) Upgrading marketing research: neuromarketing tools for understanding consumers, in *Trends and Innovations in Marketing Information Systems*, ed T Tsiakis, pp 337–57, Business Science Reference, Hershey, PA

Hutson, M (2016) [accessed 18 June 2018] Trivers' Pursuit, *Psychology Today* [Online] https://www.psychologytoday.com/articles/201601/trivers-pursuit

Kosslyn, S and Miller, G W (2013) *Top Brain, Bottom Brain: Surprising insights into how you think*, Simon and Schuster, New York

Kotler, P and Armstrong, G (2012) *Principles of Marketing*, Pearson Prentice Hall, Upper Saddle River, NJ

Levy, I, Lazzaro, S C, Rutledge, R B and Glimcher, P W (2011) Choice from non-choice: predicting consumer preferences from blood oxygenation level-dependent signals obtained during passive viewing, *Journal of Neuroscience*, **31** (1), pp 118–25

Lilienfeld, S O and Arkowitz, H (2014) [accessed 18 June 2018] Why 'Just Say No' Doesn't Work, *Scientific American* [Online] https://www.scientificamerican.com/article/why-just-say-no-doesnt-work/

Lin, P-Y, Grewal, N S, Morin, C, Johnson, W D and Zak, P J (2013) Oxytocin increases the influence of public service advertisements, *PLoS ONE*, **8** (2), e56934

Lindstrom, M (2008) [accessed 18 June 2018] Inhaling Fear, *The New York Times* [Online] http://www.nytimes.com/2008/12/12/opinion/12lindstrom.html

Lindstrom, M (2011) [accessed 18 June 2018] You Love Your iPhone. Literally., *The New York Times* [Online] http://www.nytimes.com/2011/10/01/opinion/you-love-your-iphone-literally.html

Malhotra, N K and Birks, D F (2003) *Marketing Research: An applied approach*, Pearson Education, Essex

McClure, S M, Li, J, Tomlin, D, Cypert, K S, Montague, L M and Montague, P R (2004) Neural correlates of behavioral preference for culturally familiar drinks, *Neuron*, **44** (2), pp 379–87

Murphy, E R, Illes, J and Reiner, P B (2008) Neuroethics of neuromarketing, *Journal of Consumer Behaviour*, 7 (4–5), pp 293–302

Neural Sense (2016) [accessed 18 June 2018] Creative Project: NeuroWine, *Neural Sense* [Online] www.neuralsense.com/projects

Nielsen (2016) [accessed 18 June 2018] Groundbreaking Research Shows Ability of Neuroscience Measures to Predict In-Market Sales Results [Online] http://www.nielsen.com/us/en/press-room/2016/groundbreaking-research-shows-ability-of-neuroscience-measures-to-predict-in-market-sales.html

O'Boyle, E J (2007) Requiem for *Homo economicus*, *Journal of Markets and Morality*, **10** (2), pp 321–37

Pesch, H (2002) *Lehrbuch der Nationalökonomie/Teaching Guide to Economics*, vol 3, Bk 1, trans Rupert J Ederer, Edwin Mellen, Lewiston, NY

PHYS.ORG (2016) [accessed 18 June 2018] New Wave in Tech: Hacking the Brain [Online] https://phys.org/news/2016-01-tech-hacking-brain.html

Poldrack, R (2011) [accessed 18 June 2018] NYT Op-Ed + fMRI = Complete Crap [Online] http://www.russpoldrack.org/2011/10/nyt-editorial-fmri-complete-crap.html

Renvoise, P (2013) [accessed 18 June 2018] Is There a Buy Button Inside the Brain: Patrick Renvoise at TEDxBend, *TEDx Talk* [Online] www.youtube.com/watch?v=_rKceOe-Jr0&t=9s

The Economist (2008) [accessed 18 June 2018] The Science of Shopping: The Way the Brain Buys [Online] http://www.economist.com/node/12792420

Uhl-Bien, M (2006) Relational leadership theory: exploring the social processes of leadership and organizing, *The Leadership Quarterly*, **17** (6), pp 654–76

Varan, D, Lang, A, Barwise, P, Weber, R and Bellman, S (2015) How reliable are neuromarketers' measures of advertising effectiveness? *Journal of Advertising Research*, **55** (2), pp 176–91

Venkatraman, V, Dimoka, A, Pavlou, P A, Vo, K, Hampton, W, Bollinger, B, Hershfield, H E, Ishihara, M and Winer, R S (2015) Predicting advertising success beyond traditional measures: new insights from neurophysiological methods and market response modelling, *Journal of Marketing Research*, **52** (4), pp 436–52

Predictive skills   03

Marketing and data intelligence

CHAPTER LEARNING OBJECTIVES

After studying this chapter, you will be able to:

- Appreciate that data's role in marketing is to move marketing from an art into a science.

- Appreciate that data has an important role at all stages of the marketing process, from ideation to evaluation and through the feedback loop.

- Realize that data alone is not insight and that data has to be interpreted into marketing insight for it to be valuable.

- Identify the challenges associated with analysing big data in marketing.

- Identify the analysis tools available to advanced marketing managers, as well as their advantages and disadvantages.

- Identify the behavioural environments and behavioural metrics that are required to make data analysis valuable.

- Understand the ethical concerns of applying data science to marketing research.

Advanced practice

It's time to persuade through personality profiling

What can the winning of two unpopular political campaigns mean to the future of persuasion in marketing? The short answer, a lot. Like brand marketing, election campaigns have been traditionally organized based on demographic concepts.

For instance, women receiving the same message because of their gender – or all African Americans because of their race. The process of demographic targeting, while it may seem logical, is highly flawed. The assumption that demographic similarities leads to targeted messaging is too simplistic to account for complex human behaviours and individual idiosyncrasies. An entire gender, race or age group does not think, feel or behave in the same manner.

While it is easier to segment an audience based on demographic variables, these variables only measure who your audience is. The stronger predictor of campaign success has always been to measure 'why' your audience buys, psychographic segmentation. However, it has traditionally been difficult and expensive to obtain and segment customers on psychographic data. That is, until the rise and widespread adoption of digital technologies. Now, in every interaction, every purchase and in every movement, we are being tracked; we even add to this personal data in sharing our opinions publicly through social media – and this personal data is for sale. Everything from land registries, automotive data to bonus cards and electoral rolls are up for grabs. Digital footprints can suddenly become real people with fears, needs, interests and addresses – and one company is now infamously using this data to win political campaigns.

Cambridge Analytica has been linked to Brexit, Trump and is even credited for Ted Cruz's rise to popularity (Grassegger and Krogerus, 2017). The company's core strength is in innovate political marketing – micro targeting – by measuring people's personality from their digital footprints, based on the OCEAN model. The OCEAN model, more commonly known as the Big Five traits personality model, has more traditionally been used as a predictor of future job performance outcomes. However, the model's new role in marketing is becoming popular through Cambridge Analytica's link to winning Brexit and the US presidential election, but also as an element in IBM's Watson artificial intelligence (AI) platform. Psychographic targeting through personality profiling is the next stage in targeted marketing.

The extent of this targeting is huge, Cambridge Analytica's CEO is quoted as saying they 'are able to form a model to predict the personality of every single adult in the United States of America'. The Trump campaign is said to have been won on three elements: behavioural science using the OCEAN model, big data, and ad targeting (Grassegger and Krogerus, 2017) – advertising is targeted as accurately as possible to the personality of an individual consumer, meaning that both you and your friends can receive different messages for the same brand, or in this case a political campaign.

It is believed that every message Trump shared was data driven. For instance, on the day of the third presidential debate between Trump and Clinton, the Trump team tested 175,000 different ad variations for his arguments to find the right versions in Facebook. The messages differed in microscopic details in order to target the recipients in an optimal psychological way: different headings, colours, captions, with a photo or video. Alexander Nix, Cambridge Analytica's CEO, said that this fine-tuning reaches all the way down to the smallest groups where they can 'address villages or apartment blocks in a targeted way. Even individuals' (Grassegger and Krogerus, 2017). The observation by mathematician Cathy O'Neil that Trump acted like a perfectly opportunistic algorithm following audience reaction is true – the inconsistencies in Trump's messaging turn out to be a different message for every voter (Grassegger and Krogerus, 2017).

Even today, the shock wins for Brexit and Donald Trump can still be felt across the world, but one of the biggest lessons here is for marketers. There is a new kind of data-driven communication that, in the case of Brexit, Trump and even Ted Cruz, delivered the right message to the right person at the right time – and more importantly influenced their behaviour. This is the holy grail for marketing. However, the controversy around Cambridge Analytica has continued to grow since their relationship between the Brexit and Trump campaigns was openly publicized, and marketers should seek to understand public sentiment and the ethics surrounding psychographic targeting. While the news storm surrounding Cambridge Analytica has been driven by the belief that they illegally used Facebook data to target US citizens (Cadwalladr and Graham-Harrison, 2018), their methods of targeting have been perceived as being a 'psychological warfare tool' (Cadwalladr, 2018).

It could be argued that it is customer data analysed through the lens of psychology that has won unpopular campaigns and will continue to build brands in the future. However, marketers need to discuss their stance on the ethical practices of data-driven psychological targeting via social networks. On the one hand, marketers now have the ability to profile and target users based on behavioural, emotional, personality and psychographic principles. This practice can reduce marketing spend wastage, and increase marketing effectiveness because the right messages are being sent to the right people at the right time. Additionally, psychographic targeting can also assist in increasing personalization of brand messages to consumers. For example, Netflix has reportedly increased its 'personalized recommendation engine' to include personalized artwork to pull customers into new titles based on their preferences, to decrease feelings of regret, and increase the Netflix experience (Chandrashekar *et al,* 2017).

On the other hand, just because you can does not mean you should, and the public outcry about Cambridge Analytica's profiling and targeting practices (for example, O'Hagan, 2018) suggests that many people are not comfortable with this new reality. Companies such as Facebook, Cambridge Analytica, and others who regularly create algorithms based on customer data potentially know more about us than we know ourselves, and this can be unsettling to many consumers. In fact, the public outcry over the allegations against Cambridge Analytica unlawfully harvesting an estimated 87 million Facebook profiles (Chadwick, 2018) increased the awareness of how data is collected via social networking sites and how powerful the analysis of social data can be in targeting and swaying decisions. It appeared that many consumers had been blind to the insights about their habits, preferences, decisions and opinions that they were leaving in social media. The resulting 'creepiness factor' placed pressure on Facebook with a global #DeleteFacebook campaign (Lang, 2018), and Facebook founder Mark Zuckerberg was called to question in the senate about the alleged scandal (Wong, 2018). However, it could be argued that the questioning by the senate further reinforced that many people do not understand how data can be collected and processed from social networking sites. For Cambridge Analytica, Alexander Nix was suspended and, later, Cambridge Analytica filed for bankruptcy in the United States (Ram, 2018).

The marketing challenge

What is the purpose of marketing? Seth Godin (2012) believes that marketing is 'the art of telling a story to a consumer that they want to hear that lets them persuade themselves that they want to buy something'. Seth focuses on the communicative and persuasive nature of marketing communications, but the marketing discipline is much more strategic and it impacts across the whole organization. The link to marketing and advertising has always been over-dramatized, illustrated in populist television programmes such as *Mad Men*. In today's digital age, the focus of persuasion has risen to paramount importance in the battle for the 'attention economy' (Davenport and Beck, 2002).

The marketing challenge has always been linked to creating products, brands and campaigns that grab audience attention, provoke audience interest and convert that interest into action (Nahai, 2016). However, the marketing discipline is not only linked to the output but the management process responsible for identifying, anticipating and satisfying customer requirements profitably (The Chartered Institute of Marketing, 2015). The role of data in marketing is to support the marketing management process, and to transform the marketing discipline from an art to a science. Data is pushing marketing to become more accountable. The challenge for marketers is to understand how to turn billions of data points into a process that identifies customer behaviours, and what is going to meet – and exceed – their expectations.

Getting inside our 'customers' minds' has never been so important. Crucially, two things have changed to help marketers understand their customers' needs and behaviours – the rapid pace of technological development and the widespread adoption of this technology on a global scale. Today's society is a digital one. Whether we are aware or not, much of the population is digitally connected either by choice or through the purchases we make – even registering on the electoral role. Every time we go online, every time we purchase or connect a new device we leave a digital footprint – this data is up for sale and can be traced back to our individual profiles. Data has been dubbed as 'the new oil' (Humby, 2006) and is critical to every marketing function. What you will learn in this chapter is that this data oil is worthless without processing into insight. Data-insight generation is where marketers must focus their attention. The modern marketer must have a robust insight-driven marketing strategy in place to ensure they not only capitalize on the data opportunities, but also satisfy customer requirements that are frequently being made a larger part of their remit (Ward, 2015).

The explosion of customer data

Using customer data to deliver more relevant marketing campaigns is not new. Pioneers such as Robert Kestnabaum were exploring new ways to collect and use customer data in marketing campaigns as far back as the 1960s. Data strategies, to some extent, have always existed in marketing. However, today, the data challenge is much more complex. The propitiation of connected devices, the read–write web, and move to digital transactions have increased the variety of data generated. The problem now is not that there is not enough data or data variety to understand customer preferences, it is that there is too much data. This data is commonly referred to as big data (Hopkins and Evelson, 2011).

The term big data has recently emerged to describe a range of technological and commercial trends enabling the storage and analysis of large volumes of customer data, such as that generated by social networks and mobile devices (Nunan and Di Domenico, 2013). Hopkins and Evelson (2011) argue that the challenges around big data refer to the ever-increasing volume, variety, velocity and veracity of information (Table 3.1).

Table 3.1   The four Vs of big data

Element	Description
Volume	The volume of data being produced is increasing exponentially and exceeds what can be cost-effectively stored. As the data volume expands, traditional data platforms must scale to deal with it.
Variety	The variety of different data formats is growing and makes integration between formats expensive. Integration costs grow along with the number of data formats because rules must be developed for each, and integration processes must be changed and redeployed.
Velocity	The velocity is the speed of data processing. The volume and variety of data impacts the velocity. An application processing a stream of data may enable response to critical events within hours, but if the need to take action is within minutes, it may not be met.
Veracity	As the variety of data increases the likelihood of uncertain or imprecise data rises – this is data veracity. For example, unstructured data from social media conversations is an example of natural language, and requires interpretation of complex and highly variable grammar.

SOURCE Adapted from Hopkins and Evelson (2011)

Data volume. The first V refers to the volume of data. Much of this new data has been created by 'connected' internet and mobile applications – in every online interaction, we leave behind a digital footprint. This change in human communication has also given rise to a change in human culture globally. The internet, social media and mobile applications have given more dramatic rise to individual empowerment than ever before – new technologies have reshaped our culture, how we connect with each other and how we view the world. This has resulted in more data than ever being produced. Every day, the world creates 2.5 quintillion bytes of data, and that data is doubling every 40 months or so – resulting in that 90 per cent of the world's data was created in the last two years alone (McAfee and Brynjolfsson, 2012). As more people become digitally aware, go online, or even if new technologies are created and more devices are registered, the volume of data will continue to rise exponentially. It is only now that the ability to analyse such large volumes of data exists. The good news for marketers is that the variety of data being generated means that there are literally no more consumer secrets.

Data variety. Big data takes the form of messages, updates and images posted to social networks; reading from sensors and connected devices; GPS signals from mobile phones and more (McAfee and Brynjolfsson, 2012).

As more and more business activity is becoming digitized, new sources of information are created on virtually any topic of interest to business, and crucially the marketing function. The types of data available to marketers is ever increasing (see Table 3.2).

Table 3.2 Comparing old and new types of consumer data

Old Data	New Data
Business performance data	Social media conversations
Transactional data	Consumer reviews
CRM data	Videos
Loyalty card data	Images
Internet analytics	Memes
	Engagement analytics
	App downloads
	Sensor data
	Personality data
	Internet of things

The data produced by digital devices, social media and mobile applications is becoming increasingly unstructured. Moving away from the structured data, as within transactional data or even e-mail open rates, the data collected and analysed today is highly unstructured. For instance, text, videos and images from social media require a different kind of analysis to extract contextual meaning. It is no longer about counting ones and zeroes, in the world of unstructured data, analytics will not provide meaningful insight for marketers. The marketing challenge is therefore to create actionable intelligence that is derived from an aggregation of individual and sometimes seemingly random data points (Finger and Dutta, 2013).

Data velocity. The third V refers to data velocity. For many applications, the speed of data creation is even more important than the volume (McAfee and Brynjolfsson, 2012). Data velocity is the measure of how fast the data is coming in and how fast it needs to be processed. Consider this, as of 2016 the number of active Facebook users was 1.86 billion, that is 1.86 billion users who have the potential to post content, and therefore generate data. In fact, the velocity of data produced from social media and mobile applications is rising year on year, see Figure 3.1.

Figure 3.1 What happens online in 60 seconds

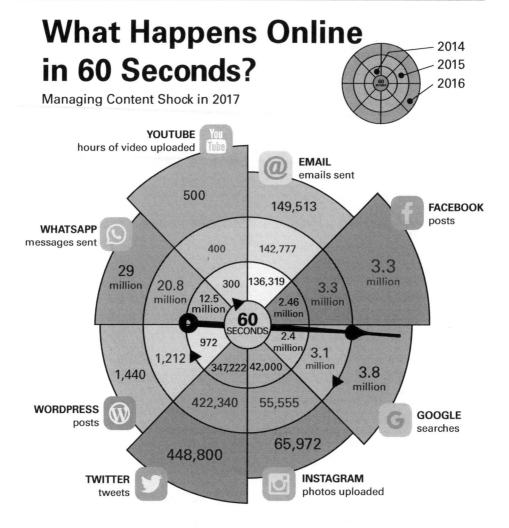

The world has fallen in love with social media and now automatically turns to online platforms to research and buy products and services. This gives fantastic opportunitites for marketers to engage audiences and encourage content sharing, but also gives huge challenges of getting cut-through and keeping up-to-date ourselves!

At Smart Insights, we look to help by focusing on the 'Must-know' platform developments and developing mind tools to help businesses review how they can best Plan, Manage and Optimize their digital marketing – see our http://bit.ly/smartlibrary

Brought to you by:

www.smartinsights.com

SOURCE Allen (2017). Reproduced with permission of digital marketing advice site www.smartinsights.com

Or think about sensor data. As the internet of things more widely penetrates digital devices and society, the more sensors will be connected in the world, transmitting data at a near constant rate – as this continues so does the flow of data. Marketers are currently obsessed with data but this data is not necessarily the right data, and over the past year the discussions around smart data have risen (Lorentz, 2013). While the data that can be analysed is big and fast there is always a necessity to have the right data, and at this stage in data strategy maturity some marketers are finding it difficult to identify the right data to analyse. A robust data strategy must include the data points for analysis and the tools to be used in the analysis of the data.

Data veracity. Data veracity is the fourth V, and this refers to the biases, noise and abnormality in data (Normandeau, 2013). The new types of data created in today's digital world are highly unstructured, and created through personal account, perception and reflection, which means the data may not necessarily be accurate or provide representative information to influence business decision making. For example, review sites have often been criticized for fake reviews and the ability to 'game' review rankings to obtain a high position, such as a story published in 2017 about how a garden shed in London became the number one restaurant in London (Butler, 2017). *The Shed at Dulwich* became an internet sensation when Oobah Butler (2017) gave insight into how he used to write fake reviews for restaurants, and decided to take it one step further by trying to get a completely fake restaurant, his garden shed, to the number-one ranked restaurant in London. Stories like *The Shed at Dulwich* highlight that the veracity of the data is too complex and untrustworthy to be used as a scoring system like the ones promoted by many review sites. The same can be said for new types of data being processed by organizations. The level of uncertainty and imprecisions varies on a case by case basis, and while there are tools to help automate data preparation and cleansing, they are still in the pre-industrial age.

Moreover, these tools can easily miss the nuance and context of human communication. Data context is important and marks the biggest challenge to data analysis. While marketers now have a wealth of data and text analysis tools, the data veracity means the analysis may have low levels of validity or accuracy, even when such tools have natural language processing ability. As a result, it is believed that one in three business leaders do not trust the information they use to make decisions (McGovern, 2014). In using data to make marketing decisions, marketers must have an understanding of the data source, cleansing process, and how the data is analysed. Many of the new data analysis software solutions offer 'black box' algorithms, which means marketers will not always be certain on the validity of the data used.

Data complexity

Further to the four Vs of big data, another fundamental consequence of the new marketing landscape, born from the digital world we now live in, is the complexity of the data produced. The data created from social media sites is different than other forms of data, such as transactional data or e-mail open rates. Data from social media sites is largely unstructured and is the product of individuals uploading their own text, images and videos. User-generated content (UGC) is the new cultural currency of the digital age. The modern marketer must be prepared to analyse and use data from a variety of different sources. For those marketers willing to take on the challenge of big data, the commercial promise is the ability to generate customer insights from the collection of new types and volumes of data in applications that were previously not economically viable. This insight can be used to predict future customer behaviour that can decrease cost and increase revenue. For example, Finger and Dutta (2013) highlighted the increased use of predictive data being used in the world and across industries:

- Google using data to predict the next wave of influenza.
- IBM using data to optimize traffic flow in the city of Stockholm and to get the best possible air quality.
- Zafu, 2style4You, and others using self-collected body data to suggest clothes that will fit you best.
- The National Centre for Academic Transformation is using data mining to help understand which college students are more likely to succeed in which courses.
- Insurance companies offering lower rates on car insurance if you place a GPS device voluntarily in your car. They use the data to predict whether you are going to have a car accident soon and then adjust your insurance policy accordingly.
- Many retailers using data for product recommendations and targeted advertisements to the point that they know if you might be pregnant.

The potential of big data is huge, and many software vendors are cashing in on the new focus of data analysis. You only need to look at a software product review site like TrustRadius (www.trustradius.com) to see the volume of software options available. The proliferation of data-related analysis tools is not an easy ecosystem for marketers to navigate. These tools are largely undifferentiated and all claim to be the 'next big thing' in data analysis and customer insights generation. However, not all of these tools live up to their own marketing claims, and this is causing unease in marketing as many marketers are finding it difficult to extract value from data analysis tools. The analysis and interpretation of data is a skill that has to be developed – you would not give an apprentice carpenter his tools and expect him to know how to use them properly. The same is true in data analysis and interpretation. The tool is not where the value lies, it is a tool. The marketer must develop data analysis and, crucially, interpretation skills in order to extract business value from the data.

The Hype Cycle and peak data complexity

The volume, velocity, variety, veracity and complexity of data will rise as the new emerging technologies are adopted by our customers. Marketers can no longer hide from the need to understand data sources, and to know which data sources to combine and technology to use. In a yearly 'Hype Cycle' Gartner Inc. (2016) demonstrates the potential for even more varied data points (for example, brain-computer interface) but also possible solutions to the data analysis challenge (for example, machine learning). It is important for marketers to continue to assess data sources and their ability to generate customer insight that will allow for better consumer targeting, conversion and product development. The good news is that we are now believed to be at peak data complexity (Goodwin, 2016). While peak data complexity is causing a collide between new and old systems today, in the future data analysis may become easier – for example, the use of an app like Slack and traditional e-mail simultaneously. For marketers, this means we will be using more applications and measures than ever before – we are one foot in the old and one foot in the new (data complexity), being led by the maturity of the other companies we work with and the technology itself. Today, marketing as a discipline is being led by customer behaviour, and the functionality of technology developed to help us deliver the right message, to the right customer at the right time. In the future, it is possible that we will lose some of the more traditional data sources, and reduce the complexity.

This technology is developed for marketers as end customers. Like every business today, technology vendors conduct research into their customer needs. Marketers are guiding the development of some technology solutions, particularly around data analysis, but marketers may not necessarily be the right people to help guide this development. If you consider the development of the Walkman and, later, the iPod, neither device was truly wanted by consumers until they were launched.

The Sony co-founder, Akio Morita

'We don't ask consumers what they want. They don't know. Instead we apply our brain power to what they need, and will want, and make sure we're there already.'

SOURCE Steel (1998)

The same applies in the development of technology, and also in the challenges for the modern marketer. Today, it is easier for marketers to build new products, services and even marketing campaigns because of the availability of data. It is the blending of seeming unrelated data points that wins the marketing challenge today. If you look closely at the right data, and interpret the data through a lens of behavioural science, you begin to see that in every interaction your customers tell you exactly what they want. Asking them directly is not an option, due to self-reflection, but analysing the patterns of their behaviour provides the strategic insight you are looking for.

However, in this world of peak data complexity, marketers may be further adding to the complexity problem by trying to fit old metrics into new technology and new behaviours. It could be argued that marketers' cognitive biases as humans may be a roadblock to their data strategy success. This is not unusual, when the motor car was first launched, for example, engine performance was not measured as engine performance but as horsepower. Horsepower was used to fit in with existing knowledge and relationships to the measurement of speed. If you like, an early form of nudge to aid in understanding and adoption of the automotive car. It is therefore possible that, due to the needs of marketers, the technology developed may not actually be sufficient to analyse the new complex behaviour of humans. There is a need in marketing to have representative metrics, but these metrics may neglect to highlight the real value from the data. Moreover, the stage in the marketing process where the data is being used may also miss new value creation from data. A word of warning to modern marketers is required.

Word of warning: data to measure attention

John Wanamaker's (1838–1922) infamous adage 'half the money I spend on advertising is wasted; the trouble is, I don't know which half' is still as true today as when it was first coined. Advertising needs to stop consumers and hold their attention in likeable ways, because when the eye stops the sale begins (Pieters, Wedel and Batra, 2010). However, understanding why advertising works is complicated because it is situation specific and it depends on the message, sender, receiver, medium and context. Yet, three elements are present in every marketing campaign: advertising content, attention and persuasion (Teixeira, 2014). While the types of content and the platforms to distribute content have changed since John Wanamaker's reign as marketer, the desire and the need for marketing campaigns to capture customer attention have not.

For marketers, attention is largely seen as a necessary ingredient for effective advertising. In recent years, a remarkable counter-argument against the need for active attention for advertising to be effective and successful has grown (Heath, 2012). There is evidence to suggest that passive attention can still be processed, memorized and is persuasive in people's minds. These arguments have merit and are in keeping with the discussions and research from neuroscience (Chapter 2). Nevertheless, for the mainstream marketer, the preoccupation continues to be measuring consumer attention or 'eyeballs' – active attention. This study has become so competitive that attention can be regarded as a currency (Teixeria, 2014). Data's role in marketing has traditionally been in the measurement of advertising effectiveness, and this trend has continued into measuring the effectiveness of online content.

In measuring the effectiveness of public relations (PR) activity the common method was to use the advertising value equivalents (AVEs). AVEs are calculated by multiplying column centimetres of editorial print media coverage and seconds of broadcast publicity by the respective media advertising rates (MacNamara, 2011). Essentially, the AVE values editorial coverage as advertising irrespective of the content and tone. AVEs are still used in the PR industry but there is a fierce debate over the appropriateness of using AVEs to measure PR effectiveness. Some of the criticism towards AVEs are weighted on the fact that all editorial is included in the calculation, no matter the context in which the editorial is found, for example sentiment or even if close competitors are mentioned, and the quality of the article (MacNamara,

2011). The AVE measure again plays into the big number fallacy without understanding the context of the PR – the potential number of views and value are taken over the quality of the communication.

Similarly, in television advertising the Broadcasters Audience Research Board (BARB) adopts a framework to measure the number of TV viewing audiences. These calculations can then be used by broadcasters where advertisers pay for the cost of views. The commonly accepted advertising effectiveness metric is gross rating point (GRP), an equation used by media planners and buyers to determine how many people within an intended audience might have seen their ads (Patel, 2016) – advertising effectiveness is essentially demonstrated through the audience size. The trend for the number of views and attention has also been widely adopted in online and digital marketing. Google Analytics (www.analytics.google.com) lets you measure your advertising ROI as well as track flash, video, and social network sites and applications quantitatively, like AVEs the context and quality of interaction is missing. Exploring marketing effectiveness in content marketing, the Content Marketing Institute argues that metrics provide deep insights into how content is performing (Cain, 2012). It advises to start tracking content performance with Google Analytics, with a specific view on six metrics: unique visitors, page views, search engine traffic, bounce rate, conversion rate and inbound links. Like all other effectiveness measures, content marketing is dictated by views, not the quality of views or their qualitative thoughts on the content they may share through social media.

In short, reach is a standard metric in measuring marketing effectiveness. This numeric view of customer data set an agenda for reductionism in measuring customer behaviours to highlight big numbers, to represent a large audience who have paid active attention to marketing campaigns. The role of data in marketing has more traditionally been applied at the end of a campaign planning process, during the campaign evaluation stage. This has not been more evident than in the measure of new types of data from social media and app download rates – where the focus is on views and growth of views. This is a very real issue of peak data complexity – retrofitting old metrics into new technology and societal behaviours.

For example, in the late 2000s marketers globally got very excited. This rise of new technology platforms, social media, had taken the world by storm. Not only did marketers now know where people – customers – 'hung out', they could also measure an outcome of their attention. Likes, shares and comments became the new marketing currency and a marked measure of capturing audience attention, and affinity to the brand (Carah, 2014). The measurement of attention did not stop there, brands could now measure the number of 'brand fans', the number of people who have willingly opted-in to allow the brand to push brand messages and brand content directly to their social media feeds. Marketers knew how many people wanted to be engaged and in constant contact with their brand. Social media literally changed the game for measuring a real behavioural consequence of customer attention online. The rise in what was termed 'social media analytics' helped marketers to demonstrate the reach of the message and the volume of customers engaged with a brand's messaging (Kietzmann *et al*, 2011).

Social media measurement literally plays into the marketers' 'big number' fallacy, and the innate desire of markets to focus on using data to prove campaign success. Social media analytics measures active customer involvement with content and campaigns – how successful a campaign was in terms of grabbing attention. The analytics do not tell you how to improve, only what content did or did not grab attention, nor do analytics tell you what customers really want. Marketers who use social media analytics alone are in a never-ending cycle of 'marking their own homework' and reproducing similar content created from 'old thinking'. In today's age, there are so many more practical applications of data analysis in marketing. Before looking at the new opportunities that data can bring to marketing, there is one more fallacy that requires a health warning to the modern marketer: research.

Word of warning: the research fallacy?

Following from the word of warning about not just using data to measure attention, comes the research fallacy. A study by Columbia Business School found that 100 per cent of marketers polled believed that successful brands must use customer data to drive marketing decisions (Davey, 2015). The Columbia study did not highlight what data or measures that marketers felt were essential to marketing decision making, but what can be taken from the study is that a shift towards using data beyond campaign evaluation is gaining traction. The most transformative role of data is at the ideation stages of campaigns or even in new product developments.

It could be argued that, to a certain extent, marketers have always conducted periods of research at the start of the campaign process. A rise in 'planners' and planning departments has ensured that research into customer preferences preceded campaign development, but in a recent article marketers have been questioned on their ability to effectively research customer preferences (Barta, 2016). The article calls out marketers for focusing on secondary desk research over primary research, including data analysis. The research fallacy is the belief that secondary research is sufficient in painting a picture of customer need and preference. Indeed, Ogilvy has taken the challenge head on after finding out that 94 per cent of its planners used the internet or other secondary research to fulfil the research phase in their pitch process, and the company is now pushing marketers to research the real lives of their customers (Chesters, 2017).

Marketers have an obligation to immerse themselves in their customers' lives – because secondary research is not enough to identify changing consumer preferences. It is also possible for marketers to fall prey to confirmation bias, where they only believe and use the information that supports their own preconceptions. Data has the power to transform marketing into predictive marketing from real customers' behaviours. In fact, GlobalDMA research suggests that the biggest factors encouraging marketers to capitalize on data is the need to become more customer-centric and maximize the effectiveness or efficiency of marketing investments. More is being asked of marketers: operating on hunches or long-held beliefs holds no business value and marketers must have the data to back up their claims.

The new marketing analytics mindset

The new marketing analytics mindset means that marketers will be forced to consider the origin of their ideas, and be prepared to defend and prove that these ideas will be successful. Data will transform the marketing discipline into both an art and a science but marketers must adopt a new mindset (and skillset) to compete, including:

- acceptance that data can and should guide the marketing process;
- acceptance that hunches, no matter how well founded, should not be the basis of campaign ideas;
- acceptance that data analysis should not focus on how the customer interacts with the brand but customer behaviours across a variety of environments;
- acceptance that the purpose of marketing is to nudge customers to make faster decisions, and therefore marketers must understand the decision-making process.

Data analysis tools

Data provides marketers with the ability to create products, services, campaigns and content with meaning and empathy. Data is critical to all marketing functions and can provide organizations with a differentiated advantage. However, the new types of data on offer from social media and sensor data may be complicated to analyse. Data itself does not provide business value, the data must be interpreted and transformed into insight. To ease the complexity of analysing big data, a host of new data-crunching solutions and applications have been created through artificial intelligence (AI) and machine learning (see Table 3.3).

Table 3.3   Examples of artificial intelligence in consumer and business

Products and Technologies	Potential Value	Relevant Industries
Augmented Reality	Cross-channel Insights, Language Translation, 3-D Maps, Virtual Shopping	Hospitality, Travel, Retail
Chatbots and Intelligent Agents	Customer Service and Customer Experience, Personal Productivity, Knowledge Management	Consumer Electronics, Travel, Retail, Beauty, B2B Sales, Legal Services
Imaging (Computer Vision)	Virtual Diagnostics, Brand Management, Quality Assurance	Medicine, Health Management, Manufacturing, Architecture and Urban Planning, Retail, Food and Beverage, Security
Machine Learning Algorithms	Forecasting Utilization, Knowledge Management, Predicative Analytics, Price/Purchase Prediction, Recommendation Engines, Software Development, Virtual Sales Assistants	City Planning, Financial Services, Legal, Travel, Retail, Consumer Electronics, Health Care, Food Safety, Security, Public Transportation, Law Enforcement
Machine Translation and Natural Language Processing	Translating Languages, Reading and Interpreting Text (unstructured data) and Converting it to Signals (structured data)	Digital Marketing, Customer Experience, Health Care (patient record analysis), Travel and Hospitality, Risk Management, Legal Service, Security and Safety

(continued)

Table 3.3 (*Continued*)

Products and Technologies	Potential Value	Relevant Industries
News Feeds	Selecting/Recommending Preferred Content, Increasing Engagement and Preference	Selecting/Recommending Preferred Content, Increasing Engagement Preference
Virtual Reality	Teleconferencing, Gaming, Entertainment, Delivering Virtual Experiences	Retail, Gaming, Media Entertainment, Medicine, Manufacturing

SOURCE Adapted from Altimeter Group, CC 3.0 (see Etlinger, 2017)

One of the most widely discussed and promoted technologies in AI has been the launch of IBM Watson – IBM's AI solution. From winning a game of jeopardy (see video https://www.youtube.com/watch?v=P0Obm0DBvwI) to suggesting strange but delicious food combinations with Chef Watson (see https://www.ibmchefwatson.com/) and assisting marketers to profile their audience's personality characteristics from social data with IBM Watson Personality Insights (https://personality-insights-livedemo.mybluemix.net/), IBM Watson has the power to help marketers turn their data into usable insight. However, IBM is not the only solution for marketers looking to generate insight from new data sources. It is reported that 70 per cent of all marketers now use social listening technologies to analyse social media conversations (Falcon Social, 2016). The social listening tool market is starting to become saturated as marketers place primary importance on their tools selection. A simple Google search on social listening tools returns 62 million articles – and most of these articles provide details of the best tool to use. There is a wide variety of tools available and with similar functionality and a lack of differentiation, making it difficult to choose amongst alternatives. Popular social listening tools include those listed in Table 3.4.

It is important to note that these social listening tools will change over time as new sources and methods of data analysis are created. The tools listed in Table 3.4 highlight a snapshot of what is available today. There is a belief that these social listening tools are the silver bullet in data analysis, and provide 'insight in the noise' (Ney, 2016), which may be why conversations regarding social data analysis start with the tool being used. However, these tools, while essential to analyse large data sets, do little more than provide a means to analyse the data – the data must still be interpreted by

Table 3.4 Popular social listening technologies

Tool	Description
Brandwatch	Brandwatch is an enterprise social intelligence platform that is designed to allow brands to listen and analyse online conversation to extract meaningful insights, inform their business decisions and understand more about the return on their marketing spend.
Crimson Hexagon	Crimson Hexagon is a high-end social monitoring platform with a strong focus on sentiment analysis using statistical analysis techniques. Customers tend to be large consumer brands and agencies.
Digimind	Digimind Social is a social listening tool that enables brands around the world to instantly understand their online presence and competitive standing, and use these insights to inform marketing, communications and engagement strategies.
Infegy Atlas	Infegy Atlas is a social monitoring tool that moves beyond simple number counting to provide answers that help researchers better understand consumers through advanced automated analysis of social media.
NetBase	NetBase is a social media analytics platform that analyses real-time and historical information on the internet. It uses proprietary Natural Language Processing along with machine learning to extract true value meaning and sentiment from online conversations.
NUVI	NUVI is a social media intelligence platform. It is designed to listen, monitor and engage the social web. NUVI's patented bubble stream visualizes the social web in real time.
Pulsar	Pulsar is an audience intelligence platform to facilitate audience understanding, category mapping, creative and planning to find the right segments and communities so that marketers can tailor content with precision.
Radarly by Linkfluence	Radarly is a social media intelligence solution offering powerful social media listening, performance measurement, community engagement and real-time management of countless daily conversations.
Salesforce Radian 6	Salesforce Radian 6 is a social listening technology that helps marketers to track the conversation in their industry to identify trends, opportunities, concerns and competitor activity.
Synthesio	Synthesio is a social media monitoring solution that mixes technology and human analysis.
Sysomos	Sysomos Heartbeat is a real-time social media monitoring and engagement platform that is designed to collect all relevant conversations happening online.
TalkWalker	TalkWalker is a social media search, monitoring and analytics tool. It delivers insights on any given search term and metrics on owned and earned media performance.

a human in order to provide business value. It appears that marketers can easily access data but struggle to transform the data into business value. In fact, PwC found that 23 per cent of businesses find no value from their data initiatives. Many senior marketers and organization C-suite executives have been left thinking that their data investments are not providing a strong return.

Gartner analyst Nick Heudecker believes that the failure rate of data initiatives is close to 85 per cent (quoted in Asay, 2017). At this point you may be asking whether the data challenge is worth the effort. The answer is, yes. One Forbes study found that leaders in data-driven marketing are more than six times more likely to report achieving competitive advantage and increasing profitability than laggards. A key reason for the failure of data initiatives is the tool-centric focus of marketers. By focusing on what tool to use instead of what business questions should be answered, the output can often be superficial due to reliance on the functionality of the tool. To increase the success rate of data initiatives, marketers should focus on identifying the questions to be answered and the metrics and measures that will be employed to answer that specific business question. Instead of being led by the capabilities of the tools, marketers must lead the tools to find new ways to help them answer the most pressing business questions.

A second reason for high failure rates is the focus of analysis. The most commonly executed data-driven activities by marketers include, targeting offers, messages and content, data-driven strategy or product development, customer experience optimization, audience analytics and measurement, and predictive analytics (GDMA and Winterberry Group, 2017). Marketers are caught in a dilemma but wanting to know more about their customers in relation to brands they work for. By focusing on the brand, instead of wider customer behaviours, marketers often find obvious insights that are already known and don't help the brand get closer to the customer. Marketers must adopt a mindset to look beyond brand data, and analyse wider customer behaviours.

Behavioural data analysis

In every other research method there are journal articles and papers to help design good research, but this is largely missing for data analysis research.

Marketers have no best practices or standard metrics to adopt in their data analysis initiatives, projects are managed through iteration and trial and error. Designing a robust methodology could be the missing link to increasing the success rate of data initiatives. For example, brands could shift their focus from their brand to analysing all five environments that their customers operate in. By synthesizing and exploring data created at a societal level, general commerce, specific industry level, competitors and finally at a brand level, marketers' can more easily understand what drives their customers' behaviours, and ultimately their preferences (Figure 3.2).

As humans, we operate in many environments and these environments have the potential to sway our behaviour, and dictate what we expect and need from the other environments. For example, the rise in digital technologies and social media has changed the way we communicate as a society. This societal change filters down into the other environments where connectivity

Figure 3.2   The five customer behaviour environments

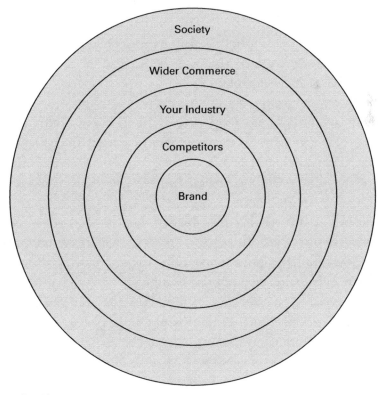

SOURCE Ney (2017)

has changed our perceptions of how we want to communicate with brands, and our expectations of how quickly we should be responded to.

Gad on technology's societal changes

'It's a fact that we have already experienced the largest change in not only the history of human communication, but also human culture globally. The internet and its mobile applications provides a greater and more dramatic empowerment of individuals than anything that has happened before. The force of this huge game-changing element is still not easy to understand or accept. Even though the impact of the internet has now matured, we simply lack the perspective needed to easily understand it, as is always the case with major changes.'

SOURCE Gad (2016)

The internet, social media and mobile technologies can have a profound impact on customer behaviour and expectation – causing business disruption. Many customers are becoming aware that in every online interaction they are leaving a data footprint. Consumers are believed to make a trade-off for data in expectation of receiving better customer experiences (van Bommel, Edelman and Ungerman, 2014). However, many brands still fail to deliver the expected experience. We are at a point in history where data means there are literally no more secrets (Finger and Dutta, 2013) but marketers are struggling to get the right data to solve their customer experience issues. Gad (2016) argues that customer experience is the last frontier in brand differentiation in the Digital Age, so what is the answer to data analysis for marketing?

The best way to answer this question is to look at disruptive innovation. Over the course of the last 10 years, markets globally have been disrupted through innovation. Disruptive innovation creates a new market and value network that eventually disrupts an existing market and value network, displacing established market-leading firms, product and alliances (Bower and Christensen, 1995). Much of this disruption has been caused by digital transformation but ultimately because data and behaviours in each of the five customer behaviour environments was considered. Disruption has become one of the most desired business goals, every brand wants to become the next Uber, Airbnb, Netflix or even SoulCycle, but their disruptive innovation does not always win the customer battle. Dav (2015) argues that disruptive brands are different from ordinary brands because they get people engaged and immersed in the brand equity. The focus for disruptive brands should be focusing on solving a consumer problem in a new way that adds more value, reduces cost or increases connectivity, not trying to disrupt a market. Market disruption is essentially caused by solving the customer's issues in an innovative way – if done correctly, the customer adopts the new provider because they address their needs better than other competitors.

The value of the five customer behaviour environments

Marketers can learn a lot from data produced in all five customer behaviour environments. For example, the 2014 Everline Future 50 competition, which searches for Britain's most disruptive start-up businesses, was not won by a start-up with a completely new business model, or anything that could really be considered disruptive. Instead CompareTheCoffin.com, an online coffin retailer, won by replicating a pre-established business model that is commonly accepted in society and running in other wider commerce industries. The Everline Future 50 competition illustrates that disruption, new product ideas and marketing ideas can be found by analysing data (and behaviour) in the five customer behaviour environments.

As Elon Musk argues: 'don't just follow the trends. Boil things down to the most fundamental truths you can imagine and reason up from there' – the five customer behaviour environments provide marketers with a framework on how to boil down customer behaviours. The output on this analysis should focus on the unmet needs, the pain points and obstacles felt by customers, and their hopes and dreams. The challenge that marketers face is to identify which data sources are of value, the data points to measure, and the metrics to use.

Behavioural metrics

In addition to the five customer behaviour environments, marketers must choose the most appropriate data points and metrics to measure. The number of data points created by new types of data has risen exponentially. As with every new challenge, some of these data points are useful and others have no business value. The immediate challenge for marketers is to decide on the best metrics and data points to measure, but this is an iterative process that may not provide immediate value. As previously mentioned, the different data analysis and social listening tools on the market offer 'standard' metrics that fall prey to the marketer's big number fallacy. The lack of real metrics that measure customer behaviour makes it difficult for marketers to really use the data effectively. We would warn that context is key, don't just count the numbers but look at everything surrounding the data.

It's not all bad news. The benefits of all this new data is that it is unprompted data. The promise of big data analytics is that studies can focus on actual behaviour and that this should supersede the outmoded approaches of focusing on behavioural intentions. If analysed properly, marketers can use big data to understand their customers' every behaviour and predict what their future behaviours will be. This is no easy task and is made substantially more complex with few best practices and known methods of analysis. In every other research method, there are accepted best practices, journal papers and books, and commonly adopted scales, metrics and methods – these largely do not exist for many of the new data sources, particularly with social media data. To have successful data initiatives, focus must shift from counting reach and views to measuring behaviour. Several organizations have taken on this challenge and are attempting to bring the rigour of traditional research into the area of big data, particularly social media data.

Ipsos has re-engineered models that it traditionally adopted in its research and insight services. The Ipsos Censydiam Framework for Social (Figure 3.3) has been developed from a long-running customer motivation framework that views motivational behaviour across two axes, the social dimension and the personal dimension. The framework assumes that there are eight primary customer motivations and it seeks to analyse social data in relation to these motivations. Ipsos (2015) argues that the Censydiam Framework for Social helps brands to uncover the nature of online conversations by revealing the motivations, emotions and the 'why' behind customer discussions.

The Ipsos Censydiam Framework for Social is operationalized on one of the commercial social listening tools (see Table 3.4, p 87), highlighting that there is more potential and value to be sought from commercial tools, and we encourage you not to discount them but build upon them with behavioural metrics. The differentiation that Ipsos provides is its segmentation and analysis framework, which is partly operationalized by human analysts. The framework is based on behaviour, in this case human motivation, and adopts both qualitative (contextual) and quantitative analysis. Ipsos has applied the Censydiam Framework for Social to the automotive industry, where they

Figure 3.3   Ipsos Censydiam Framework for Social

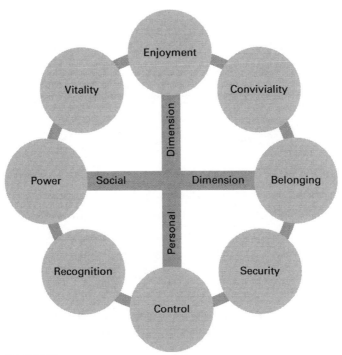

SOURCE Ipsos (SMX) 2015

were able to identify customer motivations to purchase a new car based on the eight human motivations. Adopting the framework to brand advertising, a gap analysis can be completed to spot the white space in advertising and content. The benefit of this analysis is that marketers can identify why customers purchase certain products, brands and even specific product models, and identify what these customers need to hear to help them pay attention to advertising, and the nudges required to help them make decisions faster.

Marketers are able to track how their marketing spend and customer experience management is performing in real time. The potential for big data analysis is huge and, with social media intelligence underpinning this contextual analysis of human behaviour, marketers can identify exactly what their customers need to hear, what they need to see, what they expect and how marketing and customer experience spend is performing. However, as with all research there are ethical considerations, this is particularly profound as many established research ethics do not cover the scope of these new forms of data.

Ethics in data

The use of data, particularly big data research methods, often raises complex ethical issues that intersect with technology, the social sciences, the humanities, and the law. For instance:

- Who has ownership of data and who should be granted access to this data?
- Should data be held by governments and private companies or individual citizens?
- How can data security be ensured?

Traditionally privacy concerns have been focused on the fact that a consumer had some kind of interaction with an organization, where this information was captured and used for marketing purposes. Laws and legislation existed to make it clear how marketers can use the information between the consumer and the organization but social media, sensor data and other digital data has risen the data privacy debate to a new level. The ethical issues surrounding using social media data as research data were explored in a Wisdom of the Crowd Project by Ipsos Mori and partners in 2015 (Evans, Ginnis and Bartlett, 2015). The final recommendations of the joint project concluded that social media is a valid and important research methodology but it does not always fit in easily within existing guidelines and legislation. Evans and associates (2015) advise that regulatory and legal frameworks from market research and the Data Protection Act should be considered when using social data. However, the ethical debate must also consider the other types of digital data created and analysed, like sensor data or location data. In addition to market research and data privacy, the ethical issues surrounding data science should also be considered.

Accenture (2016) has questioned whether there is anything special about data collecting, manipulating, and applying it that requires a distinct code of ethics. They go on to argue that data analytics should be viewed as a phenomenon with consequences beyond technology, and we believe that by reading this chapter you will agree that potential consequences of big data are huge. While many marketers will not be responsible for the big data analysing the data, they will be end users and it is important to understand where your role as a marketer fits into the cross section of data science, market research and marketing. Data's consequence is the blending of disciplines, and this makes it difficult to manage. Accenture (2016) laid out 12 principles of data ethics that data science professionals and practitioners should strive to perpetuate:

Principle 1. The highest priority is to respect the persons behind that data. When insights derived from data could impact the human condition, the potential harm to individuals and communities should be the paramount consideration. Big data can produce compelling insights about populations but those same insights can be used to unfairly limit an individual's possibilities.

Principle 2. Attend to the downstream uses of datasets. Data professionals should strive to use data in ways that are consistent with the intention and understanding of the disclosing party. Many regulations govern datasets on the basis of the status of the data such as 'public', 'private' or 'proprietary'. However, what is done with datasets is ultimately more consequential to subjects/users than the type of data or the context in which it is collected. Correlative uses of repurposed data in research and industry represents both the greatest promise and the greatest risk posed by data analytics.

Principle 3. Provenance of the data and analytics tools shapes the consequences of their use. There is no such thing as raw data – all datasets and accompanying analytics tools carry a history of human decision making. As much as possible, that history should be auditable, including mechanisms for tracking the context of collection, methods of consent, the chain of responsibility and assessments of quality and accuracy of data.

Principle 4. Strive to match privacy and security safeguards with privacy and security expectations. Data subjects should hold a range of expectations about the privacy and security of their data and those expectations are often context-dependent. Designers and data professionals should give due consideration to those expectations and align safeguards and expectations as much as possible.

Principle 5. Always follow the law, but understand that the law is of a minimum bar. As digital transformations have become a standard evolutionary path for business, governments and laws have largely failed to keep up with the pace of digital innovation and existing regulations are often miscalibrated to present risks. In this context, compliance means complacency. To excel in data ethics, leaders must define their own compliance frameworks that outperform legislated requirements.

Principle 6. Be wary of collecting data just for the sake of more data. The power and peril of data analytics is that collected data today will be useful for unpredictable purposes in the future. Give due consideration to the possibility that less data may result in both better analysis and less risk.

Principle 7. Data can be a tool of inclusion and exclusion. While everyone deserves the social and economic benefits of data, not everyone is equally impacted by the processes of data collection, correlation and prediction. Data professionals should strive to mitigate the disparate impacts of their products and listen to the concerns of the affected communities.

Principle 8. As much as possible, explain methods for analysis and marketing to data disclosers. Maximizing transparency at the point of data collection can minimize more significant risks as data travels through the supply chain.

Principle 9. Data scientists and practitioners should accurately represent their qualifications, limits to their experience, adhere to professional standards, and strive for peer accountability. The long-term success of the field depends on public and client trust. Data professionals should develop practices for holding themselves and peers accountable to shared standards.

Principle 10. Aspire to design practices that incorporate transparency, configurability and accountability, and auditability. Not all ethical dilemmas have design solution, but being aware of design practices can break down many of the practical barriers that stand in the way of shared, robust ethical standards.

Principle 11. Products and research practices should be subject to internal and potentially external ethical review. Organizations should prioritize establishing consistent, efficient and actionable ethics review practices for new products, services and research programmes. Internal peer-reviewed practices can mitigate risk, and an external review board can contribute to public trust.

Principle 12. Governance practices should be robust, known to all team members and reviewed regularly. Data ethics poses organizational challenges that cannot be resolved by familiarity compliance regimes alone. Because the regulatory, social and engineering terrains are so unsettled, organizations engaged in data analytics require collaborative, routine and transparent ethical governance.

While on the surface it may not appear that marketers should concern themselves with data science, research or data ethics because they are in most cases the end user, the 2018 changes to the EU General Data Protection Regulation (GDPR) means that marketers must be aware of how their data is collected, processed and used. The GDPR will replace the other data protection legislation in EU member states and will affect every business using customer data. The GDPR means that all European citizens get a new set of rights that any business conducting market, opinion and social research needs to cater for. This includes a right to be forgotten, a right to object to profiling activities, a strengthened right to prior notice before data collection, a right to data portability. European citizens now have, more than ever, a right to know before, during and after businesses collect their data. Businesses and marketers using data should be aware of the changes to data legislation.

The changes in ethics and legislation indicate that marketers must begin moving their thinking about data towards that of a researcher and adopt their ethical code. The Market Research Society (MRS) is the largest research society with 60 years of self-regulation. Their code of conduct has 10 founding principles that marketers should remember when mining data for customer insight:

Principle 1. Researchers shall ensure that participation in their activities is based on voluntary informed consent.

Principle 2. Researchers shall be straightforward and honest in all their professional and business relationships.

Principle 3. Researchers shall be transparent as to the subject and purpose of data collection.

Principle 4. Researchers shall respect the confidentiality of information collected in the professional activities.

Principle 5. Researchers shall respect the rights and wellbeing of individuals.

Principle 6. Researchers shall ensure that participants are not harmed or adversely affected by their professional activities.

Principle 7. Researchers shall balance the needs of individuals, clients, and their professional activities.

Principle 8. Researchers shall exercise independent professional judgement in the design, conduct and reporting of their professional activities.

Principle 9. Researchers shall ensure that their professional activities are conducted by persons with appropriate training, qualifications and experience.

Principle 10. Researchers shall protect the reputation and integrity of the profession.

Throughout all ethical and legislative considerations, it is evident that the act of consent is important. This may prove problematic in social media research, where many of the social listening and social analytics tools do not require social media users to confirm their consent before scraping and analysing their data. There are also calls for skilled professionals to be in control of projects. It is therefore important for marketers to keep up to date with changes in data ethics, legislation and law as well as undertake training and professional development to ensure their customer data initiatives are compliant.

Last thought

Organizations of all sizes have more data than ever at their disposal. However, converting meaningful and actionable insights from that data is difficult. The new analytical mindset required from marketers in the age of data is one that moves from 'knowing' to 'learning'. This is a difficult shift for many as it requires marketers to explore their own decision-making habits, how they generate ideas, and agree that they might not always know the right answer. The new data-driven, learning-orientated culture for marketers comes with a child's mind and treats each day like a school day. The biggest hurdle new marketers will face with big data is finding the right tools and applications to efficiently generate value through data. Both technology and data sources are still changing, and it is the role of the marketers to embrace change, and continually build an ecosystem that allows them to obtain the right data at the right time.

SUMMARY CHECKLIST

- Adopt a new analytical attitude towards the marketing discipline that moves from assumption-based marketing to evidence-based marketing.
- Avoid becoming a data-driven marketer who only uses built-in functionality of analysis tools and work to develop your own behavioural frameworks.

- Overcome the peak complexity challenge by developing your own frameworks and plugging suppliers into the framework – don't be forced to work from the vendor's development agenda.

- Avoid falling into the big numbers and research fallacy by actively analysing behaviour, not numbers, and do so throughout the full marketing process.

- Developing, presenting and applying innovative ideas are not easy steps but there are proven ways to help you become better and to succeed in challenging markets.

- Adhere to the new data legislation and work from an ethical standpoint through data science and research.

Resources to inspire you

- Dr Jillian Ney TEDx talk on social media and data: https://www.youtube.com/watch?v=ki6OhDZNDps

- The data-driven marketing playbook, panel session at SaaStock 2016: https://www.youtube.com/watch?v=8PHvExKg9aw

- Susan Etlinger talk on big data at TED@IBM: https://www.youtube.com/watch?v=AWPrOvzzqZk

Revision questions

1 What types of data would you consider using to profile your customers?

2 What types of data would you consider using to create a new marketing campaign or to create a new product?

3 What are the four Vs of big data? Explain how each one of them can impact marketing decision making.

4 How do you plan on not falling into the research fallacy?

5 If you are using social data to target customers online, what ethical considerations should you be aware of?

References

Accenture (2016) *Universal Principles of Data Ethics: 12 guidelines for developing ethics codes*, Accenture, USA

Allen, R (2017) [accessed 18 June 2018] What Happens Online In 60 Seconds?, *Smart Insights* [Online] https://www.smartinsights.com/internet-marketing-statistics/happens-online-60-seconds/

Asay, M (2017) [accessed 18 June 2018] Big Data Has Been a Big Disappointment, But There's a Way To Ensure Yours Won't Be, *Tech Republic* [Online] https://www.techrepublic.com/article/85-of-big-data-projects-fail-but-your-developers-can-help-yours-succeed/

Barta, T (2016) [accessed 18 June 2018] Marketers: Get Out of the Office, *LinkedIn Pulse* [Online] https://www.linkedin.com/pulse/marketers-get-out-office-thomas-barta?trk=v-feed&lipi=urn%3Ali%3Apage%3Ad_flagship3_detail_base%3B5d ZUC0Rl9TN2t2dMWry6rw%3D%3D

Bower, J L and Christensen, C M (1995) [accessed 18 June 2018] Disruptive Technologies: Catching the Wave, *Harvard Business Review*, January–February [Online] https://hbr.org/1995/01/disruptive-technologies-catching-the-wave

Butler, O (2017) [accessed 18 June 2018] I Made My Shed the Top Rated Restaurant on TripAdvisor, *Vice* [Online] https://www.vice.com/en_uk/article/434gqw/i-made-my-shed-the-top-rated-restaurant-on-tripadvisor

Cadwalladr, C (2018) [accessed 18 June 2018] The Cambridge Analytica Files, 'I Made Steven Bannon's Psychological Warfare Tool': Meet the Data War Whistleblower, *The Guardian* [Online] https://www.theguardian.com/news/2018/mar/17/data-war-whistleblower-christopher-wylie-faceook-nix-bannon-trump

Cadwalladr, C and Graham-Harrison, E (2018) [accessed 18 June 2018] Facebook and Cambridge Analytica Face Mounting Pressure Over Data Scandal, *The Guardian* [Online] https://www.theguardian.com/news/2018/mar/18/cambridge-analytica-and-facebook-accused-of-misleading-mps-over-data-breach

Cain, K (2012) [accessed 18 June 2018] Measuring Marketing Effectiveness: 6 Metrics You Need to Track, *Content Marketing Institute* [Online] http://contentmarketinginstitute.com/2012/10/measuring-marketing-effectiveness-metrics/

Carah, N (2014) Curators of databases: circulating images, managing attention and making value on social media, *Media International Australia*, **150** (1), pp 137–42

Chadwick, P (2018) [accessed 18 June 2018] How Many People Had Their Data Harvested By Cambridge Analytica, *The Guardian* [Online] https://www.theguardian.com/commentisfree/2018/apr/16/how-many-people-data-cambridge-analytica-facebook

Chandrashekar, A, Amat, F, Basilico, J and Jebara, T (2017) [accessed 18 June 2018] Artwork Personalization at Netflix, *The Netflix Tech Blog, Medium* [Online] https://medium.com/netflix-techblog/artwork-personalization-c589f074ad76

Chartered Institute of Marketing, The (2015) [accessed 18 June 2018] Marketing and the 7Ps: A Brief Summary of Marketing and How It Works, *The Chartered Institute of Marketing* [Online] https://www.cim.co.uk/files/7ps.pdf

Chesters, K (2017) [accessed 18 June 2018] Planning In the Wild: How Ogilvy Planners Are Getting Out To Connect With Real People, *Campaign* [Online] http://www.campaignlive.co.uk/article/planning-wild-ogilvy-planners-getting-connect-real-people/1421098#k1uLG0DfQKkRGwRS.99

Dav, A (2015) [accessed 18 June 2018] The 25 Most Disruptive Brands of 2015, *Forbes* [Online] https://www.forbes.com/sites/avidan/2015/11/29/the-25-most-disruptive-brands-of-2015/#798319e77bbd

Davenport, T H and Beck, J C (2002) *Attention Economy: Understanding the new currency of business,* Accenture, USA

Davey, N (2015) [accessed 18 June 2018] Data-Driven Marketing: What Speedbumps Are Slowing Our Progress?, *My Customer* [Online] https://www.mycustomer.com/marketing/data/data-driven-marketing-what-speedbumps-are-slowing-our-progress

Etlinger, S (2017) [accessed 18 June 2018] The Age of AI: How Artificial Intelligence Is Transforming Organizations, *Altimeter, A Prophet Company* [Online] https://www.prophet.com/2017/01/artificial-intelligence-transforming-organizations/

Evans, H, Ginnis, S and Bartlett, J (2015) [accessed 18 June 2018] #SocialEthics a Guide to Embedding Ethics in Social Media Research, Wisdom of the Crowd Report: Ipsos-Mori [Online] https://www.ipsos-mori.com/Assets/Docs/Publications/im-demos-social-ethics-in-social-media-research.pdf

Falcon Social (2016) [accessed 18 June 2018] Social Media Monitoring and Social Data Analysis, *Falcon Social* [Online] https://www.falcon.io/insights-hub/topics/social-media-monitoring/social-dataanalysis/#GEN

Finger, L and Dutta, S (2013) *Ask Measure Learn: Using social media analytics to understand and influence customer behaviour,* O'Reilly, Sebastopol, CA

Gad, T (2016) *Customer Experience Branding: Driving engagement through surprise and innovation,* Kogan Page, London

Gartner Inc. (2016) [accessed 18 June 2018] Hype Cycle for Emerging Technologies, 2016, *Gartner* [Online] http://www.gartner.com/newsroom/id/3412017

GDMA and Winterberry Group (2017) [accessed 18 June 2018] The Global Review of Data-Driven Marketing and Advertising [Online] https://dma.org.uk/uploads/misc/588f3f9e8bbd9-gdma-and-winterberry-group—the-global-review—january-2017_588f3f9e8bb1c.pdf

Godin, S (2012) [accessed 18 June 2018] *All Marketers Are Liars,* Portfolio, New York

Goodwin, T (2016) We're At Peak Complexity – And It Sucks, *TechCrunch* [Online] https://techcrunch.com/2016/09/03/were-at-peak-complexity-and-it-sucks/

Grassegger, H and Krogerus, M (2017) [accessed 18 June 2018] The Data That Turned the World Upside Down, *Motherboard* [Online] https://motherboard. vice.com/en_us/article/how-our-likes-helped-trump-win

Heath, R (2012) *Seducing the Subconscious: The psychology of emotional influence in advertising*, Wiley-Blackwell, West Sussex

Hopkins, B and Evelson, B (2011) [accessed 18 June 2018] Expand Your Digital Horizon With Big Data, *Forrester* [Online] http://www.asterdata.com/ newsletter-images/30-04-2012/resources/forrester_expand_your_digital_horiz. pdf

Humby, C (2006) [accessed 18 June 2018] Data is the New Oil, *ANA Blogs* [Online] http://ana.blogs.com/maestros/2006/11/data_is_the_new.html

Ipsos (2015) [accessed 18 June 2018] Introducing Censydiam Social, *Ipsos SMX* [Online] http://ipsossmx.com/censydiam-social-2/

Kietzmann, J H, Hermkens, K, McCarthy, I P and Silvestre, B S (2011) Social Media? Get Serious! Understanding the Functional Building Blocks of Social Media, *Business Horizons*, 54 (3), pp 241–51

Lang, C (2018) [accessed 18 June 2018] 'It's Not Good' Mark Zuckerberg Speaks About the #Deletefacebook Campaign, *Time* [Online] http://time.com/5210799/ mark-zuckerberg-addresses-delete-facebook-campaign-after-cambridge-analytica/

Lorentz, A (2013) [accessed 18 June 2018] Big Data, Fast Data, Smart Data, *Wired* [Online] https://www.wired.com/insights/2013/04/big-data-fast-data-smart-data/

MacNamara, J (2011) [accessed 18 June 2018] Advertising Values to Measure PR: Why They Are Invalid, *AMEC* [Online] http://amecorg.com/wp-content/ uploads/2011/10/Ad-Values-to-Measure-PR-Paper.pdf

McAfee, A and Brynjolfsson, E (2012) [accessed 18 June 2018] Big Data the Management Revolution, *Harvard Business Review* [Online] https://hbr.org/2012/10/ big-data-the-management-revolution

McGovern, M (2014) [accessed 18 June 2018] Big Data: A Big Focus For Procurement Organizations, *IBM blogs* [Online] https://www.ibm.com/blogs/watson-customer-engagement/2014/01/31/big-data-a-big-focus-for-procurement-organizations/

Nahai, N (2016) [accessed 18 June 2018] The Secret Psychology of Persuasive Content Video, *TheMediaFox* [Online] https://www.youtube.com/watch?v=JhyqK0nwdg8

Ney, J (2016) Social media intelligence in market research, *International Journal of Market Research*, 5 (5), pp 6–11

Ney, J (2017) [accessed 18 June 2018] Driving Growth Through eCommerce, *Crimson Hexagon Webinar Recording* [Online] https://pages.crimsonhexagon. com/WC2017-05-18-WBN-JillianNey_GatedRecordingPage.html

Normandeau, K (2013) [accessed 18 June 2018] Beyond Volume, Variety and Velocity is the Issue of Big Data Veracity, *Inside Big Data* [Online]

http:// insidebigdata.com/2013/09/12/beyond-volume-variety-velocity-issue-big-data-veracity/

Nunan, D and Di Domenico, M L (2013) Market research and the ethics of big data, *International Journal of Market Research*, 55 (4), pp 505–20

O'Hagan, E M (2018) [accessed 18 June 2018] No One Can Pretend Facebook Is Just Harmless Fun Anymore, *The Guardian* [Online] https://www.theguardian.com/commentisfree/2018/mar/18/facebook-extremist-content-user-data

Patel, S (2016) [accessed 18 June 2018] WTF is a GRP?, *Digiday* [Online] http://digiday.com/marketing/what-is-a-grp-gross-ratings-point/

Pieters, R, Wedel, M and Batra, R (2010) The stopping power of advertising: measures and effects of visual complexity, *Journal of Marketing,* 74 (5), pp 48–60

Ram, A (2018) [accessed 18 June 2018] Cambridge Analytica Reveals Finances After Filing For Bankruptcy, *The Financial Times* [Online] https://www.ft.com/content/c07fa7fe-5a84-11e8-bdb7-f6677d2e1ce8

Steel, J (1998) *Truth, Lies, and Advertising: The art of account planning*, John Wiley and Sons, Chichester

Teixeira, T S (2014) [accessed 18 June 2018] The Rising Cost of Consumer Attention: Why You Should Care, and What You Can Do About It, Working Paper [Online] http://www.economicsofattention.com/site/assets/files/1108/teixeira_t-_the_rising_cost_of_attention_working_paper-1.pdf

van Bommel, E, Edelman, D and Ungerman, K (2014) [accessed 18 June 2018] Digitizing the Consumer Decision Journey, *McKinsey* [Online] http://www.mckinsey.com/business-functions/marketing-and-sales/our-insights/digitizing-the-consumer-decision-journey

Ward, C (2015) [accessed 18 June 2018] How to Build a Data-Driven Marketing Strategy, *My Customer* [Online] http://www.mycustomer.com/marketing/data/how-to-build-a-data-driven-marketing-strategy

Wong, J C (2018) [accessed 18 June 2018] Congress Grills Facebook CEO Over Data Misuse – As It Happened, *The Guardian* [Online] https://www.theguardian.com/technology/live/2018/apr/10/mark-zuckerberg-testimony-live-congress-facebook-cambridge-analytica

Innovation skills   04

Marketing and creative thinking

CHAPTER LEARNING OBJECTIVES

After studying this chapter, you will be able to:

- Acknowledge the importance of customer loyalty in today's dynamic marketplace.
- Appreciate the value of innovation for companies and its relation to marketing.
- Recognize the challenges associated with fostering innovation and creative thinking throughout companies.
- Understand the four levels of implementing creativity for a holistic approach to innovation.
- Apply important practices for boosting innovation.

Advanced practice

Building innovation capacity... block by block

Disruption has become the most overused word in the start-up community and the business innovation arena in general (Yahoo News, 2016). If your new idea is not disrupting a whole industry it is not bold, or innovative, enough! It is not a surprise, then, that disruption and radical innovation, as concepts, have been often associated with mobile apps, online platforms and tech giants such as Facebook, Google and Amazon (Lim, 2017) that are changing drastically the way we live and work. Older companies, or incumbents as they are called, appear to be struggling to keep up with the rate of innovations introduced by start-ups and tech giants, and are increasingly afraid not to be 'disrupted' and become completely irrelevant overnight. Within this context, what seems to be a genuine surprise is the resilience of one such 'old' company that has emerged as a leader in creative thinking and innovation strategy: LEGO®.

Despite the gravitational pull that the fancy world of start-ups has on public attention, LEGO has been quietly leveraging its past and embracing the future to successfully become 'The Apple of Toys', which roughly translates to: 'a profit-generating, design-driven miracle built around premium, intuitive, highly covetable hardware that fans cannot get enough of' (Ringen, 2015). The company was founded in 1932 in Denmark by a carpenter called Ole Kirk Kristiansen. The founder made sure to engrave a few simple, but powerful, rules into the company's DNA (Robertson, 2013):

- constant experimentation with modern technologies;
- a characteristically Scandinavian obsession with quality;
- a system approach to gaming.

LEGO has had its fair share of failures in many of its new and innovative projects, especially in the early 2000s, but it eventually learnt a vital lesson in innovation that put the company firmly back into profitability. As Wharton Professor David Robertson put it (2013): 'this [return to success] occurred only after LEGO realized that simply increasing the number of new product ideas wasn't enough… LEGO learnt that boosting innovation is the easy part. What is much harder is to boost discipline at the same time, so you get not just bigger catalogues, but more profitable products.' Great new ideas and exciting new projects can only bring short-term benefits, at best, if not accompanied by new operational processes, new management, new job descriptions, new departments and a tight business ethic in creating sustainable growth (Robertson, 2013). LEGO's lesson in innovation, in short, is that a company should always be the most creative it can be, but by having a clear view of its role and values and with rigorous business support for all new product lines, projects and channels.

The relentless focus on constant experimentation in LEGO, and the acceptance of failure as a learning tool, made the company one of the most innovative companies in the world and, hands down, the most innovative toy company in the world (Basulto, 2014). At the very centre of all this, is LEGO's Future Lab. The Future Lab is the power engine of LEGO's creative leadership. Although working hard all year around to implement innovative projects, many ideas come from a retreat that takes place once per year (Ringen, 2015). On that retreat, the Future Lab people, together with internal and external diverse associates, go through a series of activities including competitions, brainstorming sessions, hackathons and more, to bring the next big idea that, according to the former LEGO Group CEO Jørgen Vig Knudstorp, is 'obviously LEGO, but has never been seen before' (Ringen, 2015).

Building such a team, and an overall culture of creative thinking and innovation, is easier said than done. But in today's unpredictable and chaotic business environment it is crucial. No need to come from the 'hot' world of start-ups. The humble LEGO brick has more to teach modern marketers about innovation than the next start-up clone that tries to copy Mark Zuckerberg's success with Facebook. The challenge? As David Gram, Marketing Director of LEGO's Future Lab, puts it: 'how to create a culture of creative confidence and exploration... You need to have a playful experimenting approach. And if companies can move in that direction, I think they become resilient to almost any change' (Howarth, 2017). Advanced marketing managers need to foster such a culture, not only in their own departments, but throughout the organization!

The marketing challenge

Customer loyalty has become an important if not *the* most important goal for marketers nowadays. In a world of increasing competition from all around the globe, of unpredictable new turns, of technological advancements and of accelerated shifts in consumer tastes, loyalty appears to be the company-saving glue that keeps customers connected to brands.

The financial value of leading corporations supports loyalty as the ultimate measure in contemporary business. In 2014 Apple managed to surpass the milestone of US $700 billion in market valuation (or market capitalization). This means that the company's total value, on a specific day in late November 2014, was US $700 billion or more (Higgins, Ciolli and Bost, 2014). Apple was the first publicly traded company in the history of western capitalism that managed to reach this valuation level. Although the number itself is impressive enough, a closer look at Apple's achievement reveals the close-knit, modern relation between financial success and customer loyalty.

Why do investors buy corporate stocks? How do they choose a company over others? Although there are numerous theories and methods for analysing stocks, a simple answer is that investors believe that the company will do well in the market and this will reflect to their stock, regardless if their motivation is to earn (US Securities and Exchange Commission, 2016):

- from regularly paid dividends, so-called income stocks;
- from the rapid increase in price of the stocks, so-called growth stocks;
- from long-term safety of the stocks, so-called blue-chip stocks;
- from the currently very low price of the stock that could soon bounce back to higher levels, so-called value stocks.

Today, in an insanely volatile business environment, what secures that a company will do well tomorrow, and will create value for its investors, is customer loyalty. It is the confidence that someone will continue buying products and services from a company that attracts many investors. If customers disappear tomorrow by easily switching to another provider or supplier then investors are in trouble. It is not by accident that the main headline in the news on 25 November 2014 for Apple reaching US $700 billion market valuation was 'Apple Tops $700 Billion Valuation, Fuelled by New Products' (Higgins, Ciolli and Bost, 2014). Thus, it is not a surprise that when Apple became the first US company to reach the US $800 billion valuation mark in 2017 (9 May), business news reports cited again the excitement built around the new iPhone as the main reason for the new market capitalization record (Webb, 2017). Coca-Cola as well cites first and foremost successful product and packaging innovations as the main reason for being evaluated as the third most valuable brand in the world in 2016 (Coca-Cola Company, 2016). Great companies have great new products that loyal fans rush to buy – and great new products need great innovation.

Customer loyalty is not only a valuable asset for attracting investors but also a strong financial indicator of a dominating brand. The presence or absence of customer loyalty, from the CFO and CEO viewpoints, can easily be detected within financial reports. As we saw in Chapter 1, advanced marketing managers need urgently to talk this language in order to win their colleagues' trust and support. Although there is some debate on the exact meaning of similar terms such as goodwill, brand calculation and brand equity (Wasserman, 2015; Pappu, Quester and Cooksey, 2005), in essence all of them try to determine the strength of a brand based on how closely attached customers are to it. The more attached, or loyal, the customers are to a brand the bigger the positive impact of the brand on the financial status of a company. This is actually the part of marketing that CEOs, CFOs and other

C-suite executives most appreciate (see, for example, the study in Chapter 1 showing higher trust for 'ROI' marketers). The bigger the part of a company's value attributed to brand value alone, the more effective marketing has been in creating loyal and eagerly awaiting customers through successful innovations. So, how much of Apple's record-breaking market valuation was attributed to brand strength?

After Apple reached the US $700 billion mark, and before getting to the $800 billion milestone, Apple retracted to the 'humble' value of US $639 billion (Colvin, 2015). The remarkable fact is that its total capital at that time was $172 billion. In comparison, Exxon Mobil's total capital at the time was US $304 billion and its market capitalization $330 billion (Colvin, 2015). Which of the two companies benefitted more from its brand? The answer is clear. Standing outside the Apple store for hours, if not days, waiting for the next gadget has a significant impact on investors' excitement with the company's stock. When the price of the company as a whole goes up, CEOs are happier and CMOs more successful.

Apple's brand value by Interbrand

According to Interbrand and its world-famous brand value ranking exercise, Apple is the leading global brand in terms of brand value for the past few years, reaching in 2016 the brand value of US $178.1 billion, 5 per cent up from the year before (Interbrand, 2016). So, it is not only Apple's skyrocketing stock price that reveals the impact of exciting innovations on a company's value but also the net contribution of the brand. These two are closely related.

The progression model shown in Figure 4.1 explains graphically how both innovation and eager, loyal customers lead to higher performance of a company's stock in the market and eventually to a happy CEO. Marketing success must be defined that way: hard financial gains leading to CEO happiness. This is how marketers will gain popularity, importance and a more strategic role in companies. The key question for determining a successful marketer should be: how much of your company's value can be attributed to your brand?

The key problem with customer loyalty today, though, is that despite the numerous photos that can be found online with people having tattooed a

Figure 4.1   Progression model: from innovation to successful marketers

brand on their body, or having shaved the shape of a company's logo on their head, loyalty has become more difficult to achieve than ever before. Schultz, Block and Viswanathan (2014) looked into consumer preferences in the US retail market and found something equally interesting and alarming. In their own words: 'findings from a large-scale survey across multiple product categories indicate a decreasing preference amongst consumers for manufacturer-originated national brands. Interestingly, this is accompanied by a nontrivial increasing preference for the No Preference option in consumer questionnaires (Schultz, Block and Viswanathan, 2014)'. This means that more customers do not go for specific brands and that they show no strong fondness towards any brand. The same researchers then compared those results with two more sources, the Customer Loyalty Engagement Index by Brand Keys and the brand value measures by BAV Consulting. Initial results were confirmed. Customers find it more difficult than ever to differentiate between brands and find them increasingly as more similar than ever. Schultz, Block and Viswanathan (2014) concluded that the risk of product commoditization is very high possibly because:

- consumers have more choices than ever, with abundant product extensions and variations;

- they have more access than ever before to information and to referral networks;

- companies introduce more incrementally improved products in the market faster than ever before.

Those findings are in accordance with research by consultancy Fidelum Partners in Europe, showing that customers do not show strong loyalty towards any of the business brands in five major European markets they conducted their study in: the UK, France, Germany, the Netherlands and Spain (Fidelum Partners, 2016). Surprisingly enough, the only brand that was consistently found to score high in loyalty was the National Mail Service in those countries, followed in most of the cases by the National Health Service. To paraphrase a famous sentence from Shakespeare's masterpiece, *Romeo and Juliet*: commercial brands... *'where art thou'*?

Commodity is the exact opposite of a brand. In overcluttered and fast-moving markets, it becomes more difficult than ever to convince customers that a product or service is unique and worth associating with. But this is exactly what determines the success of a brand. So, marketers have a monumental challenge on their hands.

The challenge for marketers today is how to create innovations that will excite customers, investors and CEOs alike. But innovation is not just about mindlessly churning out new products or projects, as we saw earlier in the chapter with LEGO during the early 2000s. It is about fostering a culture of constant creative problem solving at all levels, accompanied by corporate structures and procedures that actively support chosen innovations to create real value for customers and other stakeholders in the marketplace, especially in an era when loyalty is decreasing. How this can be achieved is explained in this chapter.

Your next McDonald's order could be a surprise

No brand nowadays, regardless of how big or small it is, can avoid being innovative in order to survive. Even globally known brands with well-established characteristics and associations are now trying new and refreshing approaches to make sure they stay relevant. McDonald's, the global fast-food giant, opened in 2017 a completely new restaurant concept in Hong Kong. The fully renovated interior is totally unrelated to the standard atmosphere and design, followed closely by a very different product offering. Apart from the known McDonald's menu, customers can find a salad bar carrying 19 ingredients including hip items such as quinoa (Haridasani, 2017). The restaurant also offers mobile phone-charging platforms, free Wi-Fi, self-ordering kiosks with Create-Your-Taste options as well as table service after 6 pm and premium coffee (Haridasani, 2017). It also has digital walls, new modern uniforms for the staff, open-plan kitchens that the company calls 'theatre kitchens' and waffles (Sheffield, 2017). The name of the concept? McDonald's Next. Why does McDonald's take such bold steps towards the future? The answer lies, again, in numbers. As it turns out, lower-than-expected results in early 2015 and trending global eating habits have pushed the brand to reconsider its concept and experiment with a different format. The company has called it the 'Deep Depression' and has taken many actions to reverse it, the latest being McDonald's Next. After visiting the new concept, one of the McDonald's Next customers stated: 'I think it's increased the value of the brand' (Haridasani, 2017). This is exactly the role of innovation: to enthuse customers, keep them coming back for more and shield the brand from competition and from wider socio-economic threats, leading to higher brand valuation.

Innovation: everyone wants it but many resist it

Marketing and innovation are two tightly interwoven terms. Marketing naturally involves innovation and innovation naturally involves marketing in return. You cannot actually have the one without the other. As ultimate business guru Peter Drucker famously said: 'Because the purpose of business is to create a customer, the business enterprise has two – and only two – basic functions: marketing and innovation. Marketing and innovation produce results; all the rest are costs' (Trout, 2006). Drucker's assertion encapsulates innovation's strategic role, to create a customer, and thus it showcases the intimate relation of innovation with marketing. If the definitive purpose of all innovation projects is not, at the end of the day, to help a company deliver better offers and experiences to its customers, then those projects need to be re-examined. Even when innovations target internal processes and problems, the end results should always impact the market, and especially customers. As *Fortune* magazine's editor-at-large Geoff Colvin (2016) emphasized in his book *Humans Are Underrated*: 'Creativity is nice. Creativity with empathy is valuable.' Empathy, for advanced marketers, is the ability to understand, feel and deliver to customers products that will directly impact their overall physical, psychological and social wellbeing (more on this in Chapter 6). In a nutshell, creative problem solving and the resulting innovations should aim to solve genuine issues and to improve, drastically in the best-case scenario, the lives of customers. Otherwise, creative thinking is just art and innovations are self-serving.

Although innovation is arguably a key business competence, if not *the* key competence together with marketing, reality in companies does not always follow through. In 2006, Jack Trout reported in *Forbes* magazine that when top management is surveyed, priorities include finance, sales, production, management, legal and people (Trout, 2006). Absent from those priorities are the two top functions of marketing and innovation. In today's turbulent environment, where incumbents are fighting with start-ups for a piece of the future, it would be expected that the situation is different. Ros Taylor, the author of the book *Creativity at Work*, conducted a survey in the UK with 1,000 professionals. She concluded that (Taylor, 2013):

- Just 30 per cent of the sample felt that their companies were doing something substantial about creative thinking.

- One of the lowest scores in the survey was achieved on the question about companies having creativity at the top of their agenda.

- Even in the industries with the highest scores in terms of creativity, like media, leisure and the arts, scores did not pass the 50 per cent mark.

- Junior staff scored their companies lower than more senior staff on creative thinking.

- Another lowest score was observed in the question regarding specific techniques used to tackle problems creatively.

These points are particularly interesting when taking into account the results of the IBM Global CEO Study in 2010. That study, which included more than 1,500 CEOs from 33 industries and 60 countries, found that the top skills for future survival are creative thinking and problem solving (IBM, 2010). CEOs globally are embracing creative thinking as a prerequisite and necessary condition for innovation but in many cases, if not in most cases, this does not trickle down to the whole organization. Also, it seems that it is not accompanied by detailed guidelines and procedures of how creativity should be executed daily. Companies want successful innovations but management has not yet found the way to deliver.

The problem is systemic and hardwired into management behaviour. In a seminar paper titled 'The bias against creativity: why people desire but reject creative ideas', researchers Mueller and her associates discovered something fascinating. By conducting two experiments they were able to show that despite people's own open-mindedness, they evaluated creative ideas and innovation breakthroughs lower when they were explicitly instructed to reduce uncertainty and when they felt generally uncertain (Mueller, Melwani and Goncalo, 2012). According to the authors of the paper these findings have immense implications for modern businesses since management can be, on the one hand, praising new ideas and innovation, and on the other, pushing people to be less creative by always asking for the best or optimum solution, and by asking employees to be vigilant of time, financial and other resources. Creative thinking and innovation need experimentation, which by default is uncertain in nature. So, management that is not fostering a sense of certainty for employees to feel comfortable to work with uncertainty will not experience the benefits of creative problem solving.

The same authors also studied a company that was considering a list of innovative product ideas. They asked executives, managers and various gatekeepers in that company to rate those ideas in terms of creativity, feasibility and profitability. They then asked both those managers and customers which of those new products they would love to see in the marketplace. Customers chose the most creative-marked ideas while managers chose the most feasible and profitable-marked ones (Mueller, 2014). In Mueller's *Harvard Business Review* article appropriately titled 'Managers reject ideas customers want' (2014) she explained that according to hers and her associate's studies, when managers get into a 'how' mindset they go more for feasible ideas, while when they get into a 'why' mindset they go more for creative solutions.

This simply means that when managers get into management shoes, asking typical managerial questions such as:

- 'Who is responsible for this?'
- 'Do we have the budget?'
- 'How does it fit into our present pipeline?'
- 'Do current skills allow for this?'
- 'What does research say?'
- 'Where is the feasibility study?'
- 'How much time will it take?'
- 'How risky is it?'

… and others, they decrease drastically the innovation potential of their decision-making process. This does not mean that all ideas are equally good, that the craziest ones are automatically the best or that managers should not be asking such questions. As we will see later in the chapter, contemporary creative thinking models factor in both idea generation and examination carefully. The main point here is that companies tend to bring into the market innovations that they are most comfortable with, NOT the ones that customers would embrace the most. No surprise then that customers struggle to identify real differences between brands. When it comes to innovation, those who dare win.

The Four Horsemen of Apocalypse that kill creativity

One of the most popular moments in our lectures and seminars is when we expose corporate executives, managers and even junior staff to what we call *The Four Horsemen of Apocalypse* and their influence against creative thinking and effective innovation in modern companies. Since at least 70 per cent of marketers face serious inefficiencies, not allowing them to apply creative thinking at work (Staples, 2015), fighting those Horsemen is vital for delivering meaningful and impactful innovations in the marketplace. The Four Horsemen are the following:

1st Horseman: meetings. How many meetings do managers have per day, week, month and even within a year? What is the effect of those meetings on significant performance indicators such as productivity and innovation? In a summary of available studies on the topic, leadership expert and author Ray Williams (2012) found out that as much as 50 per cent of meetings are a waste or misuse of valuable corporate time. He quotes Former Ernst & Young executive Al Pittampalli in saying that meetings are 'not about coordination but about a bureaucratic excuse making and the kabuki dance of company politics. We're now addicted to meetings that insulate us from the work we ought to be doing' (Williams, 2012).

2nd Horseman: presentations. This could be a variation of the 1st Horseman since many corporate meetings include presentations. However, the danger of presentations in corrupting managerial problem solving and creative thinking is so high that it deserves its own Horseman. The main case-in-point here is the fatal destruction of NASA's Space Shuttle Columbia while it was re-entering Earth's atmosphere in February 2003. When Yale University Professor, and expert on presentation of visual information, Edward Tufte, studied the case he found out that NASA engineers had indeed spotted the problem while Columbia was in orbit and presented it to their superiors. The specific information though did not have the impact it should since it was accompanied by many other slides full of bullet-points and other technical information (Judkins, 2015). The standard format of many corporate presentations does not comply with modern approaches of transmitting effectively visual information. In short, presentations make everything look and feel similar without differentiating between life-and-death points and trivial ones. They are too flat, uneventful and impersonal, and they do more harm than good. They can kill people, literally. Jeff Bezos, Amazon CEO, has even banned the use of PowerPoint in executive meetings to boost engagement (Gallo, 2018).

3rd Horseman: e-mails. On average, employees spend almost 30 per cent of their time reading and writing e-mails (Vozza, 2015). This means that almost one-third of your working time is consumed by your e-mails. This is absurd. Especially since e-mailing has been proven to increase considerably employee stress (Evans, 2014). Actually, taking breaks from checking e-mails helps employees improve both their sense of wellbeing and their focus levels (Vozza, 2015). This is the reason why companies are introducing 'no e-mails' days, where they actually observe spikes in effective time management, productivity and human interaction. E-mails tend to disconnect and isolate people, help create misunderstandings, support more bureaucracy than innovation and give a false sense of 'job well done'. Minimizing e-mail sizes and volumes, switching to more collaborative modern platforms and increasing face-to-face time can boost morale, productivity and creative problem solving in equal measures.

4th Horseman: spreadsheets. The strongest reaction we get from our audiences is probably with this last but most vicious of all Horsemen. We usually joke that: 'If it's in the spreadsheet, it happened. If it's not in the spreadsheet it never happened!' In an article with the playful title 'Microsoft's Excel might be the most dangerous software on the planet', *Forbes* contributor Tim Worstall (2013) explained how a big part of the world's financial system is running on spreadsheets, with huge risk of misuse and manipulation. This is because spreadsheets, as presentations and e-mails, portray a two-dimensional world that is too distant and too disconnected from our dynamic and chaotic reality. Numbers on a spreadsheet for many professionals look stable, controllable and as if representing absolute truths. This is a dangerous illusion. Executives' obsession with spreadsheets have caused imaginative responses, like the following one that can be found in many books: '"You can't learn this in a spreadsheet, kid", said the old man, his weather-beaten face grimacing as he swiftly removed the caribou's entrails' (BBC, 2013).

The Four Horsemen of Apocalypse roam out of control in many companies, unleashing their catastrophic menace against creative thinking and innovation. They need to be tamed urgently, not destroyed, if marketers are to boost creativity and increase the rate of successful innovation in their companies.

The new and experimental McDonald's Next format in Hong Kong was used in the previous section as an example of a well-established brand trying to respond to changes and trends by creatively offering refreshing solutions to its customers. Here McDonald's will be used as an example of what can go wrong with the creative problem-solving process in incumbents. It has to do with breakfast.

After experiencing a surge in same-store sales in the United States, from the beginning of 2011 to the first quarter of 2012, McDonald's saw a serious decrease in sales lasting from mid-2012 to mid-2015 (Griswold, 2016). This was a real blow for the finances of the company. However, the company's sales managed to recover spectacularly in the last quarter of 2015, up 5.7 per cent from the previous quarter, when McDonald's decided to make its breakfast available during the whole day (Griswold, 2016). It is impressive that one move, introducing the all-day breakfast, could put the company back on track and revitalize its finances. It must have been a real breakthrough, if not a revelation – the brilliant idea of offering the classic McDonald's breakfast all day and not only during the morning. How come this amazing insight kept itself hidden? It didn't. Customers were asking for this persistently for years but McDonald's seemed to be resisting it.

Customers frequently asked McDonald's to allow for breakfast to be served all day both through the company's website and through traditional marketing research. Here are typical responses of company officials when asked why the company initially had reservations about this request (Griswold, 2016):

- 'Well, it's not compatible with our current operating system. It's too complicated to deliver the high-quality product that we deliver at breakfast' (then CEO, Jim Skinner, 2006).

- 'It's something that we haven't really done any extensive testing on, and we would have to see how much that would stretch our capacities' (Steve Plotkin, President of McDonald's west division, 2009).

- 'Breakfast is a difficult business to be in… It takes a full commitment. It takes staffing commitment. It takes an attitude commitment about being the best you can be at that time of the morning and opening earlier and doing whatever' (Jim Skinner, 2010).

After decades of marketing science and practice, and after years of customer-centricity becoming a key theme in modern business narrative, it is rather puzzling how a consumer-driven company like McDonald's did not bring to its restaurants earlier the change its customers demanded. If companies do not respond rigorously and passionately to the 'easy' changes already demanded by their customers, sometimes even for years, how can they bring about disruptive innovations that can win the future for them? The conclusion of Nokia's CEO, Stephen Elop, in his speech on the collapse of the leading Finnish mobile brand, when Apple and Samsung smartphones changed that industry for ever, says it all: 'We didn't do anything wrong, but somehow, we lost' (Drath, 2016).

Not following the outside world closely, being too comfortable with the status quo, having too much confidence with current capabilities, not prioritizing constant learning and losing touch with customers' shifting desires can bring companies, even global brands, to their knees. To avoid such pitfalls and navigate into the future successfully through constantly reinventing products and services, advanced marketing managers need to put into practice the famous adage: 'The best way to predict the future is to create it' (Brown, 2014). The next section presents models useful to marketers to boost their creative thinking and grow the innovation potential of their companies.

Creative thinking model for advanced marketers

Innovation is king but it is also easier said than done. In order to help modern marketers decode the complexity of creative thinking and innovation capacity within organizations, and apply it successfully, we have compiled the model shown in Figure 4.2.

Figure 4.2   Four levels of creativity in transformative marketing

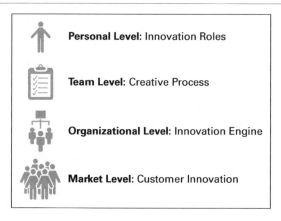

The model in Figure 4.2 comprises of four levels. All of these levels need to be taken into account for a holistic approach to innovation. Picking and mixing is not advised, apart from initial experimentation with the model. Each level is based on a specific scientific source. All levels are explained below.

Personal level: innovation roles

One of the most revered innovation companies in the world is IDEO. IDEO has worked with global brands such as Apple, Ford, IKEA, Bosch and many others, helping them to develop products, services, spaces and organizations that answer to modern human needs and wants (IDEO, 2016). The main aim of IDEO's work is to empower communities, cities and countries. Tom Kelly, a partner of IDEO and author of best-selling books on creativity and innovation, offers in his classic book *The Ten Faces of Innovation: Strategies for heightening creativity*, 10 key roles that people in organizations should play in order to cultivate a creative culture and produce innovation that matters. The 10 faces that constitute the personal level in the model, applied to the marketing profession, are (Kelly and Littman, 2008):

1 **The anthropologist.** Marketers need to experience the pains and hopes of their customers as they live them. Spending time outside the office and close to the realities of customers as these unfold is invaluable. Reports and presentations of marketing research results, and data on a laptop screen, are not enough. Reality cannot be substituted.

2 **The experimenter.** Marketers need to take calculated risks on a daily basis. Through a constant state of trial and error, marketing staff should experiment with different ideas, projects, solutions and offers until success is proven in the marketplace. The old 'best-of-the-best solution' does not apply any more, especially since yesterday's success says nothing about tomorrow's survival.

3 **The cross-pollinator.** Creative solutions to marketing problems can be found in unexpected places. Marketers need to go beyond their company, market and industry to search for ideas that can revolutionize products, services and processes. Staying for too long isolated within the box of your industry can harm creative thinking. People in other industries might have already done the work for you. Go and find it.

4 **The hurdler.** Perseverance is a key aspect for successful innovations. Not giving up and finding ways of bypassing organizational barriers to introduce

clever new ideas should always be part of marketers' plans. Don't expect that the whole organization will react enthusiastically to your proposals. Knowing this in advance and preparing adequately separates successful from failed marketing innovations. Giving up is not an option.

5 The collaborator. For marketing ideas to become market realities, a diverse group of people needs to work together and make innovations happen. Marketers need to be collaborators by securing the active partnership of people, internally and externally, to support and carry the idea forward. Innovation is not an isolation game.

6 The director. Advanced marketers collect and combine necessary talent to launch innovative projects. They act as directors gathering, coordinating, motivating and rewarding their team appropriately to achieve results through enhanced creativity. Innovation does not happen by itself.

7 The experience architect. Marketers should be focusing on delivering innovative experiences to their customers, not just new products and services. Customers value brands based on their overall experience and modern marketers should approach innovation as architects of their customers' experiences with the brand.

8 The set designer. The physical and relational context in which marketers develop innovations has strategic importance to the outcome of those innovations. Marketers should constantly create and re-create their surroundings to make sure it fosters creative thinking. Physical space, such as your office, matters. Does it make you more creative?

9 The caregiver. Customers do not want to be treated as customers but as valuable human beings. Marketers' perception of customers should shift from one based solely on economic transactions to one based on customers' long-term wellbeing. Modern marketers who are sincere caregivers have better chances of delivering winning innovations. Don't just sell, care.

10 The storyteller. Motivation is what makes creative thinking work – and motivation can stem from great stories. Marketers should use the power of storytelling both with colleagues internally in the company and with customers and partners externally, to connect and inspire. What is *your* innovation story?

Those roles are not personality traits. Although some people might find themselves more in some roles than others, the point here is that marketers should identify the impact of each role in their projects. Marketers and their partners should adopt those roles consciously to boost creativity and encourage innovation. As Kelly and Littman (2008) emphasized: 'The personas are about "being innovation" rather than merely "doing innovation".' Creative thinking cannot be faked, it has to be genuinely experienced.

Team level: creative process

Creative thinking has emerged as a major theme in today's business and thus there is a plethora of articles, books and overall scientific and practitioners' literature on the topic. The contribution of neuroscience in understanding exactly how creativity works in our brains has been particularly important in both marketing and leadership fields. Nikolaos Dimitriadis and Alexandros Psychogios published, in their 2016 book *Neuroscience for Leaders: A brain adaptive leadership approach*, a framework for creative thinking within teams that encapsulates recent science and practice. The process, consisting of six steps, ensures that teams employ a brain-based approach to delivering creative solutions to business problems. These six steps (Dimitriadis and Psychogios, 2016) are:

Step 1. Understanding. The first step has to do with the marketing team immersing itself into the problem: collecting data, talking to people, going through every piece of information. This is important for the executive, or analytical, brain to familiarize itself with the situation in as much detail as possible. Feed your team's brains with the specifics of the problem and of the wider context.

Step 2. Exploration. The executive brain has now to rest and the team needs to become as engaged as possible in exploring different possibilities, angles and scenarios. You should refrain from emphasizing responsibilities, uncertainties, failure probabilities and other information that would harm the team's ability to keep as open a mind as possible. Playfulness, excitement and a strong sense of purpose can have very positive effects in this step.

Step 3. Decision Making. When a consensus starts building around an option, or a set of options, the marketing team should not implement it automatically. In this step, the team should ask direct, tough and challenging questions for the chosen solutions. Furthermore, the team should self-reflect to make sure that biases, tiredness and even company politics do not dilute the process. Finally, asking people from the outside world, including customers, would help reveal aspects hidden from the team.

Step 4. Implementation. Implementation of innovative solutions is rarely, if ever, a straightforward affair. Marketing teams should have a clear road map of how to bring the selected ideas to life by getting personally involved, influencing others in the company, and constantly re-evaluating their assumptions. This step is as important as choosing the idea itself.

Step 5. Results. Measuring the impact of innovations in the marketplace is not as easy as it seems. Use a variety of evaluation methods on different levels, like customer, company, competition, as well as on the wider context of the industry as a whole. Apply both quantitative and qualitative measures, and make sure that your team celebrates successes and learns from failures.

Step 6. Configuration. Marketing teams should build creative processes as an integral part of their everyday job and not use creativity as an incidental firework. Empowerment, constant experimentation, passionately questioning the status quo, great team spirit, always engaging outsiders and customers, and putting specific practices and procedures in place will help the team create the necessary conditions for a constant flow of creativity.

These six steps are designed to boost neuroplasticity in the team members' brains and thus untangle learning, open-mindedness and creativity. The ultimate goal is for marketing teams to perform the steps naturally but to also safeguard the process that can be easily hijacked by habitual behaviour and an overall organizational culture that opposes real creative thinking.

Organizational level: innovation engine

 The last point above is not to be taken lightly. Marketers can do only so much if the overall corporate attitude discourages creative behaviour and genuine innovation. In such cases, marketers need to step into their transformation leadership shoes and aim at changing the culture of the company as a whole. Although not an easy task, this is actually the key role that the industry is asking marketers to play, as explained in the first chapter of this book. Tina Seelig, Professor of the Practice in the Department of Management Science and Engineering at Stanford University, and a global authority in creative thinking, introduced in her 2012 book *InGenius: A crash course in creativity*, a model for infusing and maintaining creative problem solving throughout the organization. She calls it the *Innovation Engine* and it consists of two groups: an inner one and an outer one (Seelig, 2012). Each of the two groups has three elements. Being a corporation-wide concept the engine touches some of the elements discussed in the previous levels. The Innovation Engine is as follows:

Inner Group A: imagination. There is no creativity without imagination. But imagination is restricted by corporate mental rigidity, strict rules and management unavailability for unexpected ideas. Instead of giving people problems that have single solutions, corporations should approach problems as open concepts with no single answer. Framing challenges appropriately can do miracles for unleashing the imagination capacity of the workforce. The same can be achieved by encouraging team members to connect unexpectedly distant and seemingly incompatible concepts. Companies should invest in training to help people develop such skills at all levels.

Inner Group B: knowledge. Since, according to the engine, knowledge is the toolbox for imagination, companies should enhance the ability of their employees to constantly learn new skills and to help them acquire new information from the world around them. Staying in a static box kills creativity and minimizes the capacity to solve problems differently. Companies should develop programmes by which, first, staff are exposed to new experiences, and second, build new capacities.

Inner Group C: attitude. The inner urge to innovate or not is fuelled by a corresponding mindset. According to Seelig, people can either view themselves as puzzle builders or as quiltmakers. The first try always to develop the absolute solution and if something does not fit they either abandon or get stuck in the process. The second create solutions with whatever resources they have, always trying to identify the most effective combination of those available resources. Companies should detect the current mentality and help form the appropriate one.

Outer Group A: habitat. The way companies design, organize and use their working space can benefit or harm innovation. Stimulating environments that encourage interaction, formal and informal, and empower people to co-create their own habitat in accordance with the task at hand are preferable for boosting creativity. Also, the general employment ecosystem with its rules and regulations, rewards and feedback mechanisms, management and IT infrastructure constitutes the context by which innovation will thrive or die.

Outer Group B: resources. Companies provide a number of resources to staff to use for experimentation and innovation. Financial, infrastructural and managerial resources can and should be used to foster an innovative environment. However, people should be encouraged to unlock hidden resources by utilizing people's skills, systems and internal services in ways not seen before.

Outer Group C: culture. Metaphorically, this is the background music to everyday life in a company. For example, is it a cheerful tune or a depressive one? Culture includes the values and cognitive shortcuts that drive behaviour. It is about the written, and mostly unwritten, rules that determine what is acceptable and expected. Culture is the ultimate determinant of creativity in a company and should start from the top.

The inner group is a micro view of innovation and the outer group a macro view. Seelig constructed her Innovation Engine in such a way that micro elements create couples with their macro counterparts. The As are tied together, as the Bs and the Cs are too. Looking at these couples, the engine suggests that:

- the habitat shapes our imagination potential;
- resources shape our knowledge inventory;
- corporate culture shapes our attitudes.

The Innovation Engine is a very effective tool for modern marketers in helping them to understand better creative thinking in the organization as a whole and, mainly, in giving them the right argumentation and tools for leading creative thinking throughout their companies.

Market level: customer innovation

 Innovations that do not decisively aim at improving customers' lives practically and empathically are not marketing or business innovations. Even when creative problem solving targets internal bottlenecks and inefficiencies, the end results should always be improving customers' wellbeing. As shown earlier in this chapter, marketing and innovation are two sides of the same coin, and the one cannot exist without the other. In this direction, Professor Marion Debruyne, Dean of Vlerick Business School in Belgium, developed an advanced model of customer-centric innovation explained in her 2014 award-winning book *Customer Innovation: Customer-centric strategy for enduring growth*. According to Debruyne, great companies combine customer-centricity with innovation power to discover new market opportunities by starting with the customer and designing their strategy around them. Such companies are not driven by what they are good at but by what the market says. Debruyne's core process, which represents the final level in our Advanced Marketing Management approach to innovation by adding the necessary market-driven perspective, consists of three main elements – and all three of them refer to the customer (Debruyne, 2014):

1st element: connect. True customer-driven innovation begins with the market. Marketing teams should immerse themselves into the market by establishing a variety of processes that allow them to be in touch with reality. Marketers should 'live and breathe' the market, their customers' experiences, their pains and dreams, and the wider trends that drive change. Outside-in companies work tirelessly and passionately with customers and other external stakeholders to ensure they understand current and unmet needs as well as hidden forces that will shape competition in the future. 'Connect' should be the constant or default state of doing business nowadays. It is not an option.

2nd element: convert. Being constantly connected to the market is a necessary but not a sufficient condition for delivering life-improving innovations. Companies need to convert the insights that are pouring in even on a daily basis, into concrete changes that meet real demands. For this to happen companies should not shy away from challenging current practices, processes and even entire business models. The market is unforgiving to companies that do not innovate, so sticking to old ways and being afraid of disruption is the surest path to failure.

3rd element: collaborate. No company can innovate alone long-term. Changes in the marketplace are so drastic, sudden and chaotic that in order for companies to stay relevant they need to combine their own capabilities with those of a diverse group of external people and companies. Instead of focusing solely on a single corporate system, modern marketers create ecosystems with partners, suppliers, external expert centres, agencies and other companies to transform ideas into successful market offers. Advanced marketers re-examine continuously their company's capabilities to guarantee that they always contribute immensely to the ecosystem's competitiveness. They also play a vital role in managing the ecosystem and steering it to the right direction. When it comes to innovation: divided we fall, together we stand!

In Debruyne's model, customer-centric innovation can be viewed through three lenses. The first lens refers to instantaneous changes a company can introduce to offer an improved product or service. For example, adding Wi-Fi service on a flight. The second lens refers to the total customer experience, not just to products and services. For example, understanding and optimizing the total travel experience from booking to final destination. The third, and last, lens refers to wider trends that can disrupt the whole industry. For example, are new communication and collaboration technologies going to change the way people travel for business? Marketers need to use all three lenses in combination with the three Cs described above in order to ensure a viable future for their brands and companies.

Creative problem solving and impactful innovation require personal, team, organizational and market approaches that should become integral to marketing in any industry. The four different levels in our model share elements between them in the same way that creative thinking works: by associating, not by separating. Innovation is never a linear nor a distinct affair. The same applies to our model.

Google's innovation principles

Alphabet, the owner of Google, is the second largest company, after Apple, in terms of market capitalization on the S&P 500 list (Shen, 2017). Alphabet is world famous for pursuing innovation endlessly both for disruption, like the self-driving car and the balloon-powered internet network, and for incremental changes, such as improvements on the popular Google search engine. This is why Eric Schmidt, the Executive Chairman of Alphabet Inc., and his associates wrote in their 2015 book *How Google Works*, that a more inclusive definition of innovation applies better in Google's case, since Google is after big, surprising and radically useful changes but also smaller incremental ones that, although individually cannot be considered as innovations, cumulatively can have a big impact (Schmidt, Rosenberg and Eagle, 2015). The nine principles of Google's innovation approach, the majority of which relate to various points in our four-level model described in this chapter, are (Chin Leong, 2013):

1 **Innovation is everywhere.** Everyone in the company can start a new initiative. Regardless of job titles and hierarchical level, in Google anyone can find an idea and push for its development.

2 **Focus on the user.** Customer experience should be prioritized above short-term financial gains. Even mini improvements can have collectively an enormous impact. If the solution improves customers' lives then more customers will remain loyal and new ones will join.

3 **Aim high.** People in Google are encouraged to aim as high as possible to increase the probabilities of meaningful innovations being developed. The higher you aim the more you will achieve. If you aim low then you will do even lower in the marketplace.

4 **Bet on insights.** Google staff are asked to use all possible insights and company solutions from all departments to help them accumulatively build something new. Not only internal but also external sources of insights should be used to bring about real innovation.

5 **Ship and iterate.** Include users, or your customers, as early as possible. Do not expect a new product or service to be perfect before launch. Instead, Google launches innovations and constantly works on them, incorporating feedback by users.

6 **Give employees 20 per cent time.** Experimentation and empowerment are crucial. Thus, Google allows its staff to work on their own projects on corporate time, even if those projects are outside the current company mission or scope of interest.

7 **Default to openness.** Google opts for open ecosystems rather than closed innovation platforms. Ideas from the ecosystem can many times rival and surpass ideas from the company and its close partners.

8 **Fail well.** Failure is an integral part of experimentation and creative problem solving. In Google, failure is a necessary condition for daring to be innovative so there is no stigma associated to it. Teams and people need to feel liberated to try, fail, retry and get it right.

9 **Purpose matters.** Google emphasizes its purpose and mission in every way possible. Storytelling is important and following the story closely and genuinely is even more important.

Behavioural hacks for creative problem solving

Apart from the creative thinking model for advanced marketers presented earlier in the book, which provides a holistic approach for advanced marketers, there are a number of practices that can seriously nudge a marketing team towards producing innovative ideas for products, services, experiences and processes. A summary of the most critical ones follows below in the form of Q&A:

Question: Which emotion can, above all others, boost innovation?

Answer: Surprisingly enough, it is *frustration*. Call it anger, extreme dissatisfaction or strong annoyance, it is an active negative emotion that boosts innovation. *Necessity is the mother of all invention*, the ancient Greek philosopher Plato once said, and this is now proven not to be too far from the truth. One of the most transformative products of the modern age, Apple's iPhone, was prioritized over other projects in Apple, as former head of iOS Scott Forstall revealed in an interview, because of Steve Jobs's dislike for the husband of one of his wife's friends who worked in Microsoft and was constantly boasting about Microsoft's pen-controlled devices (Gibbs, 2017). In her book *Inventology*, the columnist and author Pagan Kennedy reveals the three qualities that constructive frustration can have in boosting innovation, and especially for what she calls problem finding (Kennedy, 2016): it sustains itself for a long period and thus pushes for always better solutions; it helps reveal problems that usually remain hidden; it can help forecast the impact of the solution to people's lives, since the answer to the frustration is a relief of customer's pains. Even the well-publicized case of 3M's Post-it points to the direction of frustration: the engineer who came up with the idea had been frustrated for years with how his bookmark notes kept getting untidy while singing with a choir (Lehrer, 2012). Frustration says to our brains that a problem needs our continuous attention, mainly at the unconscious level, to be solved (Lehrer, 2012). Fittingly, the award-winning 2004 Honda advertisement, titled *Grrr*, featured a very catchy melody with the catchphrase: 'Hate something, Change something!' (Campaign, 2004). But frustration should be handled with care. Frustration works best on a personal level in providing the motivation for pushing for a solution. On a team level, the best emotions are usually positive.

Question: How better to present new ideas?

Answer: Pixar, the animation studios behind global blockbusters such as *Toy Story*, *Finding Nemo* and *Cars*, has been the go-to case for explaining innovation and creativity for the last decade. They are particularly famous in the business and marketing world for developing and applying their own proprietary process for pitching stories internally. After years in the movie business, Pixar realized that a structured way of pitching ideas helps everyone to develop better ideas in the first place, and then others to understand those ideas better when presented. The Pixar pitching process goes like this (Pink, 2013):

Once upon a time... [there was this problematic situation]; Every day... [people experienced troubles because of the problem]; One day... [solution was provided]; Because of that... [life improved]; Because of that... [wider positive implications]; Until finally... [the new normal situation].

Marketing teams should develop their own processes of pitching ideas that are engaging, exciting, motivating and relevant to their industry. Presentation matters. A lot. And it can have a very positive influence (when it is not a Horseman of Apocalypse, of course).

Question: Is there a proven method for getting to good ideas?

Answer: Toyota took the car market by storm in the 1980s because of its extreme focus on quality and the innovative ways it developed to ensure it. One of those ways was the now popular and widely applied '5 Whys' method. IDEO, the leading design studio mentioned earlier, has adopted the 5 Whys to dive into a customer problem and come up with the best possible solutions (Berger, 2009). The method boils down to asking five times 'Why?' when exploring a situation, in order to get to the real issues that need solving and not stay on the surface. The drawback of the approach is that it can annoy people who are not used to or trained in the method. Thus, a consensus should be reached before implementation. However, as IDEO claims: 'This exercise forces people to examine and express the underlying reasons for their behaviours and attitudes' (Pink, 2013). This is a very effective tool that should be used both internally and externally.

Question: How to deal with naysayers?

Answer: First of all, debating in a constructive way is necessary in the creative process. In the decision-making step of the Dimitriadis and Psychogios framework (2016) described earlier, argumentation should be fierce for making sure that promising ideas go through and unpromising ones stay put.

A study by Psychology Professor Charlan Nemeth from Berkeley University, and associates, showed that conflict techniques during idea discussion, such as debating and criticizing, had more positive effect on the outcome than more passive approaches (Nemeth *et al*, 2004). The study was conducted in two countries, the United States and France, with similar results in both cases. Pixar, the creativity powerhouse of animated movies, applies relentless, and even intimidating, examination of ideas in its famous, or more infamous, morning meetings. All these go to say that there is value to naysayers and that not all should agree immediately with everyone else. So, strategic use of naysayers at the right stage of the innovation process can be invaluable in double-checking the validity of ideas.

Second, language matters. Instead of naysaying being a static exercise it can become a constructive one when applying the right wording. Cathy Rose Salit (2016), the director of the company Performance of a Lifetime, which trains salespeople in improvisation theatre techniques, suggests the replacement of the phrase 'yes but' with the phrase 'yes and'. In that way, a negative opinion that could bring a discussion to an end, instead prompts its carrier to think constructively and help the team to carry the idea forward. For example, instead of responding 'yes, but we do not have the budget' one should respond 'yes, and if we talk to this director we could maybe get the budget'. Replacing 'yes but' with 'yes and' does not mean that all ideas will be accepted. Tough argumentation will still take place. But in the idea-generation phase of team discussion this simple technique can save many promising ideas from early death – and it will turn naysayers into valuable members of the team.

Question: Are all great ideas the same?

Answer: Olivia Fox Cabane and Judah Pollack (2017), authors of the book *The Net and The Butterfly: The art and practice of breakthrough thinking*, suggest four types of breakthrough ideas:

- Eureka are sudden ideas that form unexpectedly and create excitement.
- Metaphorical ideas are analogies requiring further interpretation as they usually connect two previously unconnected concepts.
- Intuitive ideas seem to work without obvious explanation, which usually comes later in the process.
- Paradigm ideas are the most radical of all and have the power to change the world but they are not immediately implementable.

According to the authors, knowing those types can help individuals and teams recognize the most appropriate one for the task at hand. What is also useful is the fact that teams should not be looking only for one type or form of a creative idea but should embrace the variety of idea forms.

Question: Can companies be really ignoring big things in their industries?

Answer: The revered marketing academic Theodor Levitt published his influential paper on what he called Marketing Myopia in 1960. In that paper, which became an absolute classic in the marketing world, Levitt (1960) argued that when industries fall and new ones arise it is not because of some natural law but because of management failure. The main failure of management is that when it rides on success waves it tends to focus on the product and not on the customer need. The example that he famously used was that of the decline of the US railroad business. He observed that railroad companies collapsed not because people preferred cars and airplanes but because railroad management allowed customers to use other providers. Management was being railroad-oriented not transportation-oriented. More than 50 years has passed since the publication of the article and companies continue to fall into the same trap, as Nokia did in the second half of the 2000s. Margaret Heffernan (2012), international business-woman and author, named the phenomenon of ignoring the obvious *wilful blindness*. Although a legal term from the late 19th century, Heffernan applied it in private life, business and social institutions to prove that wilful blindness is in human nature but can be addressed. Limitation in information processing in our cognition, and our inert tendency of forming habits, are the main reasons for wilful blindness. This can be dealt with effectively by adopting fierce determination against conformity and habitual weakness.

Psychologists Christopher Chabris and Daniel Simons conducted one of the most known psychological experiments, with a man in a gorilla suit walking through a basketball court as players threw the ball to each other. The fact that many observers failed to spot the gorilla when asked to focus on the players and the ball, prompted the researchers to talk about attentional, memory, confidence, knowledge, causality and potentiality-based illusions – or inattentional blindness as it is called – in our everyday lives (Chabris and Simons, 2010). Pair those with what are called blind spots, or cognitive biases that skew our perception to fit internal mental models (Banaji and Greenwald, 2016) and the answer is clear: yes, unfortunately it is *very* possible to miss out on big things!

Question: Which is a company's best innovation?

Answer: The next one. Otherwise it will soon be out of business!

Last thought

The 2017 surprising decision of Publicis, the global network of marketing services agencies, to abandon the most prestigious awards event in the industry, the Cannes Lion Festival, along with other festivals, shows that innovation needs above all transformational leadership. Publicis abandoned festivals to redirect budget and focus on its own innovative, AI-powered collaborative platform, called Marcel, that could potentially provide important advantages to the whole company by connecting talent and projects from around the world (Schultz, 2017). The move did not go without considerable backlash both from the inside and the outside of the group. But as Arthur Sadoun, President-CEO of Publicis Groupe, declared: 'I want Publicis to be on the front line. And to do that I am transforming, and to transform I need to take bold decisions' (Schultz, 2017). In order to strive to be different in an era where brands face the risk of becoming commodities, bold moves should be the standard mode of operation for any company wishing to retain and gain loyal customers. Advanced marketers need to be at the forefront of their companies' creative thinking – because successful marketing depends on it.

SUMMARY CHECKLIST

- Use LEGO's successful approach in building innovation capacity.
- Innovate constantly to stay relevant and to maintain customer loyalty.
- Focus relentlessly on market changes and customer needs to avoid resisting innovation.
- Make sure you apply all four levels of creative thinking to induce a steady flow of innovative solutions.
- Developing, presenting and applying innovative ideas are not easy steps but there are proven ways to help you become better and to succeed in challenging markets.

Resources to inspire you

- Tina Seelig TEDx talk on the innovation engine: https://www.youtube.com/watch?v=gyM6rx69iqg

- Honda advertisement 'Grrr': https://www.youtube.com/watch?v=KagSgWKaE_8

- Professor Marion Debruyne on customer-centricity: https://www.youtube.com/watch?v=LYaovtxbCX0

- The invisible gorilla test video: https://www.youtube.com/watch?v=vJG698U2Mvo

Revision questions

1 Which are the three powerful rules in LEGO's DNA that fuel its innovation approach? Why do you think that these rules are working so well?

2 Which are the most important reasons for the drop in brand loyalty and how should marketers address this? Use examples wherever possible.

3 By using the progression model, explain how effective innovation can lead to CMO success.

4 Which are the four main factors that kill creativity in companies?

5 Describe the creative thinking model for advanced marketers by highlighting its different levels.

References

Banaji, M R and Greenwald, A G (2016) *Blindspot: Hidden biases of good people*, Bantam Books, New York

Basulto, D (2014) [accessed 18 June 2018] Why LEGO is the Most Innovative Toy Company in the World [Online] https://www.washingtonpost.com/news/innovations/wp/2014/02/13/why-lego-is-the-most-innovative-toy-company-in-the-world/?utm_term=.4a9f6c452641

BBC (2013) [accessed 18 June 2018] The Mysterious Powers of Microsoft Excel, *BBC News Magazine* [Online] http://www.bbc.com/news/magazine-22213219

Berger, W (2009) *Glimmer: How design can transform your life, your business, and maybe even the world*, Penguin, New York

Brown, P B (2014) [accessed 18 June 2018] The Best Way to Predict the Future, *INC.* [Online] https://www.inc.com/paul-b-brown/the-best-way-to-predict-the-future.html

Cabane, O F and Pollack, J (2017) *The Net and the Butterfly: The art and practice of breakthrough thinking*, Penguin Random House, New York

Campaign (2004) [accessed 18 June 2018] Top Performers of 2004: Campaign of the Year, *Campaign Live* [Online] http://www.campaignlive.co.uk/article/top-performers-2004-campaign-year-honda/230473

Chabris, C and Simons, D (2010) *The Invisible Gorilla: And other ways our intuitions deceive us*, HarperCollins, New York

Chin Leong, K (2013) [accessed 18 June 2018] Google Reveals Its 9 Principles of Innovation, *Fast Company* [Online] https://www.fastcompany.com/3021956/googles-nine-principles-of-innovation

Coca-Cola Company (2016) [accessed 18 June 2018] Coca-Cola No. 3 On Most Valuable Brands Ranking [Online] http://www.coca-colacompany.com/coca-cola-unbottled/coca-cola-no-3-on-most-valuable-brands-ranking

Colvin, G (2015) [accessed 18 June 2018] Why Every Aspect of Your Business is About to Change, *Fortune* [Online] http://fortune.com/2015/10/22/the-21st-century-corporation-new-business-models/

Colvin, G (2016) *Humans are Underrated: What high achievers know that brilliant machines never will*, Portfolio/Penguin, New York

Debruyne, M (2014) *Customer Innovation: Customer-centric strategy for enduring growth*, Kogan Page, London

Dimitriadis, N and Psychogios, A (2016) *Neuroscience for Leaders: A brain adaptive leadership approach*, Kogan Page, London

Drath, K (2016) [accessed 18 June 2018] We Didn't Do Anything Wrong, But Somehow, We Lost, *Leadership Choices* [Online] http://www.leadership-choices.com/de/thinkabout/article/we-didnt-do-anything-wrong-but-somehow-we-lost.html

Evans, L (2014) [accessed 18 June 2018] You Aren't Imagining It: Email is Making You More Stressed Out, *Fast Company* [Online] https://www.fastcompany.com/3036061/the-future-of-work/you-arent-imagining-it-email-is-making-you-more-stressed-out

Fidelum Partners (2016) [accessed 18 June 2018] European Brand Warmth & Competence Study [Online] https://fidelum.com/european-brand-warmth-competence-study/

Gallo, C (2018) [accessed 18 June 2018] Jeff Bezos Banned PowerPoint in Meetings. His Replacement is Brilliant, *INC.* [Online] https://www.inc.com/carmine-gallo/jeff-bezos-bans-powerpoint-in-meetings-his-replacement-is-brilliant.html

Gibbs, S (2017) [accessed 18 June 2018] The iPhone Only Exists Because Steve Jobs 'Hated This Guy At Microsoft', *The Guardian* [Online] https://

www.theguardian.com/technology/2017/jun/21/apple-iphone-steve-jobs-hated-guy-microsoft-says-scott-forstall

Griswold, A (2016) [accessed 18 June 2018] How Did It Take McDonald's So Long To See That All It Really Needed Was All-Day Breakfast?, *Quartz* [Online] https://qz.com/602498/how-did-it-take-mcdonalds-so-long-to-see-that-all-it-really-needed-was-all-day-breakfast/

Haridasani, A (2017) [accessed 18 June 2018] McDonald's Next debuts in Hong Kong, *CNN Travel* [Online] http://edition.cnn.com/travel/article/hong-kong-mcdonalds-next/index.html

Heffernan, M (2012) *Wilful Blindness: Why we ignore the obvious at our peril*, Simon & Schuster, London

Higgins T, Ciolli, J and Bost, C (2014) [accessed 18 June 2018] Apple Tops $700 Billion Valuation, Fuelled by New Products, *Bloomberg Technology* [Online] https://www.bloomberg.com/news/articles/2014-11-25/apple-reaches-700-billion-valuation?alcmpid=breakingnews

Howarth, B (2017) [accessed 18 June 2018] How LEGO Built Its Culture of Innovation, Brick By Brick, *CMO* [Online] https://www.cmo.com.au/article/620138/how-lego-built-its-culture-innovation-brick-by-brick/

IBM (2010) [accessed 18 June 2018] IBM 2010 Global CEO Study: Creativity Selected as Most Crucial Factor for Future Success, URL: https://www-03.ibm.com/press/us/en/pressrelease/31670.wss

IDEO (2016) [accessed 18 June 2018] About, *IDEO* [Online] https://www.ideo.com/eu/about

Interbrand (2016) Best Global Brands 2016 Rankings [Online] http://interbrand.com/best-brands/best-global-brands/2016/ranking/

Judkins, R (2015) *The Art of Creative Thinking*, Sceptre, London

Kelly, T and Littman, J (2008) *The Ten Faces of Innovation: Strategies for heightening creativity*, Profile Books, London

Kennedy, P (2016) *Inventology: How we dream up things that change the world*, Houghton Mifflin Harcourt, New York

Lehrer, J (2012) *Imagine: How creativity works*, Houghton Mifflin Harcourt, New York

Levitt, T (1960) Marketing Myopia, *Harvard Business Review*, 38 (4), pp 24–47

Lim, W (2017) [accessed 18 June 2018] Opinion: Why Disruption is the Most Abused Business Word Now [Online] https://www.techinasia.com/talk/disruption-most-abused-business-word

Mueller, J (2014) [accessed 18 June 2018] Managers Reject Ideas Customers Want, *Harvard Business Review* [Online] https://hbr.org/2014/07/managers-reject-ideas-customers-want

Mueller, J S, Melwani, S and Goncalo, J A (2012) The bias against creativity: why people desire but reject creative ideas, *Psychological science*, 23 (1), pp 13–17

Nemeth, C J, Personnaz, B, Personnaz, M and Goncalo, J A (2004) The liberating role of conflict in group creativity: a study in two countries, *European Journal of Social Psychology*, **34** (4), pp 365–74

Pappu, R, Quester, P G and Cooksey, R W (2005) Consumer-based brand equity: improving the measurement–empirical evidence, *Journal of Product & Brand Management*, **14** (3), pp 143–54

Pink, D (2013) *To Sell Is Human: The surprising truth about persuasion, convincing, and influencing others*, Canongate, Edinburgh

Ringen, J (2015) [accessed 18 June 2018] How LEGO Became the Apple of Toys [Online] https://www.fastcompany.com/3040223/when-it-clicks-it-clicks

Robertson, D (2013) [accessed 18 June 2018] Building Success: How Thinking 'Inside The Brick' Saved LEGO [Online] http://www.wired.co.uk/article/building-success

Salit, C R (2016) *Performance Breakthrough: A radical approach to success at work*, Hachette Books, New York

Schmidt, E, Rosenberg, J and Eagle, A (2015) *How Google Works*, John Murray, London

Schultz, D, Block, M P and Viswanathan, V (2014) Brand preference being challenged, *Journal of Brand Management*, **21** (5), pp 408–28

Schultz, E J (2017) [accessed 18 June 2018] Publicis Groupe CEO Tries to Calm Alarm Over His Cannes Ban, *Adage* [Online] http://adage.com/article/special-report-cannes-lions/publicis-ceo-sadoun-calm-alarm-cannes-ban/309544/

Seelig, T (2012) *InGenius: A crash course in creativity*, HarperCollins, New York

Sheffield, H (2017) [accessed 18 June 2018] McDonald's Next Opens – Offering Quinoa, Touch Screens and Table Service: In Pictures, *Independent* [Online] http://www.independent.co.uk/news/business/news/mcdonalds-next-hong-kong-of-the-future-just-opened-offering-quinoa-asparagus-touch-screens-and-table-a6812611.html

Shen, L (2017) [accessed 18 June 2018] Amazon and the Race to Be the First $1 Trillion Company, *Fortune Magazine* [Online] http://fortune.com/2017/03/31/amazon-stock-trillion-dollar-company-apple-tesla-google/

Staples, J (2015) [accessed 18 June 2018] Meetings Kill Creativity – Why You Need To Rethink Your Processes, *Campaign Live* [Online] https://www.campaignlive.co.uk/article/meetings-kill-creativity-why-need-rethink-processes/1349786

Taylor, R (2013) *Creativity at Work: Supercharge your brain and make your ideas stick*, Kogan Page, London

Trout, J (2006) [accessed 18 June 2018] Peter Drucker on Marketing, *Forbes* [Online] https://www.forbes.com/2006/06/30/jack-trout-on-marketing-cx_jt_0703drucker.html

US Securities and Exchange Commission (2016) [accessed 18 June 2018] What Kind of Stock are There? [Online] https://www.investor.gov/introduction-investing/basics/investment-products/stocks

Vozza, S (2015) [accessed 18 June 2018] Why Your Company Should Consider Banning Email, *Fast Company* [Online] https://www.fastcompany.com/3042541/why-your-company-should-consider-banning-email

Wasserman, B (2015) [accessed 18 June 2018] Valuation of Intangible Assets: Should Brand Equity Be Accounted for on the Balance Sheet?, *University of Connecticut, Honors Scholar Theses*, 411 [Online] https://opencommons.uconn.edu/srhonors_theses/411/

Webb, A (2017) [accessed 18 June 2018] Apple Becomes First US Company to Top $800 Billion Value, *Bloomberg* [Online] https://www.bloomberg.com/news/articles/2017-05-09/apple-becomes-first-u-s-company-to-cross-800-billion-valuation

Williams, R (2012) [accessed 18 June 2018] Why Meetings Kill Productivity, *Psychology Today* [Online] https://www.psychologytoday.com/blog/wired-success/201204/why-meetings-kill-productivity

Worstall, T (2013) [accessed 18 June 2018] Microsoft's Excel Might Be the Most Dangerous Software on the Planet, *Forbes* [Online] https://www.forbes.com/sites/timworstall/2013/02/13/microsofts-excel-might-be-the-most-dangerous-software-on-the-planet/#14fd81fb633d

Yahoo News (2016) [accessed 18 June 2018] Disruption: The Most Abused Word in the Startup World [Online] https://sg.news.yahoo.com/disruption-most-abused-word-startup-world-094059832.html

Adaptability skills 05

Marketing and decision making

CHAPTER LEARNING OBJECTIVES

After studying this chapter, you will be able to:

- Understand what unpredictability means for modern marketers.
- Prioritize the right attitudes, mindsets and approaches for adaptive decision making before any planning and implementation.
- Apply effectively adaptive decision making in all steps of taking a decision.
- Differentiate between existing types of uncertainty and recognize actions to deal with them.
- Appreciate the importance of ethics in marketing decision making.

Advanced practice

The era of the instantly changeable product

Marketing literature is very clear about the differences between products and services, and these differences go way back in time. It was 1977 when G Lynn Shostack, the then Vice President of Citibank in the United States, published her seminal paper titled 'Breaking free from product marketing' on the need of a distinct marketing approach to services as compared with the one applied to products (Shostack, 1977). Although marketers are usually faced with a combination of products AND services when developing a brand, every company is dominated by only one, according to Shostack. The dominant force is either that of tangibility or intangibility. Intangibility, as a core element of services, is an integral part of the famous and widely accepted IHIP model that maps four service characteristics: intangibility, heterogeneity, inseparability and perishability

(Blut *et al*, 2014). Those characteristics infuse to services a certain degree of instability and unpredictability that is unknown to product marketing. Products are stable and linear, with relatively well-defined *product life cycles* and with separate roles for different actors in the value chain (producers, distributors, customers). In contrast to this, a key notion in services is that of co-creation, meaning that all those involved in services, and especially customers, are value co-creators (Grönroos and Ravald, 2011). Whatever value is to be derived from using a service, this is co-created on the process of delivering the service itself. Thus, services are much more complex than products. Is this still the case though? Are products still as rigid as they used to be? If not, what does that mean for decision making in contemporary marketing?

Tesla, the US electric car manufacturer, faced a great challenge in 2013. Cases of its popular Model S (with a retail price of approximately US $70,000 at the time) catching fire from highway debris, and hitting the battery system from underneath the car, were attracting media attention (Buss, 2013). This caused the US National Highway Traffic Safety Administration to publish a recall announcement for it. Tesla did not ask the 29,222 owners of Model S to bring their car in to be physically fixed: in response to the problem, Tesla fixed the car 'over the air', updating the software of the car over the internet and changing suspension settings to improve safety and performance (Brisbourne, 2014). Tesla's approach to the automobile is inherently different from the approach that traditional car producers had in the past. For Tesla, the car is a vessel that can be perpetually updated and upgraded through software. Its autopilot, for example, is upgraded with new algorithms for improved smoothness of driving (Etherington, 2017). Morgan Stanley's analyst Adam Jonas even went so far as to claim that the constant over-the-air (OTA) product-upgrade operating model of Tesla has the ability to make all other cars obsolete (Lambert, 2017). Tesla cars are not the rigid 'product' that traditional marketing thinking is based on. This is even more important since Shostack had used exactly this industry, automotive, to showcase the difference between stable products and dynamic services. Tesla's innovative approach renders this categorization, or separation, as a rather dysfunctional one now.

Music, as a product, was not so different from cars. For decades, musicians spent time in a studio producing an album that was then marketed to the fans. Yet music production has largely remained unchanged through the evolution of music distribution, from physical LP, cassette or CD, to digital download or streaming. It is by no accident that it is called 'production'. But Kanye West, the popular US hip-hop artist, introduced a completely new approach in 2016. His seventh studio album, *The Life of Pablo*, did not receive a normal album launch. A first version of the album was released in early February 2016, during his Yeezy Season 3 fashion show for adidas, then an upgraded version with more recordings was made available a few days later for digital streaming (Rossingol, 2016). Even after this, Kanye was reportedly still working on changes in some of the songs; changes that might become ever-lasting on an album that will be ever-changing. Jack Hamilton from *Slate Magazine*, declared that Kanye West's album is most likely 'a full-scale attack on the very ontology of the album itself: its primacy in the music industry's sales model, its status as the foremost object of music criticism, its presumed value as the supreme container for artistic expression, its existential legitimacy as anything other than a nostalgia-driven anachronism' (Hamilton, 2016). This innovative approach would not make much sense to an experienced music-industry executive. Albums were traditionally conceived, produced and released, and then supported by tours in sequential, distinct rigid phases. Song remixes certainly existed before and some significant albums received production improvement after their first release, but albums were always ready-to-market products. Kanye West has changed that, and rather successfully since it reached the number one spot on Billboard rankings and was certified Platinum in 2017 (Ahmed, 2017). With all the problems the music industry is facing nowadays, Kanye West has helped to create a new paradigm and a new hope: the never-finished, ever-changing, dynamic music album that, as a 'product', resembles more video games than the old music album (Rossingol, 2016).

Adding to the examples above is the rise of 3D printing, which allows users to print their own products based on their own or downloaded designs. This is similar to IKEA's long-term approach, asking their clients to assemble the IKEA furniture they just bought, as well as many software publisher policies that upgrade or improve their product with constant online updates and plugins after users' input. Amazon's Echo, Google Chrome and Apple's iPhones are never-quite-finished products with constant updates improving customer experience, apart from when this approach occasionally backfires – as happened with Apple slowing down older models to save battery power (Hackett, 2018). All this creates a new landscape for marketers. It is not just services that are unpredictable, dynamic and inseparable from customers (Dimitriadis, 2016a).

Products become fluid too, and the process of winning the hearts and minds of customers by creating and delivering successful products becomes more complex, unstable and inclusive than ever. In times when, as Marketing Professor Ken Bernhardt (2012) puts it, '[m]arketing is changing faster than any other aspect of business', the question for advanced marketers is this: what type of approach towards decision making should be adopted to keep up with increased complexity and adapt successfully in constantly changing conditions? When even products cannot stay as tangible or stable as they used to be, how can marketers make sure they are applying the right thinking and deciding tools?

The marketing challenge

How do marketers make sense of the world? Although such a question might seem too ambitious for providing any concrete response, there is a safe place to start looking for the answer: marketing textbooks. Generations of marketing students are taught in class that marketing is a process with few and distinct steps. The role of the marketer is to manage those steps in the best viable way to produce results that are positive for the company, the customers and even for the society as a whole. This process of marketing is better encapsulated by the model of Armstrong, Kotler and da Silva (2006), which includes the following steps in a linear logic: understand, design, construct, build and capture.

This simple model of the marketing process is usually taught at the very first stages of a student's journey into the brave world of marketing, being an integral part of the introductory lecture to marketing. The process explains that marketers need to pass through these different steps in order to execute marketing appropriately in companies. Those steps are (Armstrong, Kotler and da Silva, 2006):

1 Understanding customers and the wider context the company operates in.

2 Designing a marketing strategy with customers at its very core.

3 Constructing marketing programmes to create value for customers.

4 Building relations and making customers happy.

5 Capturing value from clients to generate profitability.

Armstrong, Kotler and da Silva (2006) also present an expanded version of the simple model including specific marketing activities for each of the steps, such as research in the first step; segmentation–targeting–positioning for the second; the 4Ps in the third; customer relationship management (CRM) in the fourth; and loyalty and lifetime value in the fifth. Although such types of modelling are invaluable for creating a basic awareness of what a discipline is all about and providing structure of thought, they can have a negative effect as well. The main downside of such models is that they make reality resemble a linear, stable-looking and predictable framework that can be easily managed and manipulated. But is this the case with the daily realities that marketers are facing in the 21st century?

In her influential TED speech on preparing for start-ups, author, consultant and keynote speaker Diana Kander describes her traumatic experience of being physically attacked on the parking lot of the restaurant where she used to work, and not being able to instinctively deploy the techniques she had learnt in taekwondo to protect herself. Although she had trained for years for situations exactly like this one, her training did not help her practically in real life. A co-worker of hers shouting her name at the parking lot saved her that night, not her training. Reflecting on her experience, Kander (2014) describes the problem like this: 'I was not really learning how to defend myself because I had no practice against realistic opponents with realistic attack moves.' She applies the same logic to business education. Creating strategies and plans in controlled, safe and linear environments in the classroom does not always prepare professionals appropriately for the dynamic, brutal and chaotic realities they will face in the marketplace. On the contrary, such protecting and simplifying environments and approaches can do a disservice to students as they can create the wrong impression and thus prepare less, not more, for the real market.

This seems particularly important for marketers since marketing is one of the company functions most affected from the various socio-economic and technological changes the world is experiencing today. In essence, marketing being in turmoil and in a constant state of uncertainty complies less with linear models than it did ever before in its history. Probably this is one of the reasons, if not the decisive one, that deems most of marketing knowledge acquired at school unrecallable at work. As reported by well-known entrepreneur and founder of Atari Inc., Nolan Bushnell, in his book *Finding the Next Steve Jobs*, research published at the *Journal of Marketing Education* shows that marketing graduates have forgotten most of their formal marketing knowledge only two years after graduating (Bushnell with Stone, 2013). Most interestingly, marketing students with A scores forgot their taught material faster than those with C scores.

The voices for adopting a different view of reality in our personal and professional lives have increased drastically during the last years. One of the most celebrated such voices is that of statistician, financial trader, risk analyst and best-selling author Nassim Nicholas Taleb. Taleb's book *The Black Swan: The impact of the highly improbable*, gave birth to what is now known as the 'Black Swan' theory, explaining that people tend to be overconfident and very comfortable about the status quo before a significant and unpredictable event wreaks havoc on current models and changes everything (Taleb, 2008). After such an event, people also tend to oversimplify the explanation of the cataclysmic event and become oversensitive to new ones, until they settle in a new comfort zone with a renewed belief in the stability of the new situation. Although Taleb stressed that we should be more aware of, and prepared for, Black Swans than we ever used to be, since Black Swan events are manifesting more often than before, it was with his next book, *Antifragile*, that he set the basics for a new behaviour. In *Antifragile: Things that gain from disorder*, Taleb supports the adoption of an approach in life and work that can help increase the positive effects that unpredictability can have on a system (Taleb, 2013). For Taleb, resilience or robustness is not the right response to disorder and chaos. This is because trying to protect oneself from unpredictability, as resilience suggests, can have serious side effects. Instead of fighting against chaos it is much better to try to benefit from it. Antifragility as an attitude, is a non-linear approach to a stressor (a potentially negative event) that increases sensitivity and variability of the response to actually derive positive outcomes from it. In marketing strategy terms, it is about turning a threat into an opportunity. This cannot happen, though, when marketers' attitude is one of rigidity, stability and predictability based on current models of understanding and responding to reality. Marketers need not only to expect chaos but to love it.

Google, physics... and marketing

Taleb's use of diverse disciplines, such as biology and financial analytics, to make sense of the world is functioning and convincing because no single scientific field alone can provide holistic answers to modern challenges. Applying diverse scientific ideas from a variety of disciplines to solve business problems can bring about surprising insights and valuable solutions. Dan Cobley, the marketing director at Google at that time, described in his eminent TED speech titled 'What Physics Taught Me About Marketing', how several laws and theories from physics can help marketers make better decisions and more sense of the world they operate in. He used (Cobley, 2010):

- Newton's law of the force equals mass times acceleration, to showcase that the bigger the brand or the challenge, the more force it needs to change or achieve something meaningful;

- Heisenberg's uncertainty principle claiming that nothing can be observed without changing, to highlight the importance of using appropriate and diverse sources of data to inform marketing decisions;

- the scientific method of trying to disprove a hypothesis in order to validate it, to pinpoint the delicateness of brands that build their reputations through expensive campaigns over time only to lose it instantly from a miscalculated move.

Most importantly, and towards the end of his talk, he focused on entropy, the tendency for disorder and uncertainty to constantly increase in every system. Echoing Taleb's concept of Antifragile, Cobley suggests that marketers should not be worrying about the increasing complexity and unpredictability they face in the process of building strong brands, because it is a positive thing. In his own words: 'This distribution of brand energy gets your brand closer to the people, more in with the people… The message for marketing is that your brand is more dispersed. You can't fight it, so embrace it and find a way to work with it' (Cobley, 2010).

In examining complexity in a business context, scholars Davis, Eisenhardt and Bingham (2007) run computer simulations trying to identify the applicability of a structured versus an unstructured approach when the level of complexity fluctuates. They found that (Davis, Eisenhardt and Bingham, 2007):

Increasing unpredictability is associated with a less structured optimum. Moreover, when environments are very unpredictable, there is a very narrow range of optimal structure and a precarious 'edge of chaos'. But when environments are very predictable, there is a broad range of optimal structures and equifinality.

Applying their findings in marketing, we can say that in stable environments, when rules are rather constant and most changes anticipated, marketers can choose between different 'optimum' solutions that increase structure in the system. For example, they can formalize their marketing research process to periodically collect customers' opinions; they can programme their new product development process to fit to projected product life cycles; and they can plan their advertising campaigns to correspond to expected product seasonality or competitors' response. But when complexity increases then increasing structure, or retaining the existing one, can have a very negative effect on performance. This means that complexity asks for less structure and more for operating at the 'edge of chaos', changing and adapting to conditions almost constantly with very little stability and organization.

Are marketers ready to work and thrive at the edge of chaos? Surely they must be if they want their brands to have a chance of surviving in turbulent times. This might sound extreme but it has been observed by others as well. In their book *A Perfect Mess: The hidden benefits of disorder*, management professor Eric Abrahamson and reporter David H Freedman provide the evidence for the serious obstacles created by too much organization and structure for companies, brands and retailers alike. As they point out, there are two main problems of systems 'in order' (Abrahamson and Freedman, 2007):

- First, there is little empirical evidence proving that more organized systems succeed long term more than less organized ones.

- Second, very rarely literature is concerned with the hidden costs of high structure both in financial terms (companies invest to create organizational systems) and in survival potential (companies hinder their adaptability skills by creating more stability).

Seeking order or high structure for the sake of it is not only outdated but also dangerous. Uncertainty is here to stay regardless of whether businesses like it or not. As Sir Martin Sorrel, marketing's global representative featured in Chapter 1, said, businesses such as his own WPP group are now faced with a 'cocktail of uncertainty' in terms of politics, economics and other factors, and that this is the one thing that keeps him up at night as a CEO (CNN, 2016). The surprising answer to uncertainty might not be a different kind of strategy as such but a different kind of thinking.

Consultant Mark Bonchek and CEO adviser Barry Libert, in their 2017 *Harvard Business Review* article 'To change your strategy, first change how you think', wrote that corporate strategy and business platforms are not the elements that can make the difference today. What does make the difference for brands is the thinking processes or mindsets that produce those strategies. This is why corporations, trying to copy business models of successful brands such as Tesla and Southwest Airlines, are deemed to fail in that they lack the wider mental processes that created those models and that make them operate successfully in the marketplace on a daily basis (Bonchek and Libert, 2017). According to Bonchek and Libert, the most valuable asset today is not a business model but a mental model. Trying to copy successful market disruption models is dangerous since it misses the main ingredient of disruption, which is not the strategy – it is thinking. Bonchek and Libert's approach to brand domination today reflects one of the most famous quotes from the late business guru Peter Drucker: 'Culture eats strategy for breakfast' (Hyken, 2015). It is not strategy, with its often pretentious stability and reliability that makes companies great. It is the power of a company's collective thinking and its people's behavioural patterns that create and deliver successful brands. Developing strategies as if they are independent of the human system within companies is a delusional and futile approach to business performance.

How you think determines what you think. Or, to put it differently, it is mindsets, not plans, that create behaviours. If you want to succeed as an advanced marketing manager you need to make sure that your internal mental processes are geared towards thriving with uncertainty. It all starts there and it is a fundamental challenge for marketers.

The mental dichotomy for succeeding in chaos

Advanced marketing managers are at the forefront of organizational transformation and market disruption. Their role internally and externally is paramount in creating new value for all stakeholders, not *despite* uncertainty but *because* of uncertainty. They do not create plans that are written in stone that no one can challenge. They do not stick to their own version of reality regardless of what is happening in the market. They are not afraid to try innovative solutions, especially as they face new problems almost every day. If things go wrong, they learn fast and change their ways to fit the new situation. They listen, interact, experiment and constantly move forward towards their brand vision without allowing mishaps and challenges to stop them. They get provable results and they inspire the whole corporation to follow in their lead. But to do all these, contemporary marketers need all the help they can get; and this help comes from various sciences.

Utilizing insights from psychology, neuroscience and the science of prediction, we have identified a certain dichotomy of attitudes that can separate success from failure in the turbulent times we live in. This dichotomy is very clear: at the extreme ends of the continuum there are two diametrically different mentalities that produce opposite thoughts and behaviours. As explained in the previous section, strategy, planning and implementation are the product of corporate mindsets and cultures. When the right attitude is adopted, solutions follow. The two opposite mentalities are explained below.

One of the most widely disseminated concepts in modern psychology, with a considerable impact on business thinking already, is that of mindsets. Carol Dweck, Professor of Psychology at Stanford University, published in 2007 her influential book *Mindset: The new psychology of success*, which was later republished with the new subtitle *How you can fulfil your potential* (Dweck, 2012). Dweck, after years of research in schools, identified two key mindsets related to opposite aptitudes for learning and personal development: growth mindset and fixed mindset. At the epicentre of her approach is the revolutionary insight that improving performance is based not on personality traits but on people's own perception of their abilities. This perception, or mindset, can either boost learning and development or hinder them. The main attributes of each mindset are presented below (Dweck, 2007):

Growth mindset:

- intelligence can be developed;
- leads to a desire to learn;
- embraces challenges;
- persists when faced with obstacles;
- effort brings success;
- learns from criticism;
- inspired by others' success;
- achieves full potential;
- free-will worldview.

Fixed mindset:

- intelligence is static;
- leads to a desire to look smart;
- avoids challenges;
- gives up when faced with obstacles;
- effort is irrelevant;
- avoids or ignores criticism;
- fears others' success;
- achieves below full potential;
- deterministic worldview.

The way that teachers treat, motivate and frame their questions to and evaluation of their students can have a huge impact on the type of mindset that students adopt and thus on their ability to learn, develop and succeed in life (Dweck, 2012). Dweck and her associate, Lisa Blackwell, have created a training and consulting company, MindsetWorks, with the mission 'to foster lifelong learning' (www.mindsetworks.com), providing a software toolkit for schools, and showcasing the science proving the effectiveness of mindset training in education. Concerning business, Dweck's book contains a whole chapter dedicated to applying her mindset analysis to understanding better issues such as: business disasters, business development, leadership, decision making, teamwork, negotiations and training.

Applying her model in organizations, Dweck and associates (HBR Staff, 2014) conducted research at seven companies from the Fortune 1000 list, including a diverse sample of employees. What they found is that the model of the two mindsets reveals two types of cultures: 1) one that fosters a 'star' system, following a fixed mindset; 2) one that fosters a 'support' system, following a growth mindset.

In 'star' systems, employees considered as natural performers are singled out and receive a star treatment while others struggle to survive and to perform to their full potential. In 'support' systems employees feel that their company 'has their backs' and thus they can be more brave and experimental. Analysis showed that employees from the 'star' system companies were less satisfied, less innovative and less engaged than those from the 'support' system companies. Google and Econsultancy conducted a study to explore what differentiates marketers that overachieve with those who lag behind, in terms of mobile marketing. Two of the top results were (Think With Google, 2017):

- **Constantly striving.** 'Leading marketers are 3X more likely to strongly agree that there will always be gaps in their ability to measure across devices and channels.' In uncertain times, there is no room for perfection. There is only room for accepting complexity as *the* status quo and working always to take advantage of what is available and helpful.

- **Constantly experimenting.** High-achieving marketers are also 'more than twice as likely to conduct strategic experiments... a culture and process flexible to strategic experimentation enables them to find the best opportunities for growth.' Remaining static in a world that accelerates change is a one-way ticket to failure.

Successful marketers are growth mindset marketers. They believe less in destiny, natural-born winners and dead-ends, and more in efforts, possibilities and responsibilities. They make their own future by perpetually learning and improving, without feeling stuck and helpless. Solutions and opportunities can be found anywhere: we just need to have the right attitude to actively look for them. The brain of people operating under a growth mindset works differently than the brain of fixed-minded people (Moser *et al*, 2011). When faced with a challenge, for example with a mistake, the brain with a growth mindset will light up in electroencephalography, demonstrating that it is working hard on multiple levels to solve the problem. It is an engaged brain. Brains with fixed mindset, on the contrary, stay inactive, not processing the problem to find a solution – they remain unengaged in relation to the challenge.

In a similar tone is an assertion made by Elaine Fox, Head of the Department of Psychology and Centre for Brain Science at the University of Essex, in her book *Rainy Brain, Sunny Brain: The new science of optimism and pessimism*. Fox highlights the fact that from the two fundamental motivational systems in the human brain (namely the *approach mechanism* and the *avoidance mechanism*) those who activate more the approach mechanism engage more with daily challenges to devise solutions and solve problems, thriving more in life than those who do not (Fox, 2013). Marketers with an engaged attitude, who do not run away from change but believe deeply in learning and development, will be more innovative, more inclusive and more motivating than others. Ultimately, they will be the winners. Marketing itself is considered by some in the start-up arena to be a mindset and not a department or function, since it lies at the very heart of start-up growth, innovation, customer understanding, flexibility and team integration (Agrawal, 2017).

Neuroscience sheds more light into the dichotomy of successful and unsuccessful attitudes. Richard J Davidson, Psychology and Psychiatry Professor at the University of Wisconsin-Madison, has discovered six basic dimensions that determine the way that the human brain reacts emotionally to situations. These are (Davidson and Begley, 2012):

1 the resilience style;

2 the outlook style;

3 the social intuition style;

4 the self-awareness style;

5 the sensitivity-to-context style;

6 the attention style.

From those six, the outlook style is of particular relevance and importance here. The outlook style determines the ability of a person to continue being energetic and engaged regardless of calamities. If this is the case then the person has a *positive outlook*, while if it is not the case then the person has a *negative outlook*. Behaviour follows the outlook. People with a positive outlook (Davidson and Begley, 2012):

- connect with others faster and more effectively;
- do not allow negativity to dominate as a mood even in the face of failure;
- focus more on the positive traits of colleagues;
- believe in, and strive for, a better future;
- rarely feel cynical and pessimistic;
- shine in social situations, and thus can be motivating and inspiring to others.

Studying brains in action, Davidson and his associates observed a delicate but significant difference between people with a positive outlook and people with a negative outlook. Although in both groups brains showed activity in the reward centre, the nucleus accumbens, when exposed to positive stimuli (such as to images of children playing happily) those with a positive outlook sustained this reward activation for much longer than those with a negative outlook. The key point here is not if people are able to feel happy or not but for how long they can sustain that feeling; a positive feeling that, by nature, is highly self-motivational and can also rub off on those around us. It is not by accident then that, according to the Digital Marketing Institute, one of the seven habits of highly effective digital marketers is self-motivation (Digital Marketing Institute, 2017). This is because digital marketing is still a relatively new field and professionals in the field need to create their own unique path by being enthusiastic, proactive and by focusing on the positive. Marketers nowadays need to create waves of change within their companies and for doing so they have to lead by positive example and with unlimited energy. Both require adopting a positive outlook, especially in unpredictable environments that constantly bring about new problems.

Apart from psychology and neuroscience, the science of prediction provides its own version of the dichotomy of successful and unsuccessful attitudes when dealing with complexity; and it has to do with foxes and hedgehogs. According to a saying widely attributed to the ancient poet Archilochus these two animals are very different: 'the fox knows many things, but the hedgehog knows one big thing'. Which one of the two has the winning attitude? According to 19th-century American theologian Ralph Waldo Emerson, the winner is clearly the hedgehog since, according to his famous take on the ancient quote, the one thing the hedgehog knows 'is the best of all' (Catlin, 2012). In a relatively stable world, with low level of complexity and unpredictability, when major players were known and the future looked rather linear, it was extreme specialization and lifelong focus on a single skill or field that was appreciated. But what about a more modern and chaotic world? In such a world, foxes have the edge. This is what Philip E Tetlock, the Annenberg University Professor at the University of Pennsylvania, found after years of studying forecasting in politics. Tetlock periodically surveyed experts with diverse backgrounds and expertise, trying to identify what made a successful forecaster of events and developments in global politics. He identified two broad attitudes in predicting the future. He called the one group *foxes* and the other *hedgehogs*. Their characteristics are described below (Silver, 2012):

Foxes as forecasters:

- Use diverse ideas from multiple disciplines.
- Pursue several solutions at the same time.
- Happily recognize mistakes in their own predictions.
- Embrace complexity and the inability to find perfect solutions.
- Make predictions probabilistically and are very cautious expressing them.
- Prefer empirical observation to theoretical certainties.
- *They are more accurate forecasters.*

Hedgehogs as forecasters:

- Are sceptical to different disciplines and specialize heavily.
- Focus on one, and the most known to them, solution.
- Always blame others or the general situation without criticizing their model.
- Expect and strive for simplistic solutions that have universal applicability.
- Are very confident about their views and rather unwilling to change them.
- Prefer applying a certain theory to many situations regardless of reality.
- *They are less accurate forecasters.*

Advanced marketing managers need to evolve from functional specialists to holistic leaders – from hedgehogs to foxes. This does not mean that less marketing specialization is needed. Quite the contrary. Marketers must make sure they have access to the best knowledge, skills and capacities the market can offer in a wide area of expertise ranging from AI to neuroscience. However, as they need to integrate marketing solutions across the organization and to navigate their brands across turbulent markets, a certain attitude emerges as more appropriate than others. Arrogance and stubbornness can prove lethal when applied to forecasting. Keeping an open mind and trying different solutions can go a long way in helping marketers play a transformational leadership role.

The 10 commandments of super-forecasting

In an updated take on prediction capacity, Tetlock and Gardner, in their book *Super-Forecasting*, offer 10 rules for becoming what they call a super-forecaster. These are (Tetlock and Gardner, 2016):

1 **Be selective**. Choose questions that can deem your efforts valuable and avoid questions that can eat up your time with very little output to show for it.

2 **Apply analytical thinking**. Break seemingly impossible-to-answer questions into manageable smaller problems.

3 **Use similar cases**. Since nothing is completely unique, try to zoom out and look globally for cases that share similar characteristics with your situation.

4 **Update your views**. The most successful forecasters constantly update their beliefs from detecting new cues in the environment and they even drastically change their opinion if reality suggests so.

5 **Apply synthesis**. No problem has a black-and-white solution so you need to make sure to include all opposing positions in your considerations.

6 **Apply granular thinking**. The more you assign probabilities to phenomena and their possible outcomes the better.

7 **Get timing right**. Being too late with a decision can be as bad as being too early, so super-forecasters consider carefully the trade-off between decisiveness and the quality of predictions.

8 **Own your results**. Rigorously analyse both successes and failures by avoiding hindsight biases and false attribution errors.

9 Work in teams. Successful forecasters inspire others and allow them to bring out their best at work, but also they are inspired by others themselves.

10 Learn by doing. You can only improve in forecasting when engaging in deep and deliberate practice, using the best feedback available.

Tetlock and Gardner have included an 11th commandment, recommending for their previous commandments to be treated carefully and mindfully. These recommendations showcase once again the importance of mental attitudes for succeeding in our modern world.

Davis, Eisenhardt and Bingham (2007), mentioned earlier in the chapter, had one more interesting finding in their study of uncertainty and structure. They found that more uncertainty deemed skills less important. In their own words: 'increasing ambiguity diminishes the value of skill' (Davis, Eisenhardt and Bingham, 2007). This is actually echoed in the global HR mantra of 'hiring for attitude and training for skill', which goes back to the mid-1990s and Southwest Airlines' approach to hiring (Carbonara, 1996) – an approach that was taken to new heights by online retailer Zappos and his CEO's assertion that a company can ensure the presence of desired employee behaviours only when it hires for values, not just skill, and when it protects its culture in the expense of everything else (Hsieh, 2010).

It seems that modern business conditions have brought about a certain level of consensus concerning mindsets. Marketers should lead by growth mindset, positive outlook and a fox attitude if brands are to have a bright future in the marketplace. Skills, strategies, plans and implementation are secondary to mental habits, thinking and culture. Having said that, when it comes to management, decision making holds a vital role. So, how can marketers improve their decision-making tactics even when applying the right mindset?

Decisions, decisions, decisions

Management is about decision making, and decision making affects directly and drastically a company's performance. A global study of executives from 760 companies, many of which exceeded US $1 billion in revenue, found that financial results correlated to decision-making effectiveness at 95 per cent confidence level or higher (Blenko, Mankins and Rogers, 2010). This was the case for every country, industry and company size that the researchers included in their sample. Results lead them to assert that: 'Ultimately, a company's value is just the sum of the decisions it makes and executes.' Since, as we saw in Chapter 4, corporate shareholder value is seriously boosted by the ability of a company to innovate constantly and to create long-lasting brand loyalty, marketing lies at the heart, if not at the very top, of all corporate decision making. Advanced marketers need to improve their decision-making approach by employing the most effective methods as well as by delving into the science of decisions. For example, Blenko and associates recommend that all managers should apply certain variables to evaluate their own decision effectiveness. These are (Blenko, Mankins and Rogers, 2010):

- Decision quality: which decisions are proven right and which not, and how often?

- Decision speed: are you deciding faster or slower than competitors and the rate of market change?

- Decision yield: are decisions usually implemented appropriately and according to intentions?

- Decision effort: what does it take to decide in terms of time, costs and trouble?

Regardless of how important decision making is for successful management and the vast amount of corporate decisions that are taken daily, managers are not particularly good at it. A study of 500 managers and executives discovered that 98 per cent of them fail to apply best available practices and methods in decision making (Larson, 2017). This is profound and it confirms our own experience working with brands from around the world. Managers, and especially marketers, do their best to take decisions that solve problems and create opportunities. They do so, though, not by applying decision-making insights and specific decision methods, but by diving into their expert knowledge and experience. While this is natural and even necessary, decision making must be treated on its own terms with its own steps and checkpoints.

The first stop in understanding better decision making concerns the different types of motivations that exist within every marketing manager when deciding A from B. Professor of Psychology Douglas T Kenrick, and Professor of Marketing and Psychology Vladas Griskevicius, in their book *The Rational*

Animal, describe seven distinct sub-selves that coexist within humans and advise our decisions. They form our internal evolutionary consultants that try to inform and improve our decisions based on their own separate goals. These sub-selves, analysed here from a managerial perspective, are the following (Kenrick and Griskevicius, 2013):

1 **Self-protection**. Decisions are often triggered by our strong motivation to protect ourselves from external threats. When active, even neutral cues can be mistaken for threats and we become overvigilant and overreliant. Managers can feel overthreatened by constant market changes and drive their decisions towards the direction of protecting themselves rather than of improving their brand position.

2 **Disease-avoidance**. Apart from our biological immune system humans have also developed a behavioural immune system that, when activated, leads to decisions that push people to avoid specific individuals or groups. Managers can wrongly exclude others from the decision-making process because of stereotyping and other cognitive biases.

3 **Affiliation-seeking**. Being social animals, people's decision making is skewed towards behaviours that can increase likeability towards them. Managers might take decisions that increase their popularity in the company, with external partners or with media – and not decisions that impact positively their company's interests in the long term.

4 **Status-seeking**. Respect is a major decision-making trigger since humans evaluate themselves and others based on a formal and informal hierarchy of relations. This is why managers sometimes take decisions that showcase dominance, and enforce behaviours on others just to demonstrate hierarchical order.

5 **Mate-getting**. Although this and the next sub-selves are explained in romantic terms by Kenrick and Griskevicius, as the titles reveal, they provide interesting analogies in a managerial context. Decision making in companies can be aiming at creating strong subgroups that serve as closed preservation clubs for their members, and less at maximizing results.

6 **Mate-keeping**. Similarly, maintaining those preservation groups drives, many times, decision making instead of issues of strategic importance.

7 **Kin-support**. Humans prioritize decisions and behaviours that aim to protect and nurture youngsters in need. Within companies, some managers will likely shape their decision-making process in such a way to ensure their prodigies will progress and thrive within the company.

The last three sub-selves might seem far-fetched when applied to management but, unfortunately, such behaviours are widely adopted in corporations, especially at the highest organizational levels. As reported by Hayman and Giles (2016), Lord Young, a prominent British figure in the world of business and politics in the UK, admitted that: 'every large company I've ever been in or known, the top two or three layers of management spend their time politicking. The business goes on without them.' Most top executives' time is dedicated to who will get promoted in order to maintain the closed-group status quo, and less on hardcore business decision making. Obviously, there is a mismatch between expectations and reality concerning decision making in companies. Marketers should be very aware of this mismatch both in themselves and in others if they are to lead transformation. Awareness can lead to avoiding using the wrong inner-voice consultant. It can also lead to provoking the one that can be of higher value in different situations. As Larson (2017) pinpointed, although many times managers feel that they exercise rigorous decision making for maximizing corporate results, they actually follow other intrinsic goals that they are not aware of. The result is ineffective decisions that harm organizations and brands.

How should marketing managers improve their decision-making process? Figure 15.1 provides a summary of best-selling authors Chip Heath and Dan Heath's framework, presented in their book *Decisive*.

Figure 5.1   Decision-making framework

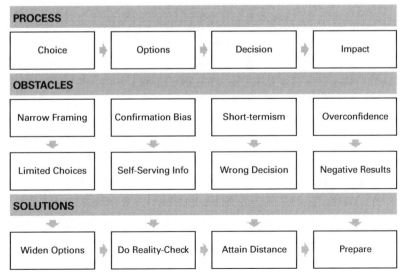

SOURCE Adapted from Heath and Heath (2013)

In the Heaths' view, the effectiveness of decision making can be seriously weakened by problems at every step of the process. When faced with a challenge, time and other constraints can lead managers to develop a restricted view of the situation and thus develop only a limited set of options. They cite research in their book showing that only 29 per cent of companies consider more than one option in their decision making, with dire consequences: 52 per cent of 'black and white' decisions failed (Heath and Heath, 2013).

When considering options, confirmation bias can lead to opting only for information that confirms what is already believed and expected. In an article for *Forbes* entitled 'Why working with people who disagree with you is good for your business', entrepreneur Tori Utley highlights the fact that surrounding yourself with people who challenge your opinion is a necessary condition for taking better decisions, because it increases transparency and variety of viewpoints (Utley, 2016). This is particularly important for marketers since they face endless streams of information from a wide variety of internal and external sources for virtually every decision they need to make.

According to Heath and Heath (2013), a major obstacle to effective decision making is short-termism: a dangerous cocktail of loss-averse feelings and too much familiarity with the situation that breed status quo-keeping decisions. Adopting a more contextual approach can help switching from a tree-only view to a whole-forest one. WARC, the marketing intelligence service, reported on a study of cases from advertising agencies, suggesting that to increase effectiveness of digital campaigns, marketers need to operate more with a long-term horizon than with a short-term one (WARC, 2017). Evidence is conclusive: 'only 3 per cent of short-term cases generated very large market share growth, whereas 38 per cent of 3+ year cases did so' (WARC, 2017). The pressure that many marketers feel nowadays to produce results fast has, many times, a negative impact on their decision making. As Jason Hawkins argued in the *Search Engine Journal*, marketers often get 'antsy, bored and impatient' when developing their campaigns, wanting to see results as fast as possible. However, a more long-term approach is advanced since research shows that customers need more time to connect and engage with a brand online (Hawkins, 2016).

The fourth and last challenge in the process for the Heaths is the unpreparedness that many decision makers demonstrate in terms of what follows after they make a decision. Overconfidence, and sometimes even arrogance, redirects attention from reality to expectations. Instead of analysing meticulously the immediate impact of their decisions to identify areas of intervention and improvement, they remain inactive waiting for everything to go as planned. The solution to this phenomenon is better preparedness, especially by developing scenarios of possible outcomes. Managers need to think and plan in advance what they can do if things go horribly wrong and what they can do if things go exceptionally well. This worst- and best-case scenario analysis has been already noted as significant for marketers. In social media marketing, where complexity is higher and success factors remain largely unknown, preparing for the worst and learning from others' mistakes can be invaluable. Viral campaigns, proven to be extremely sensitive to misunderstandings and that often backfire, ask from marketers to prepare very well before launch by studying closely viral brand disasters and developing contingency plans (DeMers, 2016). Preparing and celebrating brand victories is of equal importance for personal and team motivation but also for learning from success in order to repeat it in the future (Zetlin, 2015).

Rationality versus irrationality

One of the most prevalent dichotomies in decision making is rational versus irrational decision making: rational decisions involve analytics, while irrational ones are more impulsive. This dichotomy became even more prominent after the publication and success of psychologist Daniel Kahneman's book *Thinking, Fast and Slow*. In his book, Kahneman (2011) differentiates between what he calls Systems 1 and 2. System 1 is fast, based on emotions and more instinctive, while System 2 is slower, based on logic and more thoughtful. Kahneman's work is highly important for understanding the pitfalls of fast thinking and for avoiding dangerous biases by engaging deliberate analytical thinking in decision-making situations. There are two main criticisms, though, concerning this approach:

1 There is a certain power, or intelligence, associated with intuitive thinking that goes beyond simple, evolutionary and survival decision making. As explained in various works such as Malcom Gladwell's *Blink* (2005), Gerd Gigerenzer's *Gut Feelings* (2007) and especially Gary Klein's extensive research on the subject (2004, 2013), fast and intuitive thinking, when based on tangible experiences, deep-rooted associations, insightful heuristics and swift pattern-recognizing perception, can bring forward superior results to analytical thinking.

2 The dichotomy recommended by Kahneman, although great for simplifying decision making, might not capture the actual inner workings in our brains. There are already increasing voices suggesting that there are more than Kahneman's two systems (Gray and Lazar, 2017).

The rationality versus irrationality dichotomy might be overall counterproductive. As argued by Kenrick and Griskevicius (2013), humans have evolved to exercise what they call *deep rationality*: a combination of intuition and analytics that makes humans so different to other species. Similarly, psychologist and Professor of Social Theory and Action Barry Schwartz talks about the need of applying 'practical wisdom' to solve daily problems in our societies. Observing the general dissatisfaction of people with institutions and professionals, Schwartz calls for less rules and incentives such as carrots and sticks, and for more empowerment and personal engagement with the problems we face (Schwartz, 2010). Schwartz is using the ancient Greek philosopher and scientist Aristotle's notion of practical wisdom to argue for a tangible, inventive, passionate, applied and efficient approach to decision making and problem solving. Winning decisions are not actually an issue of rationality versus irrationality but an issue of practicality. Aristotle called this practical wisdom *phronesis* and he believed that it develops with everyday experiences, reflection, hands-on involvement and deep care for what you do (Dimitriadis and Psychogios, 2016). Phronesis is not just a skill, it is a fundamental characteristic of a person's thinking and behaviour. It is an in-built capacity of humans for better decision making but one that must be actively chosen, practised and nurtured to give optimum results. It also requires bending rigid and inefficient rules to make room for decisions that are useful and solutions that work in the real world (Schwartz, 2010).

A more interesting dichotomy to the tired 'rational versus irrational', then, is the one of the two perceptual systems our brains are using in our everyday lives: the left-brain versus the right-brain perceptual systems. Although the traditional divide of left and right brains as logical and emotional respectively is more of an urban myth than a scientific truth, the two hemispheres do apply different processes for understanding the world and for reacting to it. The two perceptual systems are briefly explained below (Dimitriadis, 2016b):

- **The right brain** perceptual system is in direct contact with reality, connects us with the world and to other people, has a more holistic view of a situation, is conceptual rather than procedural concerning language, applies metaphors, and emotionally is more mellow.

- **The left brain** perceptual system develops abstract models of reality, it does not prioritize connectivity with people, it uses only sequential logic, it is very skilful with language, it is literal not metaphorical, it is attracted by novelty, and emotionally is more joyful.

Although the 'normal' modus operandi should be right hemisphere first, left second and then right again, the corporate world seems to have long reversed the order, giving the left hemisphere the upper hand (Dimitriadis, 2016b). Marketers need to connect, empathize and conceptualise more before applying any novel analytical tool if they want to apply a more holistic and strategic approach to their decision-making process.

Good decision makers are adaptive

Decision makers should not obsess with always setting clear and consistent goals. Instead, they should discover the surprising power of following unbalanced and disordered objectives that, at the end, are better achieved. As already mentioned in this chapter, the hidden costs of always seeking clarity in decision making are, many times, much higher than initially thought of. John Kay, British economist and visiting Professor of Economics at the London School of Economics, emphasizes that: 'Problem solving is iterative and adaptive, rather than direct. Good decision makers are balancing incompatible and incommensurable objectives. They are eclectic and tend to regard consistency as a make of stubbornness, or ideological blindness, rather than a virtue' (Kay, 2010).

It is a VUCA world out there

The acronym VUCA, standing for volatility, uncertainty, complexity and ambiguity, has become a standard term in business for describing a world that is full of surprises. According to Bennet and Lemoine (2014), though, there are two major traps that managers can fall into when using it: first, they might feel that strategizing and planning is futile, and second, that all the four different words in the acronym describe the same phenomenon. To help managers avoid these traps, Bennet and Lemoine offer a comprehensive guide to VUCA, which is the following:

- **Volatility:** the situation is unstable and managers have a certain difficulty predicting its duration but variables are mostly known and easily understandable. For example, buyers increase their orders of your products drastically due to a sudden disruption of your main competitor's production. Effective response requires a level of readiness from the side of brands for such events, either by investing in stand-by capacity or by establishing extended networks that can provide additional capacity on demand. For example, cloud computing has emerged as the most accessible solution for companies worldwide to increase their agility against volatility: when workload increases companies can rent readily available additional capacity in 'the cloud' without building new infrastructure themselves (Knorr, 2017).

- **Uncertainty:** an upcoming event is known, both in terms of actors involved and cause, but the exact impact on the world is unknown. For example, two of your competitors are merging. The event is known but how it will influence various aspects of your market is not. For example, the acquisition of the large bricks-and-mortar retailer, Whole Foods, from the leading online retailer, Amazon, in the United States was a highly publicized business event in 2017 due to its high uncertainty: players and conditions were known but long-term impact on the market was not (Aziza, 2017). Effective response, according to Bennet and Lemoine, involves increased sensitivity to information, constant vigilance and expansion of your knowledge network.

- **Complexity:** the situation involves a large number of interconnected variables that cannot be grasped at any given moment in their totality or as a whole. For example, your brand is a leading one in the global market, meaning different things to different target audiences in different countries. Effective response includes engaging constantly experts from a variety of fields/places, structuring and restructuring to address challenges and building up resources devoted to dealing with complexity. For example, the Coca-Cola Company's global presence with multiple products and brands creates a high degree of complexity. The company tries to manage effectively this complexity by, among other things, restructuring in 2017 its top team to now include a Chief Growth Officer, as we saw in Chapter 1.

- **Ambiguity:** this is the trickiest situation since it is about dealing with 'unknown unknowns', or with a reality that is completely new to us. For example, when a brand extends to products that it has no experience with. Effective response is a necessary series of experiments where the brand will learn by doing. Causalities need to be discovered on-the-go and marketers need to be able to commit the time, effort and budget to deal with constant surprises as they come along. In their study of the car industry published in *Marketing Science*, marketing academic Olivier Rubel and his associates found that marketers who set aside a portion of their advertising money to deal with *Black Swans* are more successful than those who do not budget in advance for ambiguity (Rubel, Naik and Srinivasan, 2011).

Although this chapter has treated concepts such as complexity, uncertainty, chaos and unpredictability somewhat interchangeably, Bennet and Lemoine's model suggests that there are noteworthy nuances that managers need to understand. Not all difficult challenges are the same nor do they require the same response.

Ethics above all

Decisions can derive from evolutionary, neural, strategic and/or circumstantial bases but regardless the origins of a decision, modern marketers should behave ethically and constructively within the wider social, economic and physical environment they operate in. The traditional divide between the external and internal corporate worlds has grown thinner, not allowing any more for companies having different narratives inside and outside their walls (Hsieh, 2013). This means that brands cannot, and should not, try to misguide audiences and stakeholders concerning their intentions and actions.

The American Marketing Association (AMA) provides for its members and marketers in general a comprehensive Statement of Ethics that captures the main elements of ethical behaviour in marketing. The statement is separated into three brief sections: ethical norms, ethical values and implementation (AMA, 2013):

1 *Ethical norms*. There are three norms in AMA's Statement of Ethics. The first is 'Do No Harm' and refers to marketers' responsibility in following all laws, regulations and the highest ethical standards in all their decisions. The second is 'Foster Trust in the Marketing System' and refers to being fair and acting in good faith for maximizing efficiency and effectiveness in all marketing activities. The third is 'Embrace Ethical Values' and refers to actively building confidence across stakeholders for marketing's integrity by practising all values from the next part.

2 *Ethical values.* AMA describes six ethical values for all marketers to follow. These are: honesty (truthfulness of claims), responsibility (ownership of impact), fairness (avoidance of any manipulation), respect (recognition of others' dignity), transparency (clear communication to all) and citizenship (holistic approach).

3 *Implementation.* AMA encourages all marketers to proactively and force-fully lead and/or assist their brands to fulfil their promises to their various stakeholders, acknowledging the presence of more specialized ethical codes per industry and marketing subdivision.

On social media, where marketing is still exploring the basics of what works and what does not, marketers should follow strict ethical practices in order to avoid blunders and to make sure that they do not alienate their hard-earned customers. Five key pitfalls to avoid include (Vinjamuri, 2011):

1 unreported endorsements;

2 improper anonymity;

3 compromised consumer privacy;

4 unmarked employee online presence;

5 exploited online community.

The increased volatility and harshness of the environment that marketers are asked to thrive in is no excuse for unethical decision making and behaviour. True leadership will only be obtained by marketers when they prove them-selves businessworthy in achieving the best possible results in uncertain times while being, simultaneously, exceptional role models in ethics.

Last thought

The world is not set to become simpler at any time soon. On the contrary, it becomes even more complex, unpredictable and uncertain. Advanced marketers are asked to perform in a business, social and technological environment that constantly changes, providing new challenges and opportunities on-the-go. From products that are never truly completed at the moment of shipping, to brands with presence in different markets with different products, marketers should embrace complexity and lead their corporations by applying contemporary approaches to decision making. The time when marketers were educated to take only marketing-related decisions, by just using marketing science tools and matrices, is over: a new era of marketers as adaptive decision makers, with a wider reach in organizations, has begun.

SUMMARY CHECKLIST

- Abandon any belief in stability and comfort zones in marketing.
- Challenge traditional marketing models that are based on linear thinking.
- Adopt a growth mindset, a fox attitude and a right-brain perception in order to become more adaptive in decision making.
- Detect different VUCA situations in order to respond appropriately.
- Use ethics emphatically in all advanced marketing decisions.

Resources to inspire you

- Diana Kander TEDx talk on preparation versus reality: https://www.youtube.com/watch?v=pii8tTx1UYM
- Dan Cobley TED talk on physics and marketing: https://www.youtube.com/watch?v=8cwW_S29faQ
- Martin Sorrell interview on uncertainty: https://www.youtube.com/watch?v=rTt3tErCVRQ
- Carol Dweck TED talk on growth mindset: https://www.youtube.com/watch?v=_X0mgOOSpLU&t=197s
- Barry Schwartz TED talk on practical wisdom: https://www.youtube.com/watch?v=lA-zdh_bQBo
- Zappos CEO interview on corporate culture, values and employee engagement: https://www.youtube.com/watch?v=Mkyl1C5b5IQ
- Take the mindset assessment test: http://blog.mindsetworks.com/what-s-my-mindset

Revision questions

1 Use examples of instantly changeable products to discuss the role of complexity in today's business environment.

2 In your opinion, which are the biggest risks for marketers practising traditional planning and linear thinking models?

3 Which variables should marketing managers apply in order to evaluate the effectiveness of their decisions?

4 Discuss the different sub-selves, or motivators, that according to Kenrick and Griskevicius (2013) play an integral role in human decision making.

5 Which are the key barriers in every step of the decision-making process and how can marketers address them effectively?

References

Abrahamson, E and Freedman, D H (2007) *A Perfect Mess: The hidden benefits of disorder*, Phoenix, London

Agrawal, A (2017) [accessed 18 June 2018] Marketing is a Mindset, Not a Department – Here's Why, *Startup Grind* [Online] https://www.startupgrind.com/blog/marketing-is-a-mindset-not-a-department-heres-why/

Ahmed, T (2017) [accessed 18 June 2018] Kanye West's Record Label Says 'The Life of Pablo' is First Streaming-Only Album To Go Platinum, *Newsweek* [Online] http://www.newsweek.com/kanye-west-life-pablo-first-streaming-album-go-platinum-579530

AMA (2013) [accessed 18 June 2018] Statement of Ethics, *American Marketing Association* [Online] https://www.ama.org/AboutAMA/Pages/Statement-of-Ethics.aspx

Armstrong, G, Kotler, P and da Silva, G (2006) *Marketing: An introduction – an Asian perspective*, Pearson/Prentice Hall, New York

Aziza, B (2017) [accessed 18 June 2018] Amazon Buys Whole Foods. Now What? The Story Behind The Story, *Forbes* [Online] https://www.forbes.com/sites/ciocentral/2017/06/23/amazon-buys-whole-foods-now-what-the-story-behind-the-story/#1a0f330de898

Bennet, N and Lemoine, J (2014) [accessed 18 June 2018] What VUCA Really Means For You, *Harvard Business Review* [Online] https://hbr.org/2014/01/what-vuca-really-means-for-you

Bernhardt, K (2012) [accessed 18 June 2018] Challenging Times on the Marketing Front Lines, Robinson College of Business, Georgia State University [Online] http://robinson.gsu.edu/2012/06/challenging-times-on-the-marketing-front-lines-2/

Blenko, M W, Mankins, M C and Rogers, P (2010) The decision-driven organization, *Harvard Business Review*, **88** (6), pp 54–62

Blut, M, Beatty, S E, Evanschitzky, H and Brock, C (2014) The impact of service characteristics on the switching costs–customer loyalty link, *Journal of Retailing*, **90** (2), pp 275–90

Bonchek, M and Libert, B (2017) [accessed 18 June 2018] To Change Your Strategy, First Change How You Think, *Harvard Business Review*, 17 May [Online] https://hbr.org/2017/05/to-change-your-strategy-first-change-how-you-think

Brisbourne, A (2014) [accessed 18 June 2018] Tesla's Over-the-Air Fix: Best Example Yet of the Internet of Things?, *WIRED* [Online] https://www.wired com/insights/2014/02/teslas-air-fix-best-example-yet-internet-things/

Bushnell, N with Stone, G (2013) *Finding the Next Steve Jobs: How to find, hire, keep and nurture creative talent*, Simon & Schuster Paperbacks, New York

Buss, D (2013) [accessed 18 June 2018] Tesla's Fire Problem Could Be the Mother of Soft Underbellies, *Forbes* [Online] https://www.forbes.com/sites/dalebuss/2013/11/08/teslas-fire-problem-could-be-the-mother-of-soft-underbellies/#527525621683

Carbonara, P (1996) [accessed 18 June 2018] Hire for Attitude, Train for Skill, *Fast Company* [Online] https://www.fastcompany.com/26996/hire-attitude-train-skill-2

Catlin, C (2012) *The Animal Anthology Project: True tails*, Xlibris, Bloomington

CNN (2016) [accessed 18 June 2018] Advertising CEO Warns of 'Cocktail of Uncertainty', *CNN Money* [Online] http://money.cnn.com/video/news/2016/10/31/wpp-ceo-brexit.cnnmoney/index.html

Cobley, D (2010) [accessed 18 June 2018] What Physics Taught Me About Marketing, TEDGlobal [Online] https://www.ted.com/talks/dan_cobley_what_physics_taught_me_about_marketing

Davidson, R J and Begley, S (2012) *The Emotional Life of Your Brain: How to change the way you think, feel and live*, Hodder & Stoughton, London

Davis, J P, Eisenhardt, K M and Bingham, C B (2007) Complexity theory, market dynamism, and the strategy of simple rules, *Proceedings of DRUID Summer Conference*, April, pp 18–20

DeMers, J (2016) [accessed 18 June 2018] The 7 Worst (And Most Amusing) Mistakes Brands Have Ever Made On Social Media, *Forbes*

[Online] https://www.forbes.com/sites/jaysondemers/2016/05/02/
the-7-worst-and-most-amusing-mistakes-brands-have-ever-made-on-social-
media/#1d3853c36a5c

Digital Marketing Institute (2017) [accessed 18 June 2018] 7 Habits of Highly
Effective Digital Marketers, *Digital Marketing Institute: Careers* [Online]
https://digitalmarketinginstitute.com/blog/7-habits-highly-effective-digital-
marketers

Dimitriadis, N (2016a) [accessed 18 June 2018] The End of the Finished Product, *LinkedIn*
[Online] https://www.linkedin.com/pulse/end-finished-product-nikolaos-dimitriadis

Dimitriadis, N (2016b) [accessed 18 June 2018] Do We Live in the Matrix?: The
Left Brain's Great Deception, *LinkedIn* [Online] https://www.linkedin.com/
pulse/do-we-live-matrix-left-brains-great-deception-nikolaos-dimitriadis

Dimitriadis, N and Psychogios, A (2016) *Neuroscience for Leaders: A brain
adaptive leadership approach*, Kogan Page, London

Dweck, C S (2007) [accessed 18 June 2018] Fixed Mindset vs Growth Mindset –
Graph, *Stanford Alumni Magazine* [Online] https://alumni.stanford.edu/content/
magazine/artfiles/dweck_2007_2.pdf

Dweck, C S (2012) *Mindset: How you can fulfil your potential*, Robinson, London

Etherington, D (2017) [accessed 18 June 2018] Tesla's Next Autopilot Update
Is All About the Smooth Ride, *TechCrunch* [Online] https://techcrunch.
com/2017/05/23/teslas-next-autopilot-update-is-all-about-the-smooth-ride/

Fox, E (2013) *Rainy Brain, Sunny Brain: The new science of optimism and
pessimism*, Arrow, London

Gigerenzer, G (2007) *Gut Feelings: The intelligence of the unconscious*, Penguin,
New York

Gladwell, M (2005) *Blink: The power of thinking without thinking*, Little Brown,
New York

Gray, K and Lazar, N (2017) [accessed 18 June 2018] Neuroscience
and Marketing, *LinkedIn* [Online] https://www.linkedin.com/pulse/
neuroscience-marketing-kevin-gray

Grönroos, C and Ravald, A (2011) Service as business logic: implications for value
creation and marketing, *Journal of Service Management*, 22 (1), pp 5–22

Hackett, R (2018) Tech Dissatisfaction, Version 99.0, *Fortune*, 2 (February), p 9

Hamilton, J (2016) [accessed 18 June 2018] *The Life of Pablo* Is an Attack on
the Very Idea of the Album, *Slate* [Online] http://www.slate.com/articles/arts/
culturebox/2016/02/kanye_west_s_the_life_of_pablo_is_an_attack_on_the_
very_idea_of_the_album.html

Hawkins, J (2016) [accessed 18 June 2018] Is Your Brand Focusing Enough on
Developing Long-Term Campaigns?, *Search Engine Journal: SEO* [Online]

https://www.searchenginejournal.com/why-your-brand-may-not-be-focusing-enough-on-developing-long-term-campaigns/169172/

Hayman, M and Giles, M (2016) *Mission: How the best in business break through*, Penguin, London

HBR Staff (2014) [accessed 18 June 2018] How Companies Can Profit from a 'Growth Mindset', *Harvard Business Review* [Online] https://hbr.org/2014/11/how-companies-can-profit-from-a-growth-mindset

Heath, C and Heath, D (2013) *Decisive: How to make better decisions in life and work*, Crown Business, New York

Hsieh, T (2010) *Delivering Happiness: A path to profits, passion, and purpose*, Hachette, London

Hsieh, T (2013) [accessed 18 June 2018] Interview of Zappos CEO in the Documentary Film *The Naked Brand* [Online] https://www.youtube.com/watch?v=Mkyl1C5b5IQ&t=6s

Hyken, S (2015) [accessed 18 June 2018] Drucker Said 'Culture Eats Strategy For Breakfast' and Enterprise Rent-a-Car Proves It, *Forbes* [Online] https://www.forbes.com/sites/shephyken/2015/12/05/drucker-said-culture-eats-strategy-for-breakfast-and-enterprise-rent-a-car-proves-it/#415dd0f62749

Kahneman, D (2011) *Thinking, Fast and Slow*, Allen Lane, New York

Kander, D (2014) [accessed 18 June 2018] Our Approach To Innovation Is Dead Wrong, *TEDxKC Talk* [Online] https://www.youtube.com/watch?v=pii8tTx1UYM

Kay, J (2010) [accessed 18 June 2018] Think Oblique: How Our Goals Are Best Reached Indirectly, *The Independent* [Online] https://www.google.rs/amp/www.independent.co.uk/arts-entertainment/books/features/think-oblique-how-our-goals-are-best-reached-indirectly-1922948.html%3Famp

Kenrick, D T and Griskevicius, V (2013) *The Rational Animal: How evolution made us smarter than we think*, Basic Books, New York

Klein, G (2004) *The Power of Intuition: How to use your gut feelings to make better decisions at work*, Currency Books, New York

Klein, G (2013) Insight, in *Thinking: The new science of decision-making, problem-solving and prediction*, ed J Brockman, Harper Perennial, New York

Knorr, E (2017) [accessed 18 June 2018] What is Cloud Computing? Everything You Need To Know Now, *InfoWorld* [Online] http://www.infoworld.com/article/2683784/cloud-computing/what-is-cloud-computing.html

Lambert, F (2017) [accessed 18 June 2018] Tesla's Over-the-Air Software Updates Make Other Vehicles 'Highly Vulnerable to Obsolescence', Says Analyst, *Electreck* [Online] https://electrek.co/2017/07/19/tesla-software-updates-vs-auto-industry/

Larson, E (2017) [accessed 18 June 2018] Don't Fail at Decision Making Like 98% of Managers Do, *Forbes* [Online] https://www.forbes.com/sites/

eriklarson/2017/05/18/research-reveals-7-steps-to-better-faster-decision-making-for-your-business-team/#128e5ccd40ad

Moser, J S, Schroder, H S, Heeter, C, Moran, T P and Lee, Y H (2011) Mind your errors: evidence for a neural mechanism linking growth mind-set to adaptive posterror adjustments, *Psychological Science*, **22** (12), pp 1484–89

Rossingol, D (2016) [accessed 18 June 2018] Has Kanye West killed Off the Album As We Know It?, *The Guardian* [Online] https://www.theguardian.com/music/2016/feb/22/kanye-west-the-life-of-pablo-killed-off-album

Rubel, O, Naik, P A and Srinivasan, S (2011) Optimal advertising when envisioning a product-harm crisis, *Marketing Science*, **30** (6), pp 1048–65

Schwartz, B (2010) [accessed 18 June 2018] Using Our Practical Wisdom, *TEDSalon NY2011*, Talk [Online] https://www.ted.com/talks/barry_schwartz_using_our_practical_wisdom

Shostack, G L (1977) Breaking Free From Product Marketing, *The Journal of Marketing*, pp 73–80

Silver, N (2012) *The Signal and the Noise: The art and science of prediction*, Penguin, New York

Taleb, N N (2008) *The Black Swan: The impact of the highly improbable*, Penguin, London

Taleb, N N (2013) *Antifragile: Things that gain from disorder*, Penguin, London

Tetlock, P and Gardner, D (2016) *Super-Forecasting: The art & science of prediction*, Random House, London

Think With Google (2017) [accessed 18 June 2018] Mindset Matters: How Leading Marketers Are Driving Growth With Mobile Measurement, *Think With Google: Data & Measurement* [Online] https://www.thinkwithgoogle.com/marketing-resources/data-measurement/marketing-measurement-drive-growth-econsultancy/

Utley, T (2016) [accessed 18 June 2018] Why Working With People Who Disagree With You Is Good For Your Business, *Forbes* [Online] https://www.forbes.com/sites/toriutley/2016/08/25/working-with-people-who-dont-agree-with-you-and-why-your-company-needs-them/#15af967177ad

Vinjamuri, D (2011) [accessed 18 June 2018] CMO Network12 Stocks to Buy Now Ethics and the Five Deadly Sins of Social Media, *Forbes* [Online] https://www.forbes.com/sites/davidvinjamuri/2011/11/03/ethics-and-the-5-deadly-sins-of-social-media/#54905a243e1f

WARC (2017) [accessed 18 June 2018] Marketers Need To Better Balance Short and Long Term, *WARC News and Opinion* [Online] https://www.warc.com/NewsAndOpinion/News/Marketers_need_to_better_balance_short_and_long_term/38833

Zetlin, M (2015) [accessed 18 June 2018] 6 Ways You Should Prepare for the Best Instead of the Worst, *INC.COM* [Online] https://www.inc.com/minda-zetlin/6-ways-you-should-prepare-for-the-best-instead-of-the-worst.html

The 4EPs marketing mix, part 1

06

Empathic product and experiential price

CHAPTER LEARNING OBJECTIVES

After studying this chapter, you will be able to:

- Understand why the original 4Ps marketing mix model is still alive and why it needs an update instead of a total replacement.

- Question the practice of many companies globally not allowing marketers to be in control of price and place as much as they are of promotions and product.

- Appreciate the role of empathy and emotions in building and commercializing products and services.

- Emphasize the importance of psychology in shaping customers' experiences with prices.

Advanced practice

Deciem: innovating all four Ps in the skincare industry!

Skincare is considered by some insiders as an industry often troubled by overblown claims, overpromising messages and unclear product composition, and one that could benefit greatly by higher transparency in marketing and more honest brands overall (Mpinja, 2017). It is not by accident that one of the most famous quotes in business and marketing ever, according to *The Economist* (2012), is the one by Charles Revson, founder of global cosmetics company Revlon, saying that: 'In our factory we make lipstick [*lipstick* often replaced in online sources with *cosmetics*]. In our advertising we sell hope.' But how can brands break free from old, tired and misguided marketing practices and enter a new era of product transformation, market disruption and higher connectivity with consumers? Is such innovation enough when it concerns only one of the traditional Ps or should it be covering all of them simultaneously? What can innovative brands teach us for the modern application of marketing mix models?

Deciem, a disruptive Canada-based skincare brand, leads the way in applying contemporary practices through the whole spectrum of marketing mix activities. With the suggestive tagline *The Abnormal Beauty Company* and the intriguing title *The Founder Is Screwed Up!* on the company's website page on founder and CEO Brandon Truaxe (Deciem, 2018a), the brand's intention to differentiate itself as much as possible from traditional cosmetics companies is very clear. But how does it do it in practice? Is this intention just a PR exercise or is it a full-blown strategy touching upon every aspect of the brand's marketing effort? As it seems, this innovative and differentiating approach lies at the very core of Deciem's brand DNA and is manifested in its actions. Using the traditional 4Ps marketing mix model, here are some of the things Deciem is doing to disrupt the cosmetics market and to continue striving towards being 'a serious player in the beauty biz' (Mpinja, 2017):

- **Product**. Deciem is using trusted, known, simple ingredients with proved efficacy. Product ranges and individual products are straightforwardly named, like *The Ordinary* range and the *Granactive Retinoid 5 per cent in Squalane* product. Packaging is also straightforward and simple, looking more like dropper bottles out of a science lab than traditionally sleek-designed cosmetics. Labelling is white, clinical and no-nonsense looking. In its simplicity and direct appeal, Deciem is trying to be more true, uncomplicated and connected to customers' needs than traditional brands. The product's truth has now to be felt deeply through empathic processes... and not just to be bought or consumed.

- **Price**. This is the big surprise. Most of the products under Deciem's most successful range, The Ordinary, are priced under US \$10. According to *Allure Magazine*'s Mpinja (2017), Deciem is trying to reverse the mental 'programming' that the cosmetic industry has imposed on consumers to consider some products, such as serums, as premium, luxurious and thus expensive. Instead, Deciem treats its products less as cosmetics and more like health-care ones. Pricing is no simple affair: the traditional mark-up models (such as cost plus margin) and market-positioning models (such as luxury pricing) are now replaced with more complex scientific approaches based on customer experience.

- **Place**. Deciem products are available from a wide variety of channels. As the brand itself proclaimed in a post: 'we are all over the place, both literally and figuratively' (Krause, 2017). The company is using a franchise system to expand its physical locations with mono-brand stores all over the world and it makes its products widely available through its own and partnering companies' online and offline shops, such as Sephora (Deciem, 2018b). The opening statement from Deciem's 2017 Instagram post mentioned above is not at all far from the truth for modern marketing: products and services have to be available wherever and whenever customers want them. Choosing one channel over the other is a strategy of the past. Today, and tomorrow, you need to be everywhere!

- **Promotion**. Deciem is constantly present in online communications by portraying a truthful, genuine and ultimately humane face. This unpolished and gutfeel-like presence resonates deeply with people solidifying its main brand position and creating huge growth surges for its products. At the end of 2017 there was a waiting list of 75,000 people for two of Deciem's newest make-up products (Mpinja, 2017). Promotion cannot be categorized any more into one-way (old style) and two-way (new style). It goes beyond that and into creating relations and human interactions by engaging people emotionally and behaviourally. As founder Truaxe said, 'skincare purchases are driven by communication with people' (Hou, 2018), and this can be nowadays said for almost all products and services in the world!

Not all is rosy though. The backlash that the founder experienced after posting a video online, talking negatively about some online comments that were going against his very open opinions posted frequently online, led some industry commentators, and some customers, to doubt the longevity of such an *extreme transparency* approach (Hou, 2018). The situation became even more heated when Deciem's co-CEO Nicola Kilner left the company, senior members of the US team got fired, and Truaxe continued posting edgy and controversial messages on the brand's social media (Rodulfo, 2018). Nevertheless, business continued growing at a high speed (Wischhover, 2018).

The global success of the brand and the rapid growth of its sales, which are based on a more advanced and modern marketing mindset, which sometimes may not exclude or avoid controversies, show that marketers need to re-examine their ways and reapproach their marketing mix practices. Only then will advanced marketing be fully deployed, and its benefits fully ripped.

The marketing challenge

One of the most enduring concepts in marketing is the marketing mix model of the 4Ps. In Chapter 1 we discussed the concept, its historical development and some of the criticism against it. Here we will do the opposite. We will support it. This is for two reasons:

Reason 1. The need and tendency to abolish the model and to replace it with new ones did not manage to produce any alternative that took its position in global marketing literature and practice. Even the ones that claimed to just 'reinterpret' the 4Ps for specific industries, like the most recent SAVE model for business to business (B2B) tech-driven markets (Ettenson, Conrado and Knowles, 2013), SAVE standing for *Solutions–Access–Value–Education*, did not dethrone the 4Ps, regardless their certain popularity. In our understanding and experience, many times the urge to replace the 4Ps has been driven by a genuine belief that there can be a better model and many times by a more self-centred career-advancement and glory-seeking motive, sometimes from both. In any case, this urge has not really worked. Dan Bladen, co-founder and CEO of Chargifi, a wireless-charging start-up and a *Marketing Week*'s 100 Disruptive Brand, said it clearly and emphatically (Bacon, 2017): the 4Ps 'still offer a strong backbone to a marketing strategy'. The fact that he is coming from a tech start-up, which usually renounces old marketing concepts and practices, makes his statement even more interesting and important.

Reason 2. There is convincing evidence from research showing that the 4Ps are still very effective in practising marketing worldwide. In an influential article titled 'The gap between the vision for marketing and reality' in *Sloan Management Review*, Kotler *et al* (2012) reported on a global IBM study of 1,700 top marketers from a wide variety of industries. Findings indicate that the better-performing companies, and companies that find themselves more prepared to deal with future challenges, are the ones that scored higher in controlling the full pallet of their marketing mix, meaning all 4Ps. The study revealed that promotion was the P most controlled by marketers, scoring an average of 4.2 on a scale measuring intensity of control from 1 to 5; followed by product, which scored 3.4; place, with 3.2; and price with 3.1. It is obvious that marketers have not gained full control of marketing elements regardless of the 4Ps model being taught for more than 60 years! The article concludes that (Kotler *et al*, 2012): 'As organizations and markets have become more complex, the need for a less compartmentalized view of marketing is even more apparent today.' This 4Ps-related point is made not only by researchers but by marketing practitioners too. As Pete Markey, Brand Communications and Marketing Director at London-based multinational insurance company Aviva, puts it (Bacon, 2017):

> You can have the best communications in the world but if your price or product is wrong, it's not going to work... That's why the 4Ps are so relevant now, because they remind us that marketing is so much more than just advertising.

So, the marketing challenge for advanced marketing leaders is this: how to use the 4Ps today to develop their brands, connect to customers and provide business-wide value to their companies. This is not an easy task. First, the model itself seems to be constantly under attack. Second, not all companies provide the right amount of control to their marketers for dealing with all marketing elements in the mix. Third, technology has taken the focus of marketing away from a holistic approach, which included pricing and distribution, to more online community management and big data-driven customer insights. The time is right for marketers to reclaim their territory and lead their companies by integrating all crucial elements needed for brand success. To do so, they need an updated version of the 4Ps that does not change the essence of the traditional model, nor its name, but that brings it up to speed with our contemporary times by incorporating the latest science and research knowledge on how humans think, feel and do. In this direction, we recommend the 4EPs.

The 4EPs, namely the empathic product, the experiential price, the ever-present place and the engaging promotion, are the 4Ps with an addition of an E for each P. The Es are not a mere cosmetic change. They bring forward the necessary addition to traditional marketing literature and practice, upgrading each P's role, rituals and relevance. The addition of Es is not intended to reject and abolish what is written for each P up to now. On the contrary, by taking existing knowledge on the mix as something given, the Es add a more advanced layer of understanding that works well because, and not instead, of current literature. Simply put, the 4EPs do not replace the 4Ps; they provide very-much-needed upgrades with the addition of specific scientific and business issues – as in the case of Deciem, to offer companies the opportunity to experience real growth and disrupt meaningfully their industries.

The empathic product

Empathy has become one of the hottest concepts in business and marketing during the last few years. Articles in business media, with evocative titles such as 'Why your business needs more empathy' (Ellis, 2017), 'Why genuine empathy is good for business' (Booth, 2015) and 'Empathy in business is vital to an entrepreneur's success' (Pomerenke, 2014) are becoming more frequent with analysts, commentators and businesspeople alike arguing that empathy is a key human skill for advancing relationships, businesses and brands. The main premise of the argument is that business should not be just obsessing about profits and numbers. Profits and numbers are the desired outcome; the end goal. But to get there, modern leaders need to understand better and deeper the needs of their partners, employees and customers in order to respond to those needs decisively and effectively. Marketers should be playing a key role in this empathic business process, especially regarding customers. Out of the 10 most important reasons for empathy, noted by innovation and strategy consultant and business author Yoram Solomon (2017), most can be directly related to the marketing leaders' role:

- customer service;
- sales;
- negotiations;
- teamwork;
- conscious capitalism;
- design thinking.

If marketers, with all their voice-of-customer research and data analytics tools, cannot understand deeper and connect in a human level with customers, then who can within companies?

The problem with empathy

Unfortunately, marketers are not doing as well in empathy as their functional responsibilities and available tech tools would suggest. In a series of experiments with 480 experienced marketing managers, researchers Johannes Hattula and associates found an unexpected and profound paradox: the more that marketing managers tried to put themselves in the shoes of their customers the more egocentric they became by projecting their own preferences on to those of customers (Hattula *et al*, 2015). In doing so, marketing managers also decreased their dependence and usage of available marketing research in taking product, communications, pricing and endorsement decisions. Trying consciously to empathize with customers does not work and, as the study suggests, it can seriously backfire. Empathizing is not easy, and it should not only depend on marketing managers' ability or willingness to do so. Empathy should be placed at the core of the marketing function, including processes, policies, research and training on better using empathy to connect to customers.

Marketers are fighting an uphill battle. Society as a whole does not make empathy development and application easy. A recent study has found that one out of five CEOs are psychopaths (Agerholm, 2016), which means that 20 per cent of them do not activate their natural brain mechanisms that facilitate human connectivity, emotional contagion and morality-driven thinking. This percentage, according to the study, is equal to the percentage of psychopaths found in prison populations, which is alarming, since the percentage in the total population is only 1 per cent. Furthermore, the empathy deficit, which is the drop in overall empathy levels in society observed in the last 30 years (Colvin, 2015), and the parallel increase of narcissistic personality traits in the wider population (Twenge and Campbell, 2009), have been much publicized, no less by former United States President Barak Obama in his famous 2009 speech to Northwestern University graduates (Northwestern, 2006). In that speech, Obama claimed that: 'We live in a culture that discourages empathy. A culture that too often tells us our principal goal in life is to be rich, thin, young, famous, safe and entertained. A culture where those in power too often encourage these selfish impulses.' He encouraged graduates to cultivate empathy and reverse the empathy deficit by increasing their sense of concern and by promoting collective solutions that ultimately will lead to individual growth as well. In a similar note, the paper by Hattula and associates (2015) concluded that marketers can achieve higher empathy when being aware of their personal biases and by applying a more pluralistic approach in team decision making.

Marketing needs empathy. Marketers need to employ empathy, not only when communicating to clients but, most importantly, when developing products, services and experiences. It is this usage of empathy in early marketing processes that makes empathy crucial and game changing for marketers. For far too long creating products was a rather one-way approach for brands:

companies develop products and customers buy them. Regardless the occasional or systematic inclusion of research results, this was a largely ineffective process reflecting more what the company wanted or could produce and less what customers really needed. This now needs to change and move towards a more two-way approach. This means that products and services have to target core customer needs uncompromisingly, solving real problems and addressing key customer pains.

The most successful concept on applying empathy in product and service development is what is called *design thinking*. Although design thinking is an earlier concept used in diverse domains such as engineering and architecture, its application in business is generally accredited to David Kelley, co-founder of innovation consultancy IDEO (Brown, 2008). IDEO's (2018) own website explains the following in relation to the concept:

> Design thinking utilizes elements from the designer's toolkit like empathy and experimentation to arrive at innovative solutions. By using design thinking, you make decisions based on what future customers really want instead of relying only on historical data or making risky bets based on instinct instead of evidence.

For many in marketing and in other company functions, the word 'design' is associated more with graphic design and creative work, usually done by designers, and less with core marketing processes such as product and service development. Design thinking, according to IDEO, is a specific approach that borrows from the creative toolkit of designers but that applies this toolkit for creating products and services (IDEO, 2018). The main contribution and differentiation though is that it brings to those core marketing processes a more human-centric mindset, since it is placing human needs and desires at the very centre of those processes, trying to address them effectively with the best-available technology and most feasible economic means. For design thinking, customers and their emotional and functional needs should be the constant guide when developing products and services, forming the absolute benchmark both at the beginning and the end of the process.

In applying design thinking in product development, Jon Kolko (2014), a global advocate and authority on the concept, recommends four steps or questions, as presented below:

Question 1: **What is the product-market fit?** This first step is about diving deeply into the realities of your market to discover the relationship between a product and the various actors in this market. These actors are: relevant user communities, customers, competitors, trend-setters, policy and legislation makers. The aim is to understand complex, multilayered relationships but also timing and the market's readiness stage for a product or a service. Marketers should collect market signals from all possible available sources on those actors but should always have in mind that signal interpretation requires experience and time, and that it involves a certain amount of risk. The emphasis should be on user-community analysis, regardless if those users are a brand's customers or not. The end result is a map of the market with specific ideas on its constraints and its possibilities.

Question 2: **Which are the most important behavioural insights?** The second step is conducting in-depth research with potential customers. Kolko here recommends ethnographic research, which is about observing human behaviour as it happens in its natural environment. This approach also includes conversations with research participants to determine their view on what drives their behaviour. This step emphasizes synthesis and interpretation. Synthesis is about creating a simple, but not simplistic, summary of all research in a comprehensive, visual and engaging manner. This helps marketers draw data connections and reveal aspects of behaviour not easily seen in graphs, tables and Excel outputs. It is also a powerful communication tool within the marketing ecosystem when marketing leaders need to involve other people and partners into the project. Interpretation is about identifying the core needs and the core insights of the research. Interpretation in ethnography is not separate from the researcher, and being aware of your own assumptions and biases is crucial. Ethnography is a powerful research tool but the value of neuromarketing, as described in Chapter 2, cannot be denied in identifying deep and unconscious customer needs and reactions.

Question 3: **What is the product strategy?** The third step is about developing the product's or service's unique personality. Here the marketing team should use the market map and customer insights from previous steps to identify the emotional value proposition of the product. This proposition is both overt, presented to customers through open communications activities, and covert, experienced by customers while using the product. The end result is the product's stance, or personality, which portrays the product's attitude in terms of feelings experienced by customers. The process of determining the product stance includes identifying the brand's aspirational emotional traits, what the brand aspires customers to be or achieve, and the emotional requirements for the specific products, which are about the specific emotional challenges or customer pains that the product will address. It is obvious that, for design thinking, emotions are as important, if not more important, than functions when developing a product.

Question 4: **Which are the key product details?** This final step is about finalizing product design by injecting a strong product vision component to the process. This vision should be as detailed as possible and should include a comprehensive and concrete product definition, a visual mood with all emotional concerns portrayed in the overall aesthetics of the product, and how the user interacts with the product in different customer life-cycle stages. A last, but not least, action in this step includes communicating the product vision to all internal and external stakeholders in order to get them on board and ultimately deliver successfully a product to the market.

IDEO's (2018) own design-thinking process is somewhat similar to Kolko's, including the following four steps:

1 Inspiration, which is about discovering what people need.

2 Ideas, which is about thinking outside of the box to reach really innovative solutions.

3 Tangibility, which is about creating prototypes to test usability.

4 Sharing, which is about using storytelling to motivate people to take action.

Developing the empathic product through design thinking is a modern and popular way of injecting emotionality in a previously technical and rather engineering-driven process. But it is not the only way. Business psychologist Dr Mark Ingwer (2012), in his book *Empathetic Marketing*, describes how marketers can benefit greatly by looking into what he calls *the core emotional needs continuum*. This continuum includes six core, universal and deeply motivating human emotional needs: control, self-expression, growth, recognition, belonging and care. Those six emotional needs are placed on a continuum with individuality at one end and connectedness at the other. Control is the closest need to individuality and care to connectedness, although all emotional needs have a bit of both individuality and connectedness in them. Ingwer's (2012) key questions for developing empathic products are:

- **Need for control.** Are you putting your customers in the driver's seat? Are customers and prospects feeling in control throughout the whole process, including aftersales support?

- **Need for self-expression.** Are your products enabling customers to express their own, individual self-identity? Are you involving them in the developmental process by empowering them to influence tangibly the result? Is your product compatible with your customers' emotional self-identity, as this changes throughout their lives?

- **Need for growth.** Have you identified your customer's growth ambitions? Are your products necessary tools for them becoming more competent? How is your product helping them to achieve their best self-ideal?

- **Need for recognition.** Are your products and/or services personalized enough for your customers to feel recognized? Are you offering exceptional rights and privileges to recognize loyalty and commitment? Do you differentiate between customer groups with specific needs?

- **Need for belonging.** Are your products instrumental for helping customers connect more with their reference groups? Is your total product and/or service offering a platform for communities to connect or for them to facilitate their connectivity?

- **Need for care.** Are you demonstrating genuine care about their ideas and problems in tangible ways throughout the product development and product sale cycles? Are you allowing customers to showcase their care about the product and brand as well, and do you acknowledge and reward them for that?

The importance of warmth in building products

There are two variables that humans use automatically to judge other people they come in contact with. These two variables are calculated fast and automatically in our brains to deduce the right response. In the process, each of these two variables evokes different emotions. These variables are competence and warmth, and Fiske and associates have suggested that they explain more than 80 per cent of all human social behaviour (Fiske, Cuddy and Glick, 2007). Warmth is about detecting positive, caring, collaborative intentions in other people, while competence is about determining the capacity and skills other people have in collaborating or colliding with us (Malone and Fiske, 2013). Generally, warmth analysis happens faster in our brains than competence (Fiske, Cuddy and Glick, 2007). In applying this model to marketing and by doing brand research in multiple countries, Malone and Fiske (2013) found out that it explains much more of brand loyalty and purchase intention than traditional variables such as demographics and familiarity – drastically more. They also found that between warmth and competence, warmth is the top determining factor in customer attitudes towards brands.

It is too often that companies obsess over competence: procedures, quality tests, technology and functionality. What they forget or ignore is that, first, competence is easier to copy than warmth, and second, warmth impacts more on customers than competence. By building empathic products, marketers exercise more warmth towards their customers and thus connect with them better and longer.

Emotions are not, and should not be, the exclusive territory of marketing communications. Although traditionally it was the fourth P, promotions, and mainly advertising that capitalized on human emotions, nowadays emotions have to start from the very beginning in the marketing mix. The empathic product is here to stay and marketers worldwide need to understand and use emotions at the very core of their products and services portfolios. They should do so by moving away from emotionally simplistic notions of the past such as product satisfaction. Ingwer (2012) categorically argues that marketers often think that:

> Meeting needs is purely about satisfying the consumer. As it turns out, positive satisfaction surveys are neither a predictor of repurchase nor an indicator of whether more important emotional needs are met. The marketers congratulate themselves, only to find later that the same satisfied customers went elsewhere.

It is about time for marketers to become more serious about emotions.

The experiential price

The global IBM study on the 4Ps application discussed earlier showed that 'price' is the P least controlled by marketers. Why is this? Is it because of the bizarre adage that price is the only P from the marketing mix that brings revenues, while all three others induce costs (for example LearnMarketing, 2018)? If this is the case then most of marketing's work is probably considered as cost-inducing and the only revenue-bringing aspect of marketing, price, should not be left to marketers. This adage is both wrong and misleading, since all marketing elements bring revenues (no one would buy a product they do not want, they cannot find and they do not know about) and setting the right price requires investment, or cost, as well (tests and research, calculations and expert analysis, search for right vendors and suppliers etc). The point remains though: marketers are least trusted with price because this is considered too technical and too important for marketing functions to deal with; Chapter 1 explained in detail that marketers are often not considered as equal business partners as others. What is the solution to this serious problem for marketing? How can marketers reclaim price as an integral marketing tool in delivering brand value to customers? The answer, ironically enough, came from economics, and especially, behavioural economics.

The Nobel Prize in Economics went twice not to economists but to psychologists. First, in 2002, it went to psychologist Daniel Kahneman and second, in 2017, to psychologist Richard Thaler, because both of them have been instrumental in developing a better understanding of how humans make decisions, many times in relation to purchasing products and services, and thus they contributed actively in the development of the modern field of behavioural economics (Cassidy, 2017). Behavioural economics is a recent branch in economics science that challenges the long-held belief of the rational economic man (Cassidy, 2017). We have discussed in Chapter 2 the notion of *Homo economicus* and how neuroscientific discoveries have made it obsolete. However, economists are not so easy to give in. Instead of completely abolishing the concept they have accepted a variation of it through behavioural economics, which suggests that although humans are inherently irrational, by spotting biases and thinking-blind-spots science can amend the troubles created by irrationality. The obvious difference with neuromarketing is that although neuromarketing is not judgemental and accepts humans as they are, behavioural economics is almost always accompanied by a tendency to preach and restore cognitive intelligence's throne as the most effective and desired human capacity. The positive side effect of behavioural economics for marketing, though, is that it started shedding a strong spotlight on how prices affect human understanding and behaviour. This is exactly how marketers can reclaim this P as a genuine marketing mix element!

Pricing in marketing literature is typically approached as a set of strategies, most notably cost, competition or value-based for existing products and skimming or penetration pricing for new products, and as a collection of price-adjusting tactics including promotional pricing, international pricing and psychological pricing, among others (Kotler and Armstrong, 2012). But it is this last tactic, which usually receives a small part from the total pricing section in traditional textbooks, where the opportunity for marketers lies to take more control over pricing: how pricing works within the human brain and how it brings about preferences and behaviours. As business author William Poundstone (2011) highlights in his book *Priceless: The hidden psychology of value*, prices might be only numbers but they:

> Can evoke a complex set of emotions – something now visible in brain scans. Depending on the context, the same price may be perceived as a bargain or a rip-off; or it may not matter at all... [in selecting prices] we translate the desires of our hearts into the public language of numbers.

He concludes that this, unexpectedly, is not an easy process at all and that it is often proven to contain many risky turns. For Poundstone, contemporary pricing is not about using tricks, like ending a price with the number 9, but about utilizing the latest cutting-edge research from psychology and other brain-related sciences to achieve a deeper connection with, and reaction from, customers (Poundstone, 2011). Are marketers taking notice?

Academic journals and more popular books, like Poundstone's, are full of scientific research indicating the curious effects that pricing has on human attitudes and behaviours. A summary of key psychological principles concerning money and pricing is offered by renowned psychologist and behavioural economist Dan Ariely from Duke University and behavioural sciences author Jeff Kreisler (2018), and is presented below with our recommendations to modern marketers:

The relativity principle The context in which a price appears is extremely important on how this price will be perceived. This is because of the constant comparisons that are taking place at a subconscious level for our brains to determine the optimum course of action. For example, when exposed to two *Economist* subscription options, US $59 for online content only and $125 for the print version only, almost 70 per cent of the study's participants chose the first option. When a third option was inserted, with $125 for both online and print content combined, 84 per cent chose this combined offer. The difference is substantial and shows how the environment and context in which the price appears shape perceptions and choices. Marketers should carefully design price options and product comparisons to boost the value perception of the brand as a whole, and to nudge customers towards more profitable selections.

The mental accounting principle Humans use compartmentalization techniques to help them make decisions easier and faster, maximizing their emotional reward in all transactions. For example, when asked if they prefer their bonus as a $1,000 monthly instalment or as a $12,000 sum at the end of the year, most choose the second, claiming that the lump sum would allow them to spend it on something special and drastically increase their sense of wellbeing and happiness. Compartmentalisation is about mental labels and categories that customers assign to different products, services and situations, resulting in different emotional effects, regardless if they sound exactly the same to others. Marketers need to understand the emotional values their customers assign to different price options and dynamics in order to offer the one that maximizes the customers' mental accounting result.

The pain avoidance principle Brain-imaging studies have shown that what psychologists call *the pain of paying* triggers the same brain regions as when experiencing physical pain. The pain of paying exists because of a time difference that usually exists between paying for something and receiving or experiencing it, and because the process of paying has been found to receive increased attention by people's brains. Credit cards and other dynamic payment techniques can help marketers to mitigate this pain. Pain avoidance sometimes works in the opposite direction: when people are done paying for something they might change their behaviour substantially. This happened with AOL subscribers in the 1990s in the United States, who increased their usage of the internet manifold when AOL changed its pricing policy from charging per usage to a flat rate. The unexpected behavioural change created huge stress on the available AOL infrastructure, leading to loss of both profitability and clients. Marketers should be careful not to assume too much on behavioural responses to price changes and they should be ready for both good and bad scenarios.

The anchoring principle Customers put an excessive amount of trust or distrust on prices based on their own subjective experience and perception. Usually, they develop an anchor price, or reference price, of a product or service category and then compare all offers to this benchmark. Anchoring also works momentarily by factoring in often irrelevant information that might seem to our brains as influencing the final result. Looking at what other people do, using our own past memories and constantly trying to confirm what we believe to be true can influence greatly perceptions of different prices. Marketers should be aware of the anchor prices that their customers have in mind when approaching their products. Communicating social/community support for products and making sure that customers always leave with happy memories are two key ways to maintain positive anchors. For new products, where comparisons are not easy, marketers should influence anchoring by helping customers imagine the new product's emotional benefits, in contrast to older, outdated and less effective products.

The ownership principle When people feel they own something and/or they have spent considerable time and effort to experience it, they will usually value it more. The endowment effect in psychology suggests that customers will always value more something in their possession than the same thing if they do not own it; this difference apparently goes up to double the value. Companies need to give ownership of their products and services to customers before charging for them whenever possible: free monthly trials and samples can help. Experiencing the service or product with new virtual reality or augmented reality solutions can also add value.

The fairness principle The famous psychological experiment called the Ultimatum Game, including two participants separated from each other, offers an important glimpse into the inner workings of fairness in our price-related behaviour. One of the participants is offered a $5 bill and is free to share or not any of it with the second participant. However, if the second participant does not accept the shared amount, no one takes home any of the money. Results indicate that the second person considers fair something around one-third of the amount and upwards. If this is not offered, then no one wins anything. Companies have underestimated this principle in the past, with huge costs. For example, Netflix decided to replace its US $10 monthly policy for online content and DVD rental to approximately $8 for each one. Many Netflix customers revolted and dropped the company, regardless of the fact that most of them were using only one or the other, and thus were better off with the new policy. Fairness is a very strong motivator of human behaviour and marketers need to make sure they do not give wrong signals to their customers on price changes, and that they are as transparent as possible with why and what goes into pricing. The last point is particularly important for B2B marketing.

The framing principle The usage of specific words can lower or increase the perceived value, and subsequent price, of products and services. The way the products and services are presented and explained can evoke specific positive memories and associations that can increase the acceptability of the price. In that way an orange juice becomes a sunny orange juice and a trip becomes an unforgettable trip. Prices do not exist in a vacuum. Framing the offer in a desirable way will induce a desirable behaviour.

The rituals principle Research has shown that when customers are asked to go through specific rituals, or specified processes, for acquiring and consuming a product, they experience better and value more that product. Of course, rituals must be relevant, desirable and value-adding. Marketers should develop appropriate and immersive rituals when customers are acquiring and experiencing their products and services, in order for customers to increase their perception of enjoyment and delight.

The expectations principle Although the future is unknown, our survival depends to a high degree on how well we predict it. Predictions create expectations and, regardless how subjective these can be, they shape our perceptions of value. This happens in two ways: the anticipation of an event and the experience of the event itself. These are separate processes, but they can influence each other. When presenting prices, marketers should factor in the anticipation effect, meaning if their customers are going to enjoy the waiting or preparation time, and how the experience itself will measure up to their expectations. Marketers should actively both design an engaging and exciting preparatory phase and make sure they overdeliver with superior service and product quality.

The willpower principle Customers are trying to evaluate the value of a purchase now in comparison to a future possible purchase by using asymmetric emotional information: emotions now are felt and real while emotions of the future are vague and uncertain. Emotions now have a higher weight in decision making than abstract emotional value in the future. Thus, customers might give in to buying impulses now than wait for a theoretical emotional rush in the future. Marketers can induce this behaviour by emphasizing and portraying the emotional benefits that customers will immediately experience.

The money principle When customers find it difficult to make up their minds, they might use pricing as the sole piece of information to assign meaning to the product or service. So, price itself could deem a product as luxurious and of good quality or not. Prices communicate meaning and marketers need to research hard and wide for the meaning that their customers assign to prices in their product category and beyond. Only then will they be qualified to set prices that convey the right meaning to the right market segment.

Leigh Caldwell (2012), behavioural economist, business author and co-founder of London-based consumer research Irrational Agency, asserts in his book *The Psychology of Price* that:

> Understanding consumer psychology gives you the ability to improve your pricing power and increase your profits. Indeed, a business must get its approach to pricing right in order to survive and grow; it is a fundamental matter of strategy, not an optional extra.

Price in the traditional marketing mix was considered a fundamental business driver and ultimately was controlled solely by the company. Reality is now revealed to be very different. Price is not a rigid, objective and definite accounting number; it is a perception. Prices need to be experienced within their context and with all their emotional and subconscious connotations in order to be embraced or rejected. Considering the process of pricing outside the psychological forces that shape customers' interaction with prices can be devastatingly misleading for brands. The experiencing price brings pricing back to the very centre of modern marketers' responsibilities. They should be ready to seize this opportunity!

SUMMARY CHECKLIST

- Defend the original marketing mix model of 4Ps but, at the same time, recognize the value that many alternative models might be adding.

- Immerse yourself into the science of empathy and core emotional needs in order to create better products and services.

- Become an applied psychologist, or behavioural economist, in order to be able to create better pricing policies and price options through fundamental psychological principles involved in monetary transactions.

Resources to inspire you

- David Kelley, co-founder of IDEO, video on design thinking: https://www.ideou.com/pages/design-thinking

- Dr Nikolaos Dimitriadis, interview on Cannes Lions channel on how to embrace empathy: https://www.youtube.com/watch?v=bsY2gY-zrlo&t=1s

- Dr Nikolaos Dimitriadis speech on emotions, empathy and marketing at IBM: https://www.youtube.com/watch?v=p2Jj3mPrFRY&list=PLPh1DU8P4h9XHRVYpJsl8VngkhUThfAfB&index=3

Revision questions

1 Which are the main reasons for marketing academics and practitioners to try to radically change the marketing mix model of the 4Ps? In your opinion, should marketers abandon the traditional 4Ps model?

2 What is the empathy deficit and what does it mean for marketing and businesses?

3 Explain design thinking and describe the process by which marketers can apply it.

4 Discuss the core emotional needs and how they can affect product and service development decisions.

5 Which are the key psychological principles that can drastically affect pricing?

References

Agerholm, H (2016) [accessed 18 June 2018] One In Five CEOs Are Psychopaths, New Study Finds, *The Independent* [Online] http://www.independent. co.uk/news/world/australasia/psychopaths-ceos-study-statistics-one-in-five-psychopathic-traits-a7251251.html

Ariely, D and Kreisler, J (2018) *Dollars and Sense: Money mishaps and how to avoid them*, HarperCollins, New York

Bacon, J (2017) [accessed 18 June 2018] The Big Debate: Are the '4Ps of Marketing' Still Relevant?, *Marketing Week* [Online] https://www. marketingweek.com/2017/02/09/big-debate-4ps-marketing-still-relevant/

Booth, J (2015) [accessed 18 June 2018] Why Genuine Empathy is Good for Business, *Fast Company* [Online] https://www.fastcompany.com/3052337/why-genuine-empathy-is-good-for-business

Brown, T (2008) [accessed 18 June 2018] Design Thinking, *Harvard Business Review* [Online] https://hbr.org/2008/06/design-thinking

Caldwell, L (2012) *The Psychology of Price: How to use price to increase demand, profit and customer satisfaction*, Crimson Publishing, Bath

Cassidy, J (2017) [accessed 18 June 2018] The Making of Richard Thaler's Economics Nobel, *New Yorker* [Online] https://www.newyorker.com/news/john-cassidy/the-making-of-richard-thalers-economics-nobel

Colvin, G (2015) *Humans Are Underrated: What high achievers know that brilliant machines never will*, Penguin, New York

Deciem (2018a) [accessed 18 June 2018] The Founder is Screwed Up!, *Deciem* [Online] http://deciem.com/founder

Deciem (2018b) [accessed 18 June 2018] Where to Buy, *Deciem* [Online] http://store.deciem.com/crossbar/locations/hlm

Ellis, L (2017) [accessed 18 June 2018] Why Your Business Needs More Empathy, *Medium – The Startup Section* [Online] https://medium.com/swlh/why-your-business-needs-more-empathy-c578ea34e5ae

Ettenson, R, Conrado, E and Knowles, J (2013) Rethinking the 4Ps, *Harvard Business Review*, **91** (1), pp 26–27

Fiske, S T, Cuddy, A J and Glick, P (2007) Universal dimensions of social cognition: warmth and competence, *Trends in Cognitive Sciences*, **11** (2), pp 77–83

Hattula, J D, Herzog, W, Dahl, D W and Reinecke, S (2015) Managerial empathy facilitates egocentric predictions of consumer preferences, *Journal of Marketing Research*, **52** (2), pp 235–52

Hou, K (2018) [accessed 18 June 2018] Why Are People Burning the Ordinary's Products?, *The Cut* [Online] https://www.thecut.com/2018/02/brandon-truaxe-new-instagram-drama-angered-the-ordinary-fans.html

IDEO (2018) [accessed 18 June 2018] Design Thinking, *IDEO* [Online]
   https://www.ideou.com/pages/design-thinking

Ingwer, M (2012) *Empathetic Marketing: How to satisfy the 6 core emotional
   needs of your customers*, Palgrave Macmillan, New York

Kolko, J (2014) *Well-Designed: How to use empathy to create products people
   love*, Harvard Business Press, Boston

Kotler, P and Armstrong, G (2012) *Principles of Marketing*, 14th edn, Pearson
   Prentice Hall, New Jersey

Kotler, P, Calder, B, Malthouse, E and Korsten, P (2012) The gap between the
   vision for marketing and reality, *MIT Sloan Management Review*, 54, pp 13–14

Krause, B (2017) [accessed 18 June 2018] The Skin-Care Brand With an Insane
   Cult Following is Finally Coming to the US, *Refinery29* [Online] https://www.
   refinery29.com/2017/07/163827/deciem-store-opening-new-locations

LearnMarketing (2018) [accessed 18 June 2018] Marketing Mix: Price and Pricing
   Strategies, *LearnMarketing* [Online] http://www.learnmarketing.net/price.htm

Malone, C and Fiske, S T (2013) *The Human Brand: How we relate to people,
   products, and companies*, Jossey-Bass, Hoboken

Mpinja, B (2017) [accessed 18 June 2018] Meet Deciem, the Industry-Changing
   Company Behind the Ordinary Skincare, *Allure* [Online] https://www.allure.
   com/story/everything-you-wanted-to-know-about-deciem

Northwestern (2006) [accessed 18 June 2018] Obama to Graduates: Cultivate
   Empathy, *Northwestern University* [Online] http://www.northwestern.edu/
   newscenter/stories/2006/06/barack.html

Pomerenke, J (2014) [accessed 18 June 2018] Empathy in Business is Vital to an
   Entrepreneur's Success, *Entrepreneur* [Online] https://www.entrepreneur.com/
   article/238935

Poundstone, W (2011) *Priceless: The hidden psychology of value*, Oneworld,
   London

Rodulfo, K (2018) [accessed 18 June 2018] An Extremely Detailed Timeline
   of All the Deciem Drama, *ELLE* [Online] https://www.elle.com/beauty/
   makeup-skin-care/g19723451/timeline-deciem-brandon-truaxe-drama/

Solomon, Y (2017) [accessed 18 June 2018] Why Empathy is the Most Important
   Skill You'll Ever Need to Succeed, *INC.COM* [Online] https://www.inc.com/
   yoram-solomon/10-reasons-empathy-is-most-important-business-skill-you-will-
   ever-need.html

The Economist (2012) [accessed 18 June 2018] An A-Z of Business Quotations:
   Advertising, *The Economist* [Online] https://www.economist.com/blogs/
   schumpeter/2012/06/z-business-quotations

Twenge, J M and Campbell, W K (2009) *The Narcissism Epidemic: Living in the age of entitlement*, Simon and Schuster, New York

Wischhover, C (2018) [accessed 18 June 2018] The Ordinary Founder Brandon Truaxe to Company: 'I'm Done With Deciem', *Racked* [Online] https://www.racked.com/2018/4/27/17289876/deciem-brandon-truaxe-instagram

The 4EPs marketing mix, part 2

07

Ever-present place and engaging promotion

CHAPTER LEARNING OBJECTIVES

After studying this chapter, you will be able to:

- Apprehend the strategic role of synergies in orchestrating different channels while optimizing customers' purchasing journeys.

- Utilize engaging communications in inviting and interacting with customers, and other stakeholders, for co-creating various key aspects of the brand.

- Argue convincingly for the need of integration of all 4EPs in achieving higher brand value and business success.

The ever-present place

Amazon and the new groceries war

One of the biggest business stories in 2017 has been Amazon, the online retailer giant, buying Whole Foods, the upscale US supermarket chain, for US $13.7 billion (Aziza, 2017). This surprising move made immediate waves in the business world, with some claiming that it terrified the entire food market (Kowitt, 2017) simply because it single-handedly shattered the invisible divide between online and offline sales models. Although all major bricks-and-mortar shops had already offered online shopping options to their customers and online behemoth Amazon had already moved into the real world with experimental mini-shops such as Amazon Go and Amazon Fresh (Aziza, 2017), the divide was mostly there. Not any more. These waves got to tsunami level towards the end of 2017 when rumours claimed that Amazon is also planning to buy Target, another well-known retail chain in the United States. The interest in Amazon's expansion in the real world was so intense that it provoked an almost minute-by-minute coverage of the story, with competing story titles such as: '3 Reasons Amazon Will Buy Target This Year' (Munster, 2018), 'No, Amazon Isn't Buying Target In 2018' (Kestenbaum, 2018) and the more flexible 'Here's Why Amazon May Not Buy Target' (Hirsch, 2018). All these stories appeared in business media within the first week of January 2018. Regardless of whether Amazon finally bought Target or not, the company's move into real-world retail is substantial and is expected to disrupt the industry inside out. As data entrepreneur and Forbes contributor Bruno Aziza (2017) explains, Amazon will benefit in two major ways: first, it will get the opportunity 'to reinvent and re-engineer the process of buying, moving and selling goods' because of 'a trove of [retail] data that it can mine to write the future' from Whole Foods's 460 stores, and second, 'Whole Foods has higher margins than Amazon's retail business (5 per cent versus 3 per cent)'. So, Amazon is tapping in to a higher-profitability channel and at the same time it is using its advanced data-analytics and habit-creating experience to disrupt the groceries market as well.

It is interesting that a few months before Amazon acquired Whole Foods, the globally famous investor Warren Buffet exited Walmart, the US's leading bricks-and-mortar retailer, by selling US $900 million worth of Walmart stocks and indicating for some the end of traditional retail models (Lutz, 2017). Walmart, as an answer to Amazon's moves, partnered with Google in order for the Walmart product range to be accessed through Google Express, Google's online shopping mall (Wakabayashi and Corkery, 2017).

In the meantime, major brand owners in the UK signed a deal with an app that promises to offer products directly to consumers, bypassing supermarket chains, and lowering prices by up to 30 per cent (Morley, 2017). Having on board major brand owners such as Mars, Unilever and Reckitt Benckiser, the move is expected to change the face of retail, challenging the traditional retail model to its core.

Regardless the fears, excitement and overall uncertainty that all these moves bring about in the marketplace, it seems that the third P, place, is undergoing a major shift. The question is not any more should a brand be online or offline, but how can brands be everywhere, always enhancing customers' experiences?

The IBM worldwide study mentioned previously found that place was the second P, after price, that was the least controlled by marketing departments. As with price, place is traditionally considered as too technical, too engineering-based and too complex for marketers to deal with. Transportation, logistics, delivery systems, supply chain management and other concepts and methods became a separate function in business due to globalization and the advent of worldwide markets in the last 30 years. Increased complexity of global trade, and of the flow of products and services around the world, created the need for new systems and new managerial approaches to ensure successful transactions and access. These changes took the second P, place, further away from marketers and closer to specialized experts in other, many times newly created, departments. As with price, though, place is integral to achieving brand growth and delivering the brand vision in the market, and marketers need to reclaim it. Changes in technology, buying habits and market conditions make product and service accessibility more important than ever. Are customers encountered in an efficient and effective way whenever and wherever they are? This is the main promise of the ever-present place.

Take Hasbro, the toy company behind global brands such as Play-Doh and Monopoly. Initially, the company found out from its own research that it was not leveraging new technologies and channels effectively to follow the customer shopping journey and to be where customers were. However, as VP of Integrated Media and Promotions, Ginny McCormick, said, the company eventually 'started really understanding where consumers were shopping' and it was now 'leveraging analytics to create a frictionless and relevant experience for the consumer' (Heine, 2017). This is the essence of the ever-present place. New technologies, social media, smartphones and the merge of offline and online tools and marketplaces are creating a unique opportunity for brands: to seamlessly incorporate their products and services in every step of their customers' lives and shopping trips, in order to maximize exposure in a relevant and meaningful way for their customers. While a multichannel approach is more about using different channels to achieve different goals, the ever-present place is about creating a unique, integrated and powerful experience regardless the channels used by customers. In this sense, it is closer to the concept of omnipresence and the omnichannel approach than to the multichannel one; the first being about the immersive brand experience that removes barriers between channels while the second being the rather simple approach of products and services being available through different channels in different ways (Orendorff, 2017). However, ever-presence, apart from fitting the 4EPs acronym better than omnipresence, puts an emphasis on *EVER*, as in wherever, whenever and whatever customers prefer and are doing in their lives, rather than in *ALL*. This is a small but important difference since *EVER* does not necessarily mean *ALL* as in *all the time*, and *all of them equally*. Ever-presence allows for distinction, focus and prioritization more than omnipresence, the latter being a major criticism towards the omni model (Denis, 2017). By applying such an ever-present approach as a key aspect of its overall marketing transformation effort, Hasbro, the toy company, managed to reach US $5 billion in sales in 2016, the highest point in its 93-year history, and saw a surge in its stock price by 140 per cent within four years (Heine, 2017). Hasbro's McCormick emphasizes, for all marketers to hear, that: 'There is not a linear path to purchase [any more] – consumers are coming in at different points' (Heine, 2017).

In order for advanced marketers to develop the right ever-present strategy they need to have a thorough understanding of the following elements (Agius, 2017):

- **Product/service.** What is offered by the company, in terms of products, services and experiences, will influence the strategy. Disney and Bank of America both implement such strategies but in different manners in order to better fit their customers' needs, journeys and expectations: the former by integrating online content with access to its physical assets in theme parks, and the latter by doing everything to remove the hassle from acquiring many banking services.

- **Communications.** The main brand message and the overall brand personality have to shine through the choice of channel strategy. Customers should never be confused about the brand appearing in incongruent channels.

- **Sales.** Sales objectives influence the channel mix and overall customer channel experience, since seasonality, product launches, promotional offers, bundles and other sales-oriented activities can determine channel priority and focus.

- **Customer support.** Traditionally customer support was scarce and incidental. Nowadays it is continuous and strategic. Customers are reaching out for help, recommendations and guidance constantly and also companies should be reaching out to customers constantly too. Building a trustful relation is the key success factor and, to do so, contact points should be frequent, honest and impactful.

- **Customer success.** In a true empathic approach, marketers should always have in mind that the ultimate goal of making their products and service widely accessible, and their customers' experience seamless and integrated, is the deep satisfaction of the customers' emotional needs. This is the main benchmark that marketers should adhere to in developing ever-present strategies.

The ever-present strategy itself should include the following five steps, as suggested by Shore and Jauk (2017) and adapted for the purposes of this book:

1 **Start with the team.** Ever-presence requires teams and mindsets alignment before everything else. Is everyone driven by the same purpose? Furthermore, it needs a supportive organizational structure and clear direction of which teams focus on which brand touchpoints. Leadership should be strong, inspiring and geared towards affirmative action.

2 **Integrate systems and data.** Ever-presence requires the ability to analyse and synthesize data coming from different channels quickly and effectively in order to draw real-time insights and proceed fast in enhancing, resolving and concluding customer journeys. The role of both technology and analytical skills present in the team cannot be overemphasized here.

3 **Be relentlessly customer-centric.** As already mentioned, customers do not bother about channels and company strategies: they want to have access to their preferred products and services in simple and meaningful ways. The team should make sure they understand the emotional drivers behind their customers' wishes and actions. Also, marketers must map carefully their customers' journeys to ensure they have a clear picture of interaction points, of the challenges for each point and their impact in the total customer delight.

4 **Create channel synergy.** First, when customers take a purchase action in one of the available channels, for example on their mobile phones, they need to see this action registered in all the other channels, both online and offline. Second, rich experience-based actions taken by brands to engage their customers in one channel should have traces in other channels too to create a seamless transition. This high level of channel synergy, and its coordination, requires the right vision, the right team and right tech working closely together.

5 Build enduring brand–customer relations. The ultimate goal is that when customers interact with the brand through different channels they have a fulfilling customer experience that leads them to become loyal and to connect even deeper emotionally with the brand. Checking and testing constantly the effects of various channels is paramount in staying ahead of the game and working towards improving customer experience every day.

Being always present: start-up and small business edition

Small businesses and start-ups need – probably even more so than bigger companies – to be everywhere, in order to push for growth and further development in all directions. For smaller businesses, omnipresence is as much about the real faces, the people behind the brand, as it is for their products and services. This is because success in start-ups and small companies depends a lot on their ability to build trust and connect with partners that can help them to grow fast and with confidence. In this direction, owners, co-founders and top managers in such companies need to be ever-present in the following three ways (Cardone, 2016):

- **Engage. Engage. Engage.** Entrepreneurs should always try to do their best to be present at relevant events in their business communities. Attending conferences, gala dinners, award ceremonies, networking events and training seminars, as well as professional associations' and interest group meetings is essential for placing themselves into the heart of action. Attending is necessary, but not sufficient though. Interacting is of equal importance for developing relations and acquiring contacts that can prove very beneficial in the future.

- **Seize every opportunity.** Entrepreneurs should not lose any opportunity to be present everywhere possible. This means that they should always say 'yes' to invitations to write articles, blog entries, opinions as well as give talks, lectures and participate at panel discussions online and offline.

- **Have a big vision.** Start-ups and small businesses should be driven by a big vision of impacting the entire world. Big visions can lead to strong commitments and to relentless actions. Every opportunity to present the company and its portfolio is seen as one more step towards achieving this big vision. No event can be skipped, and no external meeting can be postponed, if there is a chance to make the big vision a reality and change the world for the better.

Brands, entrepreneurs, products and services cannot afford to be hidden any more in the world of extreme speed, abundance of choice and short attention spans we live and operate in. The ever-present place suggests that, based on the brand strategy, marketers should strive to make sure that their products and services, and their overall brand message, are present where customers are: and nowadays this means anywhere and any time they want it. Ultimately, the mere discussion about channels can be rather misleading for marketers. As strategic adviser and Forbes contributor Steve Denis (2017) highlights: '[marketers'] problem is somehow thinking that customers care about channels. Customers care about experiences, about solutions, about shopping with ease and simplicity.'

The engaging promotion

'Baking in' engaging promotion

Is it possible to amass 14,000 active weekly users to a new product without spending a penny on marketing or advertising? In a word, yes. While UK advertising spend amassed £21.4 billion in 2016 (Hobbs, 2017), there is a rise of small, nimble brands using disruptive promotional methods with little to no cost. These disruptive promotional practices are designed to utilize peer-to-peer influence and drive awareness to attract thousands of new customers who systematically retain loyalty and influence others to participate. The era of 'engaging promotion' is colliding the elements of product and promotion to 'bake' promotion into product design at the start of the process.

It is these principles that Zest, a content distillation platform, has adopted. In a year and a half since launching, Zest has attracted and retained 14,000 active weekly users without spending any money on paid promotion. Zest founder, Yam Regev, explains that by understanding his customers' needs and unmet needs he was able to develop the content distribution platform that has now inspired marketers all over the world to use as their trusted content source. Many of Zest's customers (users) even offer their free time to help further develop the platform. So, how did Zest achieve such impressive growth, retention, customer advocacy and a desire for customer co-create?

Regev explains that it starts by building something that solves a problem for the audience and then putting the audience 'to work' to attract more customers. In the case of Zest, the problem is content shock for marketers. Zest seeks to fix the way professional marketing content is being consumed, making the content useful and actionable – every time. Zest solves this problem by using a combination of human checking and artificial intelligence to ensure that the articles are useful and of a high quality. The result, Regev explains, is 'users are surprised about the quality of the articles, they constantly get good content easily and they stick around'. The team at Zest created an experience that has three 'WOW moments':

- **Installation:** install Zest and understand the proposition and receive a product that is well designed, intuitive and has the ability to be personalized.
- **User journey:** set up Zest to your preferences and locate more high-quality relevant content.
- **Suggest content:** become invested in the product by suggesting content and sharing high-quality content with own networks.

The WOW moments are designed to take users through a journey, get them to invest in the product and start to share their experiences with their own networks online – essentially, baking promotion into the product by designing triggers to prompt customers to share user-generated-content with their networks. Customers are rewarded by using Zest through the content they receive from the content but also through sharing the same value with their online networks – making the Zest experience addictive and creating a self-perpetuating promotion machine.

SOURCE Zest (2017)

The promotional mix refers to one of the traditional marketing mix's 4Ps. The promotional mix is considered to be all the forms of communication that a brand uses to establish meaning for its product or service, as well as a way to influence the buying behaviour of targeted customers. It is traditionally believed that there are five main promotional tools (Kotler *et al*, 2002):

- **Advertising:** any paid form of non-personal presentation and promotion of ideas of products or services.
- **Personal selling:** personal presentation by a brand's sales force for the purpose of making sales.
- **Sales promotion:** short-term incentives to encourage the purchase of products and services.
- **Public relations:** building good relations with a brand's various publics by obtaining favourable publicity.

- **Direct marketing:** direct connections with carefully targeted individual consumers to obtain an immediate response and cultivate consumer relationships.

These promotional tools are often discussed as falling above or below a metaphorical line in advertising. In 1954 Procter & Gamble made the decision to pay their advertising agencies a different rate from the agencies who undertook other promotional activities on their behalf (Baker, 2002). This led to the creation of above the line (ATL) and below the line (BTL) advertising and, more recently, the concept of through the line (TTL) advertising (Table 7.1).

Table 7.1   The metaphorical line in advertising

Advertising Type	Description
Above the line (ATL)	The use of mass media to promote the brand in a non-targeted manner that is focused on building brand awareness.
Below the line (BTL)	The use of targeted direct advertising activities aimed at a specific group of customers that is focused on increasing conversions.
Through the line (TTL)	A combination of ATL and BTL to maximize brand building and conversion results.

Traditionally, these marketing initiatives were designed to interrupt consumers and grab their attention. For example, television advertising. When we watch television programmes they are often interrupted by advertising breaks and we are forced to watch advertising, because the brand paid money. It doesn't matter if the commercial is interesting, relevant or engaging – it only matters that it sells the brand. To explain such tactics, Seth Godin (cited in Taylor, 1998) coined the term interruption marketing (or interruption promotion) due to their interruptive nature.

However, with the advent and mass adoption of digital technologies and social media consumers are now exposed to up to 10,000 brand messages a day, across multiple devices (Saxon, 2017). This results in shifting consumer attention and in an increase in distraction from many different types of sources, including brands, thought leaders and even other customers. The nature of promotion is also changing from one of interruption to one of permission. Permission marketing is where consumers will 'opt-in' and

Table 7.2   Evolution of promotional activities

Traditional Promotion	Digital Promotion	Engaging Promotion
TV advertising	Search engine optimization	Social media marketing
Newspaper advertising	Display advertising	Content marketing
Magazine advertising	Paid search	Personalization
PR	E-mail marketing	Webinar/virtual events
Direct marketing	Mobile marketing	Social selling
Sales promotions	Lead generation	Chat bots
Sponsorship	Affiliate marketing	Influencer marketing
Word of mouth	Multi-level marketing	User-generated content
Outdoor	Video marketing	Growth hacking

provide marketers with permission to promote to them. For example, a newsletter subscription, chat bot opt-in or a Twitter follow. Promotion is no longer regarded as a one-way mass communication vehicle to promote the brand but offers marketers the opportunity for a two-way conversation with customers and between customers. As such, a new range of promotional activities can be utilized to capitalize on the concept of engaging promotion, and reduce the frequency of interruptive marketing (Table 7.2).

Marketers are now presented with more and more channels to reach their customers, and that number is growing rapidly (Saxon, 2017). Not every channel or every activity are appropriate for every brand, campaign or budget. Nevertheless, it is still common for brands to plan marketing activity through the line (TTL), including traditional, digital and engaging promotion practices. Consider airline company Cathay Pacific with their investment in traditional television advertising, digital website and engaging social media and customer care (Brandwatch, 2017). However, there are a number of smaller, nimble, disruptive brands such as Tesla who reportedly do not pay for advertising to make sales, instead they concentrate on media stories, word of mouth and user-generated content (Schultz, 2017). As a result, technological change and engaging promotion has pressured marketers to adopt a new mindset. A perceived illusion of control had traditionally existed in the mind of the marketer, one that believed marketing messages were under the control of the brand. The adoption and use of social media has eroded this perceived illusion due to interactivity between peers, resulting in increased consumer power and empowerment.

Research conducted by Labrecque and associates (2013) outlines a framework documenting the consumer power sources that have risen as a result of the internet and social media. Marketers must be aware of such power sources and the move from individual-based sources to a more networked-based source where consumers band together to assert power and inform change. These power sources are described below:

- **Power source 1: demand.** Demand-based power resides in the aggregated impact of consumption and purchase behaviours arising out of internet and social media technologies.

- **Power source 2: information.** Information-based power is composed of two areas, grounded in the abilities to consume and produce content: information-based power through content consumption relates to the ease of access to product or service information, which reduces information asymmetry, expedites market diffusion of information and shortens product life cycles. Information-based power through content production is the ability to produce user-generated content. It enables empowerment by providing an outlet for self-expression, extending individual reach and elevating the potential for individual opinion to influence markets.

- **Power source 3: network.** Network-based power is the metamorphosis of content through network actions designed to build personal reputation and influence markets through the distribution, remixing and enhancement of digital content.

- **Power source 4: crowd.** Crowd-based power is the ability to pool, mobilize and structure resources in a way that will benefit both individuals and the group. Notable examples include Wikipedia or Kickstarter.

All four consumer power sources still exist on the internet today and exist to complement rather than compete with previous sources. Labrecque *et al* (2013) warn that consumers can draw power from multiple sources, and each source's boundaries are fluid and permeable. The challenge for marketers is to develop marketing strategies and tactics that work with the founding principles of engaging promotion – interaction and influence. For marketers, the new challenge of engaging promotion is a deep understanding of human behaviour and the use of behavioural biases to increase consumer propensity to share brand-related messages.

Today, much like traditional word of mouth, user-generated content is shown to be more influential on customer behaviour, beliefs, attitudes and purchase intent than brand-owned content. For example, 83 per cent of people trust the advertising that comes from people they know (Nielsen, 2015) and 84 per cent of consumers trust online reviews from anonymous authors (Bloem, 2017). As a result, today's promotional activity is moving away from interruption marketing to one that creates shared meaning and value to customers and brand alike. As such, the new founding principles of engaging promotion are interaction and deep understanding of human behaviour. To explain, Casanova and Casanova (2013) argue that marketing is no longer about crafting a strong message or choosing colours, rather marketers have to know about content propagation, social media, user experience, user expectations, customer behaviour and consumer psychology. In other words, to succeed in engaging promotion, marketers must leverage behavioural biases in human behaviour to reach and nudge consumer behaviour.

As humans, we all have a tendency to think of ourselves as individuals, and our behaviour is guided and decided upon by us. However, this in fact is not the case. There are outside influences where our choices and decisions are engineered for us, giving us the impression of free choice. For example, the governmental department, The Behavioural Insights Team, commonly referred to as 'The Nudge Unit' applies psychological theory and experimental design into governmental policy. As a result, the nudge unit has successfully changed citizen behaviour to save money and extend their lives with healthy behaviours. Brands across the world are also seeking to utilize behavioural science into their product design and promotional activities. A new genre of marketing book has risen that combines the principles of marketing with behavioural sciences to assist marketers to navigate human behaviours and 'put customers to work' to influence their friends, family and wider connections. One such book is HERD: *How to change mass behaviour by harnessing our true nature*. The author Mark Earls explains how to change behaviour through an understanding of the true nature of human behaviour – that, as humans, we have an inbuilt desire to connect. Our need to connect can change our behaviour to follow 'the herd'. Earls (2009) introduces the seven principles of herd marketing where marketers can use the nature of human behaviour to influence mass consumer-behaviour change. These are:

1 Interaction: the act of interaction between individuals within a given context.

2 Influence: the act of influencing behaviour beyond persuasion.

3 Us-talk: the act of brand word of mouth.

4 Just believe: the act of creating and sharing purpose through human interaction, influence and word of mouth.

5 (Re)lighting the fire: the act of aligning behaviour to belief.

6 Co-creating: the act of co-creating meaning and value with customers, employees and citizens.

7 Letting go: the act of letting go of the illusion of certainty and control.

Earls's (2009) herd-marketing principles reaffirm the founding principles of engaging content – interaction and influence. The power of engaging promotion is the interaction and influence of individuals – consumers' influence on each other.

Engaging promotion dictates that brand messages are no longer transmitted one way, that every actor – including brands, employees, consumers, customers, competitors and other stakeholders – can co-create their own brand meaning or work together to co-create meaning. However, some messages have a more persuasive and further-reaching lifespan than others, and this has prompted much research to understand why some messages affect change beyond other competing messages. After analysing hundreds of messages, products and ideas, Berger (2013) found that the most viral or 'contagious' messages had the same six principles, which make the STEPPS method. Berger (2013) argues that STEPPS cause things to be discussed, shared and imitated. These principles are outlined below:

1 Social currency: design messages that help people achieve their desired impressions, make them feel like insiders, and give them visible symbols of status that they can show to others.

2 Triggers: design products and ideas that are frequently triggered by the environment and create new triggers by linking products and ideas to prevalent cues in the environment.

3 Emotion: don't always talk about function, focus on emotions.

4 Public: create products and ideas that are observable to increase the likelihood of imitation. Achieve this by designing products that advertise themselves and create behavioural residue.

5 Practical value: package knowledge and experience so that people can easily pass it on. Highlight the value of what is on offer.

6 Stories: make stories surrounding the brand valuable. Make stories integral to the narrative so people cannot tell the story without it.

The STEPPS method builds upon the nature of human behaviour, for marketers to create communications and marketing promotion that allows their customer to connect and follow 'the herd'. Other researchers have also found that the addition of customer engagement in a brand's promotional activities increases influence on 'stickiness' of brand stories (for example Zhang *et al*, 2017). Stickiness can be defined as the messages and stories related to the brand, which stick with audiences long after they have been exposed to the communication. In the new era of engaging promotion, influence (and marketing success) is moderated by the co-creation of value between consumers, not the brand alone (Zhang *et al*, 2017). It is the power of interaction and influence that has led to a new way of thinking about brand and product (or service) promotion, one where the mechanisms of peer-to-peer promotion are baked into the product design.

Due to the mass adoption of digital technologies and the knowledge that peer-to-peer communication is more influential than brand communication alone, smart brands and product designers have begun to 'bake in' promotion into their design. Instead of creating new marketing campaigns, television adverts or sales promotions, there has been a steady flow of marketers converting to 'growth hacking' practices and leveraging the consumer's power to influence other consumers and create marketing interventions at each stage of the sales journey.

Growth hacking is a new marketing mindset with the goal of 'building a self-perpetuating marketing machine that reaches millions by itself' (Ginn, 2013). Growth hackers seek to create 'viral loops' that bring consumers back and influence other consumers to join in. Jeffryes (2010) explains that a viral loop is a self-fuelling action loop that drives users to create more users, which increases engagement and existing users. In effect, this happens by using the principles set out by Earls in his book *HERD*. The process starts at the conception of a new product and promotion is considered from the start of product development – it starts by making a product that consumers need. Holiday (2014) argues that: 'isolating who your customers are, figuring out their needs, designing a product that will blow their minds – are marketing decisions, not just development and design choices'. While growth hacking is more closely associated with the development of digital products and services, there are useful methodologies that can help any marketer in any industry. By better understanding and using the principles of engaging promotion, marketers can increase awareness, customer acquisition and, importantly, customer retention and subsequent peer-to-peer influence.

The idea behind growth hacking is to find a way to cut through the clutter and reach the target audience through non-traditional promotion techniques and product design (Casanova and Casanova, 2013). Growth hackers create experiments across marketing channels and product development in order to identify the quickest and most efficient ways to grow a business. The process therefore sees a growing linkage between product, promotion – and sales. To accomplish their goal of increased conversion, growth hackers create built-in, scalable marketing features in a product and ensure that every aspect of each user's experience is custom tailored to lead them to the next stage in the funnel (Casanova and Casanova, 2013). As explained by McClure (2007) in his AARRR system (Table 7.3), the purpose of promotion is to get the consumer to move from one stage of the system to another.

In the age of engaging promotion, marketers should consider where their promotion efforts sit within the system. In this direction, it is important to think about the purpose of the promotion. For example, promotion initiatives that sit at the top of the system will be considerably different to those towards the bottom of the system, as consumer information needs to change. Moreover, marketers must find the right trigger to nudge customers to share the brand with their own networks.

Table 7.3 The AARRR growth-hacking system

Principle	Description
Acquisition	Optimize acquisition by attracting the right type of customer through a deep understanding of their needs.
Activation	Speed up customer engagement by providing them with the right information to make an action or purchase decision.
Retention	Find the behaviour that all promotion (and product design) should encourage the customer to complete to increase the likelihood of customer loyalty (retention).
Referral	Create a value-driven mechanism that encourages customers to refer the product to other customers.
Revenue	You have turned your prospect into a paying customer.

SOURCE Adapted from McClure (2007)

Last thought

The 4Ps is a robust and resilient model that managed to survive decades of criticism and attacks, both from academics and practitioners alike. Resisting the common urge to dismiss and replace the 4Ps completely with new letters and acronyms, we instead opted for a cosmetic change that updates them appropriately for the 21st century. The 4Ps become 4EPs, in an attempt to reflect the changes that occur in the business and marketing landscape; and are now ready to assist marketers become the company leaders we envision them to be. Although the 4EPs are presented in chapters 6 and 7 as separate from each other, mainly for educational purposes, this separation is not as clear-cut as it seems. The empathic product, the experiential price, the ever-present place and the engaging promotion, from a marketing-practice perspective, are morphing into one, being the everyday reality in a marketer's job. Naming them and separating them is less important than integrating them in cutting-edge marketing strategies and tactics that can give meaningful advantages to brands and win over customers in the marketplace.

SUMMARY CHECKLIST

- Integrate teams, systems, data and channels to deliver seamless customer experiences through all brand touchpoints, online and offline.
- Use herd marketing and growth-hacking communications techniques to engage customers and create active communities around the brand.
- Spread the word of the 4EPs marketing mix model as an evolved version of the original and world-famous 4Ps!

Resources to inspire you

- *Today* show report on Amazon–Whole Foods merger: https://www.youtube.com/watch?v=CHT9VVL22NM
- Mark Earls video on *Homo mimicus*: https://www.youtube.com/watch?v=dpPizW3_iVg
- Dave McClure's slideshow presentation on the AARRR model: https://www.slideshare.net/dmc500hats/startup-metrics-for-pirates-long-version
- Buenavente, growth-hacking interview series: https://www.buenavente.com/all-growth-hacking-interviews/

Revision questions

1 What does Amazon's move to buy Whole Foods mean for modern marketers and for the future of retail?

2 What are the steps for developing an ever-present strategy? In your opinion, what are the key challenges that marketers face in each of these steps?

3 Discuss the consumer power sources that have emerged as a result of the internet and social media. Use examples for each one.

4 Describe the seven principles of herd marketing and analyse how they can be used to enhance engaging promotion.

5 Describe the STEPPS method for creating viral and contagious messages. Give examples of existing brands to illustrate how the method works in practice.

References

Agius, A (2017) [accessed 18 June 2018] 7 Outstanding Examples of Omni-Channel Experience, *HubSpot* [Online] https://blog.hubspot.com/customer-success/omni-channel-experience

Aziza, B (2017) [accessed 18 June 2018] Amazon Buys Whole Foods. Now What? The Story Behind the Story, *Forbes* [Online] https://www.forbes.com/sites/ciocentral/2017/06/23/amazon-buys-whole-foods-now-what-the-story-behind-the-story/#ae35cbee8986

Baker, M J (2002) *The Marketing Book*, Taylor and Francis, London

Berger, J (2013) *Contagious: How to build word of mouth in the digital age*, Simon & Schuster, London

Bloem, C (2017) [accessed 18 June 2018] 84 Percent of People Trust Online Reviews As Much As Friends. Here's How To Manage What They See, *Inc* [Online] https://www.inc.com/craig-bloem/84-percent-of-people-trust-online-reviews-as-much-.html

Brandwatch (2017) [accessed 18 June 2018] Cathay Pacific: How Social Analytics is Used at Scale at Cathay Pacific, *Brandwatch* [Online] https://www.brandwatch.com/case-studies/cathay-pacific/

Cardone, G (2016) [accessed 18 June 2018] 3 Steps to Omnipresence, *Entrepreneur* [Online] https://www.entrepreneur.com/article/269786

Casanova, J and Casanova, J (2013) *Growth Hacking: A how to guide on becoming a growth hacker*, CSNV Books, Miami

Denis, S (2017) [accessed 18 June 2018] Omnichannel Is Dead. Long Live Omnichannel, *Forbes* [Online] https://www.forbes.com/sites/stevendennis/2017/03/23/omni-channel-is-dead-long-live-omni-channel/#309aa7fe5215

Earls, M (2009) *HERD: How to change mass behaviour by harnessing our true nature,* Wiley, Chichester

Ginn, A (2013) [accessed 18 June 2018] What is a Growth Hacker?, *Aaron Ginn's Thoughts* [Online] http://www.aginnt.com/growth-hacker#.WnhrVJOFjjA

Heine, C (2017) [accessed 18 June 2018] Inside Hasbro's Digital Transformation Into a Modern Toymaker and Advertiser, *AdWeek* [Online] http://www.adweek.com/brand-marketing/inside-hasbros-digital-transformation-into-a-modern-toymaker-and-advertiser/

Hirsch, L (2018) [accessed 18 June 2018] Here's Why Amazon May not Buy Target, *CNBC* [Online] https://www.cnbc.com/2018/01/03/heres-why-amazon-may-not-buy-target.html

Hobbs, T (2017) [accessed 18 June 2018] UK ad spend hits record £21.4bn as digital dominates again, *Marketing Week* [Online] https://www.marketingweek.com/2017/04/25/uk-ad-spend-digital/

Holiday, R (2014) *Growth Hacker Marketing Revised and Expanded*, Profile Books, London

Jeffryes, J (2010) [accessed 18 June 2018] Viral Loop: A Self-Fuelling Action That Drives Users To Create More Users, *Slideshare* [Online] https://www.slideshare.net/jjeffryes/viral-loops-making-selfmarketing-apps/12-Viral_Loopbr_A_selffueling_action

Kestenbaum, R (2018) [accessed 18 June 2018] No, Amazon Isn't Buying Target In 2018, *Forbes* [Online] https://www.forbes.com/sites/richardkestenbaum/2018/01/03/no-amazon-isnt-buying-target-in-2018/#52401dd33134

Kotler, P, Armstrong, V, Saunders, J and Wong, V (2002) *Principles of Marketing,* Pearson Education Limited, Harlow

Kowitt, B (2017) [accessed 18 June 2018] Why Amazon's Whole Foods Deal Is Terrifying Food Makers, *Fortune* [Online] http://fortune.com/2017/06/22/amazon-buying-whole-foods-disruption/

Labrecque, L I, vor dem Esche, J, Mathwick, C, Novak, T P and Hofacker, C F (2013) Consumer power: evolution in the digital age, *Journal of Interactive Marketing*, **27** (4), pp 257–69

Lutz, A (2017) [accessed 18 June 2018] Warren Buffett Just Dropped Walmart and Signalled the Death of Retail as We Know It, *BusinessInsider* [Online] http://www.businessinsider.com/warren-buffett-drops-walmart-stock-2017-2

McClure, D (2007) [accessed 18 June 2018] Startup Metrics for Pirates: AARRR!!!, *Slideshare* [Online] https://www.slideshare.net/dmc500hats/startup-metrics-for-pirates-long-version

Morley, K (2017) [accessed 18 June 2018] End of the Supermarket? Big Brands Sign Up for High-Tech Service That Could Cut Prices By A Third, *Telegraph* [Online] www.telegraph.co.uk/news/2017/10/31/end-supermarket-britains-biggest-brands-sign-direct-selling/amp

Munster, G (2018) [accessed 18 June 2018] Commentary: 3 Reasons Amazon Will Buy Target This Year, *Fortune* [Online] http://fortune.com/2018/01/05/amazon-target-buy-walmart-whole-foods/

Nielsen (2015) [accessed 18 June 2018] Recommendations From Friends Remain Most Credible Form of Advertising Among Consumers; Branded Websites are the Second Highest Rated Form, *Nielsen Press Room* [Online] http://www.nielsen.com/eu/en/press-room/2015/recommendations-from-friends-remain-most-credible-form-of-advertising.html

Orendorff, A (2017) [accessed 18 June 2018] Omni-Channel vs Multi-Channel: What is the Difference and Why Does It Matter?, *Shopify Plus* [Online] https://www.shopify.com/enterprise/omni-channel-vs-multi-channel

Saxon, J (2017) [accessed 18 June 2018] Why Your Customers' Attention is The Scarcest Resource in 2017, *American Marketing Association* [Online] https://www.ama.org/partners/content/Pages/why-customers-attention-scarcest-resources-2017.aspx

Schultz, E J (2017) [accessed 18 June 2018] Tesla Still Doesn't Need Paid Advertising To Make Sales, *AdAge* [Online] http://adage.com/article/cmo-strategy/tesla-paid-advertising/310008/

Shore, A and Jauk, D (2017) [accessed 18 June 2018] Five Tips for Developing an Omnichannel Strategy, *edx*, Blog [Online] https://blog.edx.org/five-tips-for-developing-an-omnichannel-strategy

Taylor, W C (1998) [accessed 18 June 2018] Permission Marketing, *Fast Company* [Online] https://www.fastcompany.com/34360/permission-marketing

Wakabayashi, D and Corkery, M (2017) [accessed 18 June 2018] Google and Walmart Partner With Eye on Amazon, *New York Times* [Online] https://www.nytimes.com/2017/08/23/technology/google-walmart-e-commerce-partnership.html

Zest (2017) [accessed 18 June 2018] Zest Content Platform [Online] http://zest.is/

Zhang, M, Guo, L, Hu, M and Liu, W (2017) Influence of customer engagement with company social on stickiness: mediating effect of customer value creation, *International Journal of Management*, 37 (3), pp 229–40

Reorganizing the marketing function 08

CHAPTER LEARNING OBJECTIVES

After studying this chapter, you will be able to:

- Appreciate the fact that traditional marketing structures do not fit the new vision of advanced marketing.

- Understand the contemporary landscape of emerging marketing skill sets.

- Separate effectively between strategic, tactical and operational levels of new marketers.

- Highlight the key differences between traditional, box-like marketing structures and more modern, circular ones.

- Explore the variety of new roles that the modern marketing department needs.

- Adopt more innovative, adventurous and constructive hiring approaches for marketers.

Advanced practice

Do it like the brain does!

How should marketers organize their departments, to actively assist their companies to survive, and thrive, in the modern business landscape? Does the current marketing organization suffice for the challenges of the new business environment? What kind of professionals does the new marketing function need in order to be effective in achieving its ambitious goals? Academics, consultants and marketers the world over search for convincing answers.

Chapter 1 touched upon various changes undergoing the marketing profession, including the new positions created at the highest corporate levels to deal more effectively with the far-reaching and strategic role of modern marketing. Such changes do not stay only on the surface though. They continue deeper inside the organization, altering drastically the ways the marketing function configures its resources to align with new market realities and achieve better results. In this direction, in their *Harvard Business Review* article titled 'The ultimate marketing machine', de Swaan Arons and associates describe a comprehensive new approach for organizing marketing within organizations (de Swaan Arons, van den Driest and Weed, 2014). Their approach suggests a radical review of the marketing function, which should be organized around specific capabilities. Their model includes three main capabilities that should represent the three main focus areas of new marketing teams:

- **THINK**. The first one concerns data and analytics. Marketing professionals belonging to this focus area consist of data professionals, web analysts, media planners and modellers, and ROI experts and optimizers. Their role is to collect and crunch data that led to modelling for guiding further action.

- **FEEL**. The second one is about consumer engagement. Here, marketing professionals include all those directly interacting with customers and other stakeholders: customer service professionals, community and membership managers and PR executives. Their role is to create, keep and grow customer relations actively through constant interaction and engagement.

- **DO**. The third one is about content and production. Marketing professionals with this focus include all types of content developers such as creatives, digital, web and production managers. Their main role is to ensure that the right content will be produced and delivered to customers through multiple channels.

According to the authors of the article, marketing teams dealing with any marketing project should consist of a unique combination of thinkers, feelers and doers who best serve the purpose of the project: some projects might consist of more thinkers than doers and feelers, while others might have more feelers than thinkers and doers. Such interdepartmental teams are headed by what the authors call the Orchestrator, who could be the Chief Marketing Officer, the Chief Experience Officer or any other major marketing leader. According to them: 'Complex matrixed organizational structures – like those captured in traditional, rigid "Christmas tree" org charts – are giving way to networked organizations characterized by flexible words, fluid responsibilities, and more-relaxed sign-off processes designed for speed' (de Swaan Arons, van den Driest and Weed, 2014).

The foundations of this approach are remarkably similar to the Triune Brain Theory, developed by the late neuroscientist Paul MacLean and the popular notion of three main aspects of human existence: thinking, feeling and doing – or cognition, emotions and behaviour. MacLean's theory, first stated in the 1960s, views the evolution of the human brain as a linear progression, from bottom to further up the skull, of three distinct structures: the old or reptilian brain; the mammalian or limbic system; and the primate or neocortex (Baars and Gage, 2010). According to the theory, each of these different structures, or brains, has a separate function that is, respectively, behavioural, emotional and cognitive: the reptilian brain does, the mammalian feels and the primate thinks. The theory has received considerable criticism but its educational/informative role still stands, mainly due to its clarity and wider resonance (Dimitriadis and Psychogios, 2016). In popular culture, the think–feel–do model, which the Triune Brain Theory tried to explain in a neuroscientific manner, is ever-present, from religious leaders' speeches to management and marketing consulting (Osorio, 2015). Its origins in marketing can be traced back to the so-called hierarchy of effects models, such as AIDA or attention–interest–desire–action, which go back to the late 19th century but were popularized in the 1960s, mainly through the work of Lavidge and Steiner (Vakratsas and Ambler, 1999). These models tried to explain customer behaviour as an advancement from thinking processes to actual purchasing choices. Although we have seen in Chapter 2 that the advancement is not as linear as those hierarchy of effect models would like it to be, these models pointed successfully to separate human capacities and the complexity of human nature that marketers needed to consider when delivering marketing campaigns.

The efforts of taking these neuroscientific and psychological models internally, and using them for restructuring the marketing function, portray the obvious and profound need of new solutions to the marketing organization. Nevertheless, the think–feel–do model, or the Triune Brain one, have already been used in some form in the marketing ecosystem. Advertising agencies, for decades, have included planning/analytical, account/client management, creative/content and production departments (Suggett, 2017) that correspond quite accurately to the aforementioned recommended model of internal marketing organization.

New marketing realities ask for a new marketing organization. In order to determine the format of this new organization, its internal staffing and its relations to the wider marketing ecosystem, advanced marketers need to ask some tough questions concerning the skills and capabilities needed. Ultimately, they need to define not just job descriptions, roles and organograms of their department, but the overall attitude of the modern marketing function.

The marketing challenge

What kind of professionals do advanced marketers need to staff their function with? What skills and capabilities are needed in the modern business landscape for marketing departments to succeed in their strategic role? What type of structure best fits those skills and the overall environment? The first of these two problem areas, new marketing skills, is discussed in this section. Structural challenges and organizational solutions follow in the next part of this chapter.

A report by global consulting firm McKinsey, on hiring trends in marketing for 2017, stated the key findings as follows (McKinsey, 2017):

- Demand for marketing talent far exceeds supply in key areas.
- 44 per cent of companies will hire more marketers (up from 28 per cent).
- Cutbacks will be minimal.
- Over half of relevant hires will be digital.

The first and second findings formulate the first main challenge of Advanced Marketing Management nowadays. Although companies are hungry to improve and increase their marketing function, available top talent is not in equal supply. Another study, based on data from 314 marketing professionals in a wide range of industries, revealed that 56 per cent of participants would look for staff with digital marketing expertise, 35 per cent would look for creative services expertise, and 27 per cent would look for marketing operations expertise (Nanji, 2017). It is worth noting that only 19 per cent of respondents would be interested to hire people with traditional marketing expertise!

An earlier report by leading professional online network LinkedIn in 2015, titled 'Announcing the Marketing Skills Handbook: A deep dive into today's most in-demand marketing jobs', had already highlighted the importance of new technical skills in marketing. Two of the report's main conclusions were that (Callahan, 2015):

- The top three skills named in recruiter searches for marketing skills are SEO/ SEM marketing; digital and online marketing; and marketing campaign management.
- The three marketing job titles with outstanding growth in the past decade were: Digital Marketing Manager (+248 per cent); Brand Ambassador (+147.5 per cent); and CMO (+62.4 per cent).

The first point is consistent with the overall trend of 'technicalization' of the marketing profession, at least at an operational level, as is the impressive 248 per cent increase of Digital Marketing Managers on the LinkedIn platform from 2004 to 2015. The 147.5 per cent and 62.4 per cent increases of Brand Ambassadors and CMOs respectively portray the parallel need for better high-level, strategic marketers and brand professionals. The increasing 'technicalization' of the marketing operations can be seen in almost all lists of essential marketing skills, including the list from the online advertising platform, Wordstream. That list, consisting of 14 key skills for marketing personnel, included 13 technical-oriented skills such as content, content management system (CMS), customer relationship management (CRM), mobile, data, user experience (UX), video and e-mail marketing... and only one, the last one, as the non-technical, consumer behaviourist skill (Marrs, 2015).

These findings showcase the pains of modern companies and their marketing efforts. Since a lot of business is directed online and every company has, in one way or another, digital presence, they expect to achieve faster and stronger growth than before with the new tools. However, this is not always happening. The 2017 State of Inbound study report stated the following top marketing challenges and priorities (State of Inbound, 2017):

- generating traffic and leads (63 per cent);
- providing the ROI of our marketing activities (40 per cent);
- securing enough budget (28 per cent).

If the top challenge and priority today is generating traffic and leads online then it is only logical that marketing personnel who can make this happen and possess the right digital skills would be in high demand. The year 2016 has been the first one that digital (desktop and mobile together) advertising revenue surpassed that of TV (Slefo, 2017). All this new marketing activity online needs new methods and skills, and this is something that is subsequently shown on numerous marketing trends lists, such as the State of Inbound. The second and third priorities on that list, ROI and sufficient budget for marketing activities, are strongly linked with The Marketing Paradox issues discussed in depth in Chapter 1.

The marketing challenge of our day, based on all the data presented above, seems to be the inability for many marketing functions to secure the appropriate, quantitatively and qualitatively, marketing personnel with advanced data and technology-related skills. This is why this book has already included data skills, in Chapter 3, as one of the four key marketing skills for Advanced Marketing Management. An interesting phenomenon for marketing is that the gap in technical skills is not served only by new marketers becoming more technical but from engineers becoming more marketing-savvy. In his blogpost titled 'Engineers are becoming a lot like marketers too', Scott Brinker from the Chief Marketing Technologist Blog observed that as marketers become more technical, engineers have started learning marketing and are becoming more important in the marketing function (Brinker, 2012). This phenomenon opens new opportunities for advanced marketers in finding the right personnel for their functions, looking at more diverse scientific and academic fields than ever before.

There has been, however, an unbalanced rush for recruiting marketing staff who are too tech-savvy. Undeniably, technology and data are and will be extremely important in any present and future marketing effort. As if a fear of missing out (FOMO) fever grabbed marketers, they looked more on engaging advanced tech skills, internally or outsourced, without an equal focus on content and the big picture. *HOW* brands communicate, mainly through digital channels, became more important than *WHAT* they communicate, and the actual results achieved.

FOMO in the marketing function

FOMO is an acronym for fear of missing out, initially used in relation to social media usage. FOMO is a form of social anxiety experienced when a person feels excluded from something great that is happening and that can be beneficial for those 'in the know'. In order not to be excluded from this potential rewarding happening, a person's FOMO anxiety pushes for constant online connectivity and relentless social media checking (Przybylski *et al*, 2013). In the marketing function, FOMO relates to marketing leaders trying to keep up with or to outpace competition in the digital arena with high online spending, intense engagement of tech consultants and agencies, and laser focus on digital capabilities instead of digital deliverables.

FOMO as a marketing function has two main negative implications:

- **Narrowness**. Joe Pulizzi, the founder of the Content Marketing Institute, described in his 2017 article 'One thing is killing content marketing and everyone is ignoring it', how marketers from different industries, including consultants, usually employ a variety of digital tools and channels but they are rarely happy with the results. According to Pulizzi, this is because marketers usually focus too narrowly on the techniques and variety of online actions that are being used and not on what is communicated. As he emphatically stated: 'Our job, as marketers, is not to create more content… It's about creating the minimum amount of content with the maximum amount of behaviour change in our customers… For that to be possible, what you are creating has to be valuable, useful, compelling and, yes, different' (Pulizzi, 2017). It is a delusion that if marketers tick a long checklist of digital tools employed that results will somehow appear. Being present in many digital channels is a competitive necessity, but winning because of that fact alone is not a competitive fact. So, hiring an army of internal and external tech-savvy marketers to increase digital presence and output cannot win the day if this is not accompanied by creative and targeted content that resonates with your customers' brains. This is well-documented throughout the previous chapters in this book.

- **Short-termism**. Many digital channels are highly skewed towards short-term results: another 'like', another 'share', another 'comment', another 'subscription'. Although those measures by themselves are not harmful for marketing, marketers' obsessive and one-sided focus on them is. As observed as early as 2010 by Peter Field, short-termism is a significant threat to modern marketing because it pushes marketers to forget about building strong and long-lasting relations with customers that can help brands develop and grow (Field, 2010). More recently, George Musi has argued in an article of his in *Adweek* that, despite the fact that CMOs are too much pressured for short-term results, they should: 'begin looking at marketing as a financial investment, with a measured, balanced and logical investment strategy, investigating the risk potential, growth expectations, and their portfolio as a whole, in order to meet the goals of the business' (Musi, 2017). According to Musi, short-termism is the biggest downside of the explosive growth of digital marketing in our modern business age.

Staffing the marketing function with qualified tech-savvy marketing personnel is a big challenge for marketing today. At the same time though, an equally big challenge is not to be driven only by FOMO and overdo it on the technical side, forgetting and harming the strategic, holistic and ultimate marketing purpose. This is why new types of marketers are needed, in all levels: the strategic, tactical and operational ones (Table 8.1).

Table 8.1 New types of marketers

STRATEGIC	TACTICAL	OPERATIONAL
Transformational Marketers	Hybrid Marketers	Specialized Marketers
VP and C-suite	Managerial and Directorial	Employee and Supervisory
New breed of marketing leaders that understand the holistic role of marketing for the success of the organization as a whole. They lead other top-level colleagues in creating strong brands, adopt an unconditional customer focus, and deliver superior experiences.	New breed of middle-level marketers that, regardless of their specialized background, speak fluently both tech and content, channels and creativity, digital and real world. They lead their teams of experts by providing them with the big picture and by being able to balance short-term results with long-term brand building.	New breed of marketing specialists that span a wide range of academic, scientific and practical backgrounds. Based on the role they might be more tech-oriented or more traditional marketing-oriented. In both cases they understand each other on a basic level and they collaborate for achieving the team's goals.

The need for and role of transformational marketers at the strategic level of companies has been thoroughly explained in Chapter 1. The need for specialized marketers, either thinkers, feelers or doers with the skills described earlier in this chapter, will always be evident at the operational level due to all the different expert tasks that have to be performed within complex and dynamic marketing processes. The hybrid marketer, a term coined by Jason Miller in his LinkedIn post titled 'Are you ready for the rise of the hybrid marketer?' (Miller, 2017), fits best the tactical level where marketers need to lead teams with expert precision but also with a universal marketing language and a big-picture understanding of how different channels and short-term efforts contribute to a wider marketing vision and long-term success for the brand. As reported by Charlotte Rogers in *Marketing Week*, this new breed of marketers, who also constantly rebrand their careers to achieve maximum learning and personal development impacting positively the brands they work for, is on the rise (Rogers, 2017).

A study of 315 senior marketers by the agency 3Q Digital in the United States, reported in *Forbes*, stated that the top challenges for marketing leaders are (Whitler, 2017):

- alignment and integration;
- innovation and modern strategies;
- data and decision making;
- client–agency relations.

A careful look at the list showcases that in order for those challenges to be addressed effectively, all three levels of new breeds of marketers need to get actively involved. Alignment and integration refers more to the role of the transformational marketers, while innovation and modern strategies needs a close partnership of all three levels due to the highly interwoven and cross-boundaries nature of innovation today, as described in Chapter 4. Data and decision making, and especially the inability of companies to use data appropriately, as reported in the study, concerns more the hybrid marketers and of course those who produce data, usually the specialized marketers. Client–agency relations, and especially the somewhat widespread dissatisfaction of clients with their agencies that the study found, is primarily the responsibility of hybrid marketers since, more often than not, they manage these relationships, and again, the specialized marketers that interact operationally with their agency counterparts even on a daily basis.

New marketing needs new marketers – and new marketers need new ways to organize their work internally and externally. How relevant are the traditional marketing structures to today's marketing challenges and what does the marketing organization of the future look like?

The new marketing structure

Traditional marketing literature and thinking offers a rather consistent view of how companies used to organize their marketing function. In an always pyramid-like shape of hierarchical organization, marketers used to group their marketing resources in the following ways (Hollensen, 2003; Kotler, 2000):

- **Functional structure.** This is probably the most classic marketing organization approach, where the CMO leads a team of functional experts: public relations, advertising, marketing research, products, distribution and retail etc. Each of these functional expert leaders, like the PR Director, have their own teams of specialized experts that deal exclusively with their focused scope of work. In this structure, the same specialized team deals with all brands, customer groups and geographical markets. This is the main reason why such structures work better in smaller than bigger companies.

- **Product or brand structure.** This approach emphasizes the different product lines or brands that a company holds instead of marketing specializations. Here, the CMO leads a team of products or brand leaders, and those leaders often utilize shared marketing-expertise resources to help their products and brands be marketed successfully. Companies usually adopt such a structure when their growth leads to creating and/or acquiring too many products or brands that are quite distinct from each other.

- **Geographical structure.** When companies operate in diverse geographical markets, locally, regionally or internationally, with distinct customer and market needs, they often opt for this type of structure. The CMO here leads a team of geographic-oriented marketing directors representing regions within a country, whole countries or groups of countries. This type of structure became very popular with the advent of globalization and the worldwide expansion of many large companies.

- **Customer or market structure.** Companies that serve dissimilar customer groups, or markets, choose to organize their marketing function around such groups. For example, companies can separate business from consumer segments, large from smaller clients and government buyers from business buyers. Or they can go for more specialized customer groups. For example, a cleaning products company can differentiate between the medical premises market, the business premises market and the household market.

- The most widespread structure, especially in larger corporations, is the **Complicated Structure**, which is actually a combination of two or more of the above approaches. Although such an approach is many times necessary to deal effectively with the complexity of market conditions globally, the main problem is the resulting unclear, and/or too complicated authority and communications lines that such systems usually produce. The *Silo Effect* is also a serious problem of rigid and overcomplicated structures, where people in one department/unit/team/group have the belief that what they do is totally unique and has very little similarity with what others do (Trefler, 2014). This inevitably leads to an isolative mindset where everything is kept within the group, and willingness for collaboration and information exchange is kept to a minimum. There is no shared purpose, no unifying values and no inspiring cross-departmental leadership. The *Silo Effect* slows down corporate and marketing reactions and harms flexibility, creativity and widespread passion. New marketing-organization approaches need to move away from such barriers to become more successful and reliable business-wide. Especially since a study, by global consulting group BCG published in 2015, showed that the top struggle reported by 30 CMOs and senior marketing executives in major corporations was the *Silo Effect* and its resulting ownership issues (Vesser, Field and Sheerin, 2015).

The common thread between all the above structures is the box-like and linear organogram that they create. Regardless of whether companies organize around markets, products, functions, geographies or a combination of those, they end up looking very similar on paper with individual boxes indicating roles, lines indicating relations and an overall pyramid form indicating authority. Even in more recent approaches, where technological change has forced the creation of digital channel departments versus traditional channel departments, with the CMO sitting above and overviewing both of them (Scott, 2015), the same basic top-down philosophy is applied. Figures 8.1 and 8.2 show this philosophy in its simple and more complicated versions.

Regardless of the small or large number of boxes, lines and roles, the fundamental similarities between these two structures are so obvious that it makes

Figure 8.1 Simple marketing structure

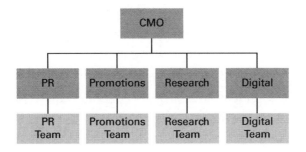

Figure 8.2 Complicated marketing structure

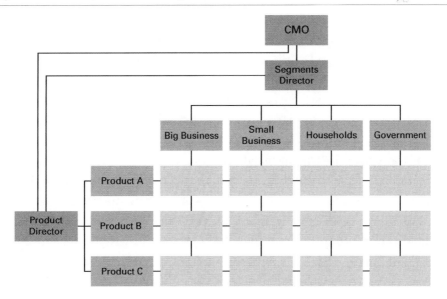

it easy to understand why they belong to the same, outdated organizational models. At the beginning of the new millennium, celebrated marketing minds started foreseeing the end of such hierarchical and neatly developed models and their replacement with more evolved models. As discussed extensively in Chapters 4 and 5, business and marketing realities rarely, if ever, fit into well-defined boxes and well-drawn lines. Evolved models are needed in order for marketers to respond better to the newly emerging challenges of technology, globalization and early market disruptions. One of those minds, the late marketing professor Peter Doyle, wrote at the end of the 20th century (Doyle, 2003):

> The rapidly changing business environment makes existing products and marketing strategies obsolete. Companies have to become faster, more flexible, more innovative and capable of forging new partnerships with customers and suppliers. To put in place such strategies, however, requires sweeping organizational changes… [many traditional companies] have proved to be too bureaucratic, slow moving and production oriented to adapt their strategies to the momentum of their markets.

What are these 'sweeping organizational changes'? What does the marketing function of the present, and probably the immediate future, look like? Although Doyle touched upon some of the key characteristics of modern marketing functions, such as breaking hierarchies, self-management teams, a learning culture and network-like formats (Doyle, 2003), it is much later that the new marketing organization started taking a more visible shape. The need for new marketing structures only grew stronger and stronger leading to more than four out of five marketers believing that marketing needs restructuring, and at least one-third of them to claim that this is urgent (Sinclair, 2016).

A glimpse of this new structure was offered at the opening vignette of this chapter, 'Advanced practice: Do it like the brain does'. The role of the marketing leader as an Orchestrator marks a stark difference with the old role of the CMO as a position at the very top of a hierarchical pyramid. In their think–feel–do model of what they call 'The Ultimate Marketing Machine', de Swaan Arons and associates place the marketing leader at the very centre of the marketing function, surrounded by an interdisciplinary group of professionals both internal and external (de Swaan Arons, van den Driest and Weed, 2014): 1) **internal**: marketing, sales, customer care, IT, analytics, finance; 2) **external**: agencies, consultancies, partners.

The role of the CMO at the centre of all marketing operations, and not on top of them, has emerged as the main alternative to the traditional pyramid-shaped marketing and corporate hierarchies. Almost a year before the influential de Swaan Arons and associates article in the *Harvard Business Review*, Jennifer Rooney, of *Forbes*, published her article titled 'Here's what the marketing organization of the future should look like', presenting an earlier version of the de Swaan Arons and associates research results. Rooney (2013) opens her article with the emphatic realization that: 'Marketing organizations that aren't restructuring to meet the demands of 2020 – of today, for that matter – will be left by the wayside.' She then lists the most important, *non-negotiable* as she calls them, characteristics of new marketing structures based on the Marketing2020 research project (Rooney, 2013):

- business growth orientation;
- strong and shared purpose;
- clear alignment of internal functions;
- defined roles and responsibilities;
- vibrant research and data-driven activities;
- a web of partnering agencies;
- internal agency-like teams;
- cross-platform online efforts;
- a tied CEO–CMO relation.

The *circular* rather than the *linear* view of the modern marketing function and ecosystem, with many of these characteristics, is also supported in a 2017 McKinsey report titled 'Building a marketing organization that drives growth today'. The McKinsey report cites survey results indicating that (Buck *et al*, 2017):

- 71 per cent of high-growth companies have adopted agile processes such as cross-functional collaboration and co-located teams.
- Top-performing marketers are more likely to be part of a networked organization and meet more frequently with colleagues from different functions to create and deliver successfully customer journeys.

In order for CMOs to be able to collaborate often with other colleagues and for marketing teams to break silos and become more inter-functional, allowing for better alignment and integration of all departments towards

Figure 8.3   The new circular and networked marketing structure

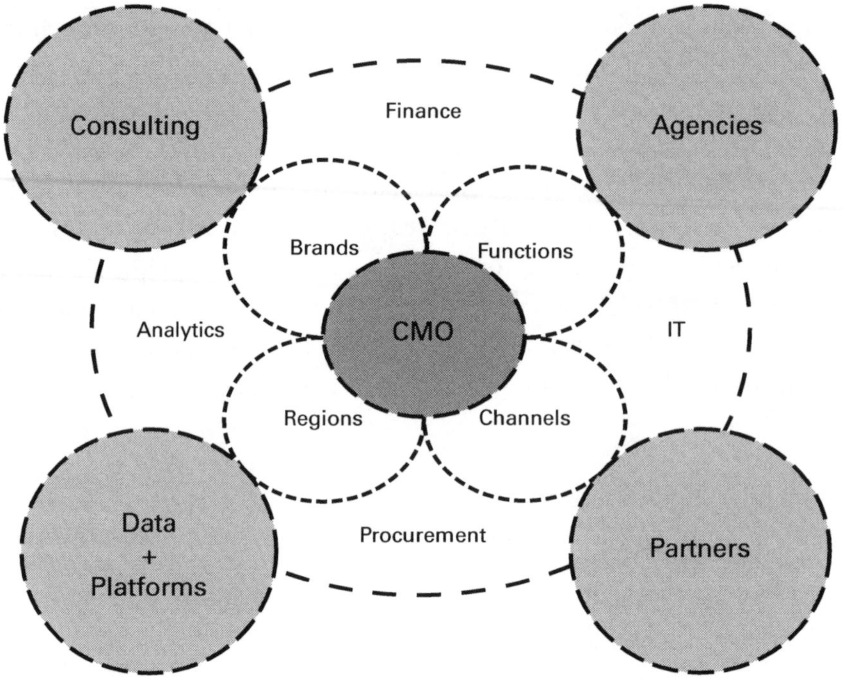

one common brand goal, a new structure is necessary. This seems to be the overwhelming consensus in both marketing industry and academia. The emerging new model, which is more circular and networked than the old one, can be seen in Figure 8.3.

The main characteristic of Figure 8.3 is that there are no solid lines: neither internally nor externally. Every unit is open to its immediate surroundings, creating multidisciplinary, multipurpose teams with members from both inside and outside the company. The CMO is at the very centre, overviewing and orchestrating teams of experts, marketers and others. The model allows for the more traditional structures of markets, channels and marketing function, such as PR and promotions, to exist but this happens in a more dynamic, collaborative and open manner than ever before. The models' network-like format is also evident in the unlimited opportunities for creating, maintaining and nurturing nods, or interaction points, throughout the open system. The main units are known and well-defined but the connection, interactions and partnerships between them are not. The latter ones are formed, dissolved and reformed based on projects, campaigns and strategic intentions.

This structure is definitely not for the faint-hearted. It is not for marketers seeking stability, comfort, predictability and a linear career. It is for those who embrace the challenges of the new Advanced Marketing Management and aim at becoming the true transformational leaders of their organizations!

The marketing function: trading room or assembly line?

The Economist Intelligence Unit, in an effort to reveal the key success factors of marketing in the near future, conducted in-depth interviews with six leading marketing thinkers. One of the major findings was that the modern marketing function should not only prepare for major marketing activities, like campaigns, events and product launches, but it should connect and interact on a real-time basis with customers and other stakeholders. The days when marketers went through the marketing process linearly and with certainty are long gone, and are replaced with dynamic, unpredictable and interactive days that never really end. The Economist report highlights that, in a 24/7 mode of working, marketing cannot continue applying an assembly-line mentality: 'Now [marketing] it is more like a trading room that responds to the ebbs and flows of the market as they occur. Although marketers will always have to manage the equivalent of an iPhone launch, there will also be day-in and day-out efforts to build a relationship with customers' (EIU, 2015). This is already happening. *Fortune* magazine reported in 2016 that Mastercard has created a *Command Centre* at its New York headquarters where 'product managers gaze at a 40-foot display that broadcasts feeds, visualizations and performance metrics for more than 60 markets', and which the company calls the Conversation Suite (Clancy, 2016). According to the article, this command-centre or trading-room approach provides significant advantages to the company for real-time marketing decision making. A notable example was the 2015 Rugby World Cup, when Mastercard found that its Apple Pay promotional activity was more successful in reaching its targeted population on social media than on the web, and changed its approach on the spot to increase its social media presence (Clancy, 2016). The assembly line is a time-consuming, flexibility-decreasing and authority-protecting model. Marketing deserves better. Although the assembly-line approach will not completely disappear from marketing projects any time soon, the leading mentality will be one that promotes fast connectivity, dynamic relations and real-time decision making.

The new organizational approach for Advanced Marketing Management described in this chapter is somewhat adjacent with a number of contemporary structural approaches for companies as a whole. In an era of constant disruption, technological uncertainty and global competition, companies cannot afford to stand still. Like with the marketing function, corporations search for new ways to organize their resources in order to remain ahead of the curve and win in the marketplace. Three such approaches, popular in their own right, are presented below: Holacracy, dual organizational system and Teal organization.

Holacracy

Holacracy is the brainchild of Brian Robertson, a tech entrepreneur, first described in his 2007 article titled 'Organization at the leading edge: introducing Holacracy™'. Robertson (2007) laid down in that article the main characteristics of Holacracy: replacing 'artificial hierarchy' with self-organizing teams, called *circles*, with specific roles assigned to appropriate members to achieve the goals of the circle as best as possible; allowing members in the circle to take decisions with full responsibility and ownership of the result, even in uncertain situations with limited information; creating two types of processes, core ones that include regular 'governance' and 'operational' meetings among its members, and supportive processes, or 'modules', that have to do with shared resources such as HR or budgeting; inducing a new organizational mental mode, with specific language and shared meaning that help communication between members go 'beyond ego'. Although Holacracy sounds like another version of a network and circular organization, as discussed earlier in this chapter, it is not. It is an extreme version with very tight rules and very detailed procedures that ultimately lead to a rigid vertical hierarchical system (Denning, 2014). This has led to serious criticisms against the model, regardless of the fact, or because of the fact, that Zappos, the online shoe and accessories online retailer, has adopted it. The Zappos experience has been questionable and, combined with the fact that other companies have dropped it, like the social media company Medium, has created some doubts on its actual feasibility and overall effectiveness (Bernstein *et al*, 2016). The tight monitoring of the system as a whole, the very rigid procedures and the relentless cultural moulding that the model induces can create the opposite effect: freedom from one type of control and subjugation in another (Denning, 2014). The main differences between

Holacracy and the new marketing model suggested in this chapter are that the latter retains the firm role of individual leadership within the structure, it does not abolish functional or other traditional organizational units, and it allows for more flexibility concerning organizational subcultures. A high degree of empowerment is preferred in our model over extreme self-management teams.

Dual organizational system

John P Kotter, a global influencer in the area of corporate leadership, has developed and tried his own approach in how to create organizational structures that are stable and highly innovative at the same time. In his 2014 book *XLR8*, or Accelerate, he expresses his view that modern companies should combine the operational continuity and excellence of traditional corporations with the creativity, agility and adaptability of dynamic technology start-ups (Kotter, 2014). In order to achieve this near-impossible Herculean task, Kotter suggests a dual system of two structures that run in parallel: the stable, predictable, operational system that takes care of everyday business and helps the company survive today; and the passionate, creative, flexible and engaging system that leads to drastic innovations that can help the company stay competitive and to thrive in the future. The first system is hierarchical and logical, following all the known rules and regulations, while the second is rather chaotic and emotional, making its own rules as and when needed. As Kotter mentions in his book, his dual organizational system resembles somewhat the dual thinking system in humans suggested by the Nobel of Economics prize-winner Daniel Kahneman in his globally influential book *Thinking, Fast and Slow* (Kahneman, 2012). The *Accelerator networks*, as Kotter (2014) names his initiative-based, interdepartmental, creative-thinking teams, come to life because of a big opportunity and a sense of strategic urgency; they do not have typical operational plans; they use looser measurements methods that fit their ephemeral purpose; they are staffed with volunteers or/and near-volunteers from across the organization; they are *led* rather than *managed*; they are fully governed by the *Guiding Coalition*, which is the core, passionate starting team behind an initiative; and their ultimate goal is to institutionalize the winning innovations they create. Kotter's approach has the advantage of not jeopardizing existing processes and thus ensuring endurance of the business in the mid-term, while allowing for highly engaged and highly driven people to form working groups, in addition to their everyday job, which can lead to breakthrough innovations and market-disruptive outcomes. This model is actually very close to the one recommended in this chapter and probably one stage before its full implementation.

The Teal organization

Business coach and author Frederic Laloux has overviewed the evolution of organizational models in human history, coming to the conclusion that our current times are ripe for the next stage of organizations, what he calls the Teal organizations. In Laloux's model, every stage of organizational evolution in history is marked with a colour and a metaphor (Laloux, 2015): red organizations, or wolf packs, are all about the strong leader and the followers, who collectively react fast to achieve tribal, short-term objectives; amber organizations, or armies, are about command and control in rigid hierarchies, which aim at the perpetual survival of a stable system; orange organizations, or machines, are management systems trying to win the competition through innovation and accountability, controlling tightly the *What* of the system but less tightly the *How*; green organizations, or families, have a wider purpose that includes multistakeholder wellbeing, and focus heavily on engaging corporate cultures, self-motivation and flatter hierarchies; teal organizations, or living organisms, use self-managed teams to achieve their true evolutionary purpose through a shared feeling of wholeness. The Teal organization concept is very similar to Holacracy, at least in principle, and this is something that Laloux believes himself since he included Holacracy in the list of 12 companies, one of which was the worldwide clothing brand Patagonia, which he considers to be a truly Teal organization (Laloux, 2015). Of course, Holacracy is not a company, it is an organizational model, but this fact did not deter Laloux from adding it to his list. His somewhat unusual terminology in relation to companies, such as 'the next stage of human consciousness' and 'soulful organizations' (Laloux, 2014), resembles more spiritual literature than business. Self-managing teams is at the very heart of Teal organizations, as is Holacracy, but without the stiff rules and extremely detailed execution procedures.

Although there are some performance benefits of self-managing teams found in academic literature, especially when they are implemented under favourable conditions, there are still serious knowledge gaps that need to be addressed by scientific research on the subject to firmly establish its credibility (Magpili and Pazos, 2017). Concerning marketing though, the most important caveat for a pure self-managing team structure is the trend towards more centralization, and not decentralization, observed in modern marketing systems (Vesser *et al*, 2015). This is because high budgets are becoming scarcer, the provable ROI is becoming more dominant as a metric, and outside complexity is becoming more difficult to predict and control. Marketing departments are regrouping to make sure they respond to new challenges with conviction, bold moves and verifiable results. Strong transformational leadership, a network and circular structure, empowered workforce, skilful experts and hybrid managers are necessary conditions for marketing success today.

Design an effective marketing system the Coca-Cola way

David Butler, VP for Innovation and Entrepreneurship at the Coca-Cola Company, and Linda Tischler from Fast Company, offer in their book *Design to Grow: How Coca-Cola learned to combine scale and agility*, their three most valuable lessons for designing a holistic system (Butler and Tischler, 2015), adjusted for the themes of this chapter:

1 **Align your system design with your growth strategy** Systems exist for a purpose. Unfortunately, organizational systems with a long history sometimes forget the reason for their very existence, or this reason is hidden underneath tons of rules, procedures and processes. Such systems end up operating for the sole sake of operating, thus the system's uninterrupted continuity and perpetual survival becomes the de facto embodied purpose. Modern marketing departments should make sure that the system they design is fully aligned with the overall brand vision and with the brand's growth strategy. Advanced marketers often ask *why* questions and encourage their team to do the same, in order to make sure the system is always kept updated, fresh, vibrant and aligned.

2 **Be mindful of your design process** There is a difference between the end product of designing a system, which is the structure, roles and lines of the system, and the process of getting there. Although designing and redesigning the marketing system is now an ongoing process, and not a well-defined 'project' with clear beginning and end, marketers should have a clear approach and attitude when deciding on the *how* of designing their system. Questions such as 'Who is involved in the process?', 'What are the design team's

members' responsibilities?', 'Are there any timeframes?', 'What are the available resources?' and 'Which are the team's priorities?' are key to performing the task successfully. The system design process should also adhere to corporate-wide design codes and approaches to ensure the marketing system's compatibility with the overall system it belongs to.

3   **All the system's outputs should be connected** A marketing system's most important outputs are the products, services, conversations and experiences that aim to create satisfied and loyal customers. Every brand touchpoint is calibrated to serve customer needs, conscious and unconscious, contributing emphatically to the long-term business success of the company. Again, many companies have forgotten the fact that marketing outputs should not only achieve short-term wins and instant sales but also enable the company to achieve its long-term growth strategy and wider vision. Every action of the new marketing function, internally and especially externally, should be a living proof of the company's existential purpose.

All these are necessary for ensuring the success of the new marketing function. Few key questions remain though. First, what kind of roles should new marketers employ in order to make the new structure work in the best possible way? Second, what type of hiring approaches and techniques should modern marketing leaders adopt in order to select great marketers for their new structure?

Hiring for the new marketing function

Chapter 4 included a list of different roles to be performed within the creative process. Those roles are crucial for creativity to exist and transform into valuable innovation. In the same direction, there are a number of crucial roles that the new marketing function should contain to perform successfully its tasks. According to marketing tech entrepreneur and consultant Anita Breaton (2017), those roles, adapted for the purpose of this chapter, are:

- **Strategist**: this role includes the following tasks – setting different types of goals, defining strategic directions, establishing positioning objectives and developing tactical plans to ensure appropriate implementation of the marketing vision.

- **Comunicator**: this is a very important role because it entails the crucial task of articulating throughout the company and its different departments all major marketing initiatives and main messages to ensure that the organization speaks with a single tone of voice.

- **Creative**: translating marketing strategy goals into effective messaging and imaging is essential for every marketing project and therefore marketers engage creative agencies to help them communicate better to their target audiences. This role though cannot be fully outsourced because marketing departments need to brief, evaluate and choose the right solutions for the right situation.

- **Technologist, operator and integrator**: all three roles are tech-oriented. The first role is about defining the total technological framework for the marketing function and helping its development and management. In order for the role to be successful, plug-and-play technology is many times purchased from various vendors from the global marketplace and/or proprietary solutions are developed in-house or with the help of consultants. The second role, the operator, is an adjacent role to the technologist, involved in running the everyday marketing technology infrastructure. It is also involved in helping all marketing personnel get accustomed to and utilize the benefits of new marketing tech. The third tech-oriented role is that of the integrator, who makes sure that all tech is connected, aligned and works perfectly together. The integrator works very close to the corporate-level tech department.

- **Liaison**: this role is particularly important for companies with larger marketing operations in more than one location/country. The liaison works hard to create a mutually beneficial environment across the organization for marketing personnel, and many times other professionals connected to marketing, spread in different offices. It also integrates internal and external marketing resources across boundaries.

- **Hunter**: in an era where creating and utilizing leads is at the top of the agenda for marketers around the world, the hunter is the one to organize and deliver the process of attracting leads and to manage it on a daily basis.

- **Sales assistant**: the sales assistant monitors the various leads along the sales funnel and creates the right motivation to move them towards an actual purchase. This role works closely with the creative to develop and communicate the content that will make leads go forward in the funnel and towards the purchase.

- **Concierge:** the concierge oversees the total customer journey to ensure a customer experience across all brand touchpoints. The main goal is to convert buyers into loyal life-long customers. The concierge uses a variety of resources to formulate and utilize the right insights for delivering a superior customer experience, currently and in the future.

- **Analyst:** the analyst is the main marketing research-oriented role in the list. It concerns the planning, organization and daily supply of useful and actionable insights from a wide variety of sources, methods and vendors. Insights are not raw data but processed, integrated and purposeful data that fit the information needs of the marketing strategy and brand vision.

- **Financier:** the financier role is about coordinating the creation and spending of the marketing budget in accordance with plans and available resources. Due to the complex nature of the contemporary business environment this is not any more a linear and predictable process. The financier is a dynamic and adaptable role that needs to follow less set goals and more emerging needs for unplanned but necessary marketing activities. It informs the other roles about important metrics such as customer lifetime value (CLTV) and cost of acquisition (COA) to ensure that all marketing actions are within the financial capabilities and the long-term brand objectives of the function.

- **Coordinator:** the coordinator role resembles the traditional role of the traffic manager in advertising companies. It is about making sure that the flow of work, deadlines, delivery of campaigns and general marketing activities are coordinated and finalized as promised. The coordinator identifies procedural bottlenecks and resolves them, fast-track opportunities and takes advantage of them, resource and skills shortcomings and informs leadership about them, and keeps a watchful eye on all interactions and workloads within marketing and beyond.

- **Futurist:** this is the role of constantly asking questions about the future direction of markets, technologies, customer needs, competition and the world in general. It keeps track of major macro and micro trends in the wider socio-economic landscape and actively facilitates discussions within the function about marketing in the future of the company.

These roles are NOT necessarily distinct job descriptions. Marketing managers should consider them as key competences that every marketing department should contain internally. External expertise might and should be needed to obtain the full scope of some of those competences, but internal advanced understanding must exist as well. Advanced marketers should have in mind those roles and who in their team is performing them, when they design and develop their functions. Most importantly, they have to be aware of any gaps and seek actively new candidates to fill them as best they can.

This brings to the foreground the significance of the hiring process for advanced marketers. It is no longer the case that marketers can rely solely on the services of the HR department in creating a function that will fulfil their complex and dynamic requirements in human capital. According to our experience, marketers that are 100 per cent involved in the hiring process, leading their HR colleagues through the process and creating unique to the marketing function tasks can achieve much better results in attracting and recruiting great marketing talent than those that do not. The main reasons for that are:

1 **Attracting great marketing talent is becoming more difficult than ever.** Unless you are one of the top global companies that people want to work for, such as Google, the BCG Group, Salesforce and KPMG (Fortune, 2017) competition is getting harder than ever. According to the August 2017 CMO Survey, 6.4 per cent more marketers would be hired in 2018, the highest percentage improvement reported since 2012 (CMO Survey, 2017). The assertion by Christine Moorman, Business Administration Professor at Duke University – that if you want to hire a marketer in 2018 you need to 'join the crowd!' – seems quite fitting to the situation (Moorman, 2017).

2 **The diversity of marketing skills, roles, knowledge and attitudes needed for the modern marketing department is higher than ever before.** This makes the hiring process extremely demanding and multifaceted, and thus great attention to detail and personal involvement is needed. As Adele Sweetwood (2014), SVP of Global Marketing in analytics firm SAS and member of the University of East Carolina, emphasized in her article 'How to find, assess, and hire the modern marketer', the marketer of today needs to be competent in: 'campaign design, multichannel integration, content performance, personalization and digital marketing. The marketers I am referring to have a distinct blend of creativity and reasoning talents; they are inquisitive, inventive, and enthused by a culture that is advanced and agile.' This type of advanced professional cannot be easily identified through traditional CV submissions and standardized job interviews.

The new marketing hiring process needs to be adventurous and multi-levelled. It has to use the newest available tools, channels and ideas. One of these is hiring through neurotesting. Chapter 2 analysed in depth the nature and value of neuroscience for marketing from a consumer behaviour perspective. However, neuroscience can be also used for hiring new members of the marketing team. This is because neuro and bio-feedback methods can reveal unconscious brain processes that are crucial in building a modern marketing team, such as empathy and intentionality of behaviour (Dimitriadis, 2017). Notable examples globally include the Royal Bank of Scotland and Unilever. The Royal Bank of Scotland used EEG devices to test attention span of tech students in early recruitment stages (Turner, 2016) while Unilever, the world's leading FMCG giant, used neuroscience-based gaming and bio-feedback technology to screen all entry-level employees (Feloni, 2017). Although such methods are still work in progress and have attracted some criticism in terms of accuracy and scientific rigour (Chivers, 2017), the companies using them have reported satisfaction and continue with their implementation (Feloni, 2017). Trizma Neuro, the neuromarketing and neuroHR company headed by one of us, Dr Nikolaos Dimitriadis, has performed extensive studies in what the company calls neuro-competence testing and has identified indeed that neuro and bio-feedback offer unique benefits in personal and team evaluation in the areas of empathy, resilience, influence, diversity and mindset. Such tests are going to be used more extensively in the future and are going to improve drastically the selection, hiring and onboarding of new employees (Zak, 2013).

But the introduction of such disruptive approaches will not be easy nor smooth. As brain-savvy business consultant and author Jan Hills highlights (De Pape, 2016): 'One thing that gets in the way of using neuroscience in business is that science kind of scares people... [and recruiters will] probably not go off and read the kind of neuroscience articles from the scientists who carried out the research'. However, as she concludes, today there is 'a lot of good quality interpretation of that science available'. Since advanced marketers are the ones who use neuroscience to decode consumer behaviour and unconscious brain reactions to brands, they should be the first ones in their companies to use the same techniques in staffing the marketing department with recruits who portray appropriate brain patterns – those being empathy, emotional agility, growth mindset, creative problem solving or others.

Staffing the new marketing function: the hiring process

Apart from neuroscience, there are few additional innovative ways to identify and select the most promising members for your contemporary marketing team. Kevin Daum (2013), an *Inc. 500 Entrepreneur* and best-selling author in sales and marketing, suggests the following three-step approach for hiring great marketers:

1 **Advertising the position** The easier the ad for the job the less challenging it will be for top marketing talent – this means that easy job ads will attract many 'easy' candidates, those who apply casually and/or possess low-calibre skills. The ad should be teasing, asking for more than simply sending a CV, and helping marketing leaders to see beyond the obvious in the process. For example, the ad could ask candidates to do some preliminary reading or search before submitting their application, like your company's values, history and portfolio, and to include an unusual element such as making a joke. This approach will help marketing recruiters understand if the candidates do their homework, are empathic and can create basic human connection, can market themselves based on insights, and their overall professionalism and commitment.

2 **Conducting the interview** When calling the selected candidates for the personal interview, marketing recruiters can include one more layer of evaluation by asking them to submit, prior to the interview, a short video, an infographic or brochure, and a slide deck on a topic of your choice. This could be something like: how can you contribute to our brand growth? How is *your* personal brand different and better than the other applicants? What are our key brand challenges and what can you do about them? Such an approach can reveal both content-related and selling-related skills: creativity, advanced marketing sense, data analytics and competence for successful delivery, among others. The way the candidate juggles all those during the interview will also show interpersonal, negotiation and persuasion skills.

3 **Project-testing the candidate** The final stage, for the very few who have made it so far, includes a project related to a real brand or marketing activity of the company. Usually in a short timeframe, up to a couple of weeks, candidates will perform the role of the project manager and will have to interact with actual members of the marketing team they wish to join, in order to deliver their analysis and recommendations. Apart from checking their actual project management skills and core marketing competences, recruiters can see the candidates' problem-solving approach in real time, collaboration and communication with team members and self-motivation for completing the task.

The overall hiring process for marketing should be Fun, Fair and Futuristic. Fun, in order to be engaging, inviting and creative both for the recruiter and the candidates. Fair, in order to ensure procedural integrity, meritocracy and trustworthiness of results. Futuristic in order to utilize the latest available approaches such as neuroscience, gamification and real-word project delivery, to maximize the effectiveness of the process for all involved.

Key dilemmas in deciding the new marketing function

Building the marketing function of the future will not be an easy task, especially since there is rarely a one-size-fits-all solution to structuring a marketing system. Within the many structural decisions marketers have to take, as described in this chapter, there are two additional dilemmas that seem to be central in the conversation of organizing modern marketing departments. Those are: 1) in-house versus external expertise; and 2) machines versus human resources.

The *Marketing Week Vision 100* roundtable on the topic of *Building the Marketing Team of the Future*, featuring prominent marketers in the UK, included the discussion on in-house versus external expertise as a key theme for the future of marketing departments. The views expressed in that panel can be summarized as follows (Hemsley, 2017):

- Internal teams are easier controlled, and many times are more flexible and agile than external ones.

- The decision to outsource or not will have to touch upon data ownership and location issues, not just old criteria such as cost/benefit analysis.

- Some very specialized tasks and projects of large scope will always need external assistance.

- Using external sources has to bring the add-on advantage of fresh perspectives and outside-in mindsets.

- In the case of utilizing external expertise, brands nowadays have more options than ever, especially in going directly to a very specialized provider, skipping agencies' middleman function.

- Timely reaction to unpredicted real-world events and to changing customer moods, as well as the need for fast content output, force companies to internalize roles that traditionally belonged to agencies such as copywriters, video producers and photographers.

- In the case of using agencies, a very close relationship is nowadays mandatory with both parties contributing to it: companies, by sharing brand information appropriately and welcoming agencies as members of the brand team, and agencies, by doing their best to understand the brand and its intentions in an in-depth manner by bringing hard-to-find, necessary expertise into the mix.

Recent academic research on the integration process in the buyer–supplier relation has highlighted the fact that integration needs time and that emphasizing quality over cost enables the integration process to start earlier in the evolutionary progress of the relation (Kaipia and Turkulainen, 2017). This means that shifting attention from a strict cost/benefit approach of choosing external marketing partners to a more long-term strategy-oriented one will help marketers develop better relations with their external resources and achieve more.

The second debate concerns the increasing use of automated technology both internally and externally in the marketing function. The digital transformation craze has engulfed companies worldwide, leading to various degrees of restructuring and restaffing of key business functions. Many of those digital transformation projects led to downsizing: by one estimation published in *Fortune*, more than 60,000 jobs were lost in the United States within one year because of such projects (Vanian, 2016). Although many of the eliminated jobs come from the IT sector itself and especially from hardware-related jobs (Vanian, 2016) this is not always the case. The move by Microsoft in 2017 to downsize its global sales and marketing operations because of automation, mainly outside the United States, by cutting 3,000 jobs (Phys.org, 2017) sent a shockwave throughout the marketing industry. Technology replacing real jobs in marketing and sales is a reality. It is perhaps comforting then for marketers that, compared with other professions, marketing jobs have been found to have a lower possibility to be replaced by machines. An Oxford University and Deloitte study has suggested that marketing associate professionals are fairly unlikely, at 33 per cent probability, to be replaced by automations in the next 20 years, while marketing and sales directors are very unlikely to be replaced, at 1 per cent probability (Chahal, 2017). In the opposite direction, an Oracle survey of 800 senior marketing and sales professionals, showed that (Chahal, 2017):

- By 2020, 78 per cent of brands will provide customer experiences through virtual reality.

- By 2020, 80 per cent of brands will utilize the power of chat bots for customer interactivity.

- 48 per cent of brands have already implemented automated solutions in sales, marketing and customer service.

- An additional 40 per cent is planning to do the same by 2020.

The somewhat contradicting facts of, on the one hand, more marketers needed in general, and on the other, more automations introduced in marketing and sales, highlight the transitional period in which modern marketers operate. Marketing is becoming more important than ever for companies in all industries and markets, and this sometimes might lead to fast introduction of innovative automations (resulting in job cuts) or/and to new expertise and marketing roles that are in high demand. Regardless the rise of AI, machines and robots, human presence in the marketing function will not disappear any time soon. On the contrary, human leadership and intervention will always be crucial, even more than ever, for developing engaged marketing departments and meaningful customer relations. In any case, the marketing function of the future will have very little in common with that of the past, in terms of leadership, structure and roles. Companies need to prepare well for these changes and, even, lead the way in transforming their marketing functions into contemporary market-winning organizations.

Last thought

The new marketing leader needs a new marketing department, organized around new marketing roles. Although there is no one solution or one strict model to be applied in all companies everywhere in the world, the traditional 'boxes and lines' marketing structure is being replaced by a more circular and network-like model that allows for higher flexibility, better collaboration and faster implementation of ideas and projects. Additionally, advanced marketers need to take control of the hiring process for their function and make sure they select and recruit the best available talent based on innovative and adventurous solutions. The marketing function of the future, part internal, part external, part human, part machine, but always moving and changing, will be the living and breathing centre of the whole corporation. It is this new marketing function that will lead companies into their brand-dominated future. Advanced marketers will be ready to take over!

SUMMARY CHECKLIST

- Explore fresh and diverse approaches to organizing teams such as the brain-based think–feel–do model.
- Regardless of how important it might be, do not overemphasize the role of technical over other, more human, marketing skills in your team.
- Move away from box-like marketing structures and closer to circle and network-like ones.
- Remember that self-organized teams with strong leadership and a shared sense of purpose form the basis of many modern organizational approaches.
- Create a hiring process that is adventurous and experiential rather than static and old-fashioned.

Resources to inspire you

- Holacracy TED: https://www.youtube.com/watch?v=tJxfJGo-vkl
- Reinventing organizations, speech by Frederic Laloux: https://www.youtube.com/watch?v=gcS04Bl2sbk
- Paul Zak interview on how neuroscience can improve hiring: https://vimeo.com/78269333

Revision questions

1 Discuss how narrowness and short-termism affect decision making concerning the organization of the marketing function.

2 Critically compare the traditional 'boxes and lines' marketing structure with the modern circular and network-like one.

3 Which are the steps by which Coca-Cola designs its effective marketing systems? In your opinion, how easy is it for these steps to be applied in any marketing system?

4 Which are the different roles that every marketing department should include? In your opinion, which of these should be always internal and which can be outsourced?

5 Discuss the steps of the contemporary marketing hiring process. From the candidates' point of view, how does each step help them unfold and demonstrate their true potential?

References

Baars, B J and Gage, N M (2010) *Cognition, Brain, and Consciousness: Introduction to cognitive neuroscience*, 2nd edn, Academic Press, Burlington

Bernstein, E, Bunch, J, Canner, N and Lee, M (2016) Beyond the holacracy hype: the overwrought claims – and actual promise – of the next generation of self-managed teams, *Harvard Business Review*, **94** (7–8) (July–August), pp 38–49

Breaton, A (2017) [accessed 18 June 2018] Building the Perfect Marketing Organization, *CMSWire* [Online] https://www.cmswire.com/digital-marketing/building-the-perfect-marketing-organization/

Brinker, S (2012) [accessed 18 June 2018] Engineers Are Becoming a Lot Like Marketers Too, *Chief Marketing Technologist Blog* [Online] http://chiefmartec.com/2012/05/engineers-are-becoming-a-lot-like-marketers-too/

Buck, R, Cvetanovski, B, Harper, A and Timelin, B (2017) [accessed 18 June 2018] Building a Marketing Organization that Drives Growth Today, *McKinsey* [Online] https://www.mckinsey.com/business-functions/marketing-and-sales/our-insights/building-a-marketing-organization-that-drives-growth-today

Butler, D and Tischler, L (2015) *Design to Grow: How Coca-Cola learned to combine scale and agility (and how you can too)*, Portfolio Penguin, London

Callahan, S (2015) [accessed 18 June 2018] Announcing The Marketing Skills Handbook: A Deep Dive Into Today's Most In-Demand Marketing Jobs, *LinkedIn* [Online] https://business.linkedin.com/marketing-solutions/blog/a/announcing-the-marketing-skills-handbook-a-deep-dive-into-todays-most-in-demand-marketing-jobs

Chahal, M (2017) [accessed 18 June 2018] Rise of the Machines: Are Robots After Your Job?, *Marketing Week* [Online] https://www.marketingweek.com/2017/01/12/rise-of-the-machines/

Chivers, T (2017) [accessed 18 June 2018] No, RBS Can't Read Your Mind and Tell You If You Ought To Work In Banking, *BuzzFeed* [Online]

https:// www.buzzfeed.com/tomchivers/the-magic-hat-said-rbs-but-i-was-really-hoping-for-slytherin?utm_term=.wdnKxwR2#.qi8EoNdK

Clancy, H (2016) [accessed 18 June 2018] MasterCard Uses a Command Center to Track Its Marketing Spend, *Fortune* [Online] http://fortune.com/2016/01/29/mastercard-data-analytics/

CMO Survey (2017) [accessed 18 June 2018] August 2017, *The CMO Survey* [Online] https://cmosurvey.org/results/august-2017/

Daum, K (2013) [accessed 18 June 2018] How to Hire a Great Marketer, *INC. COM* [Online] https://www.inc.com/kevin-daum/how-to-hire-a-great-marketer.html

De Pape, C (2016) [accessed 18 June 2018] What Neuroscience Says About Your Hiring Practices: Q&A with Jan Hills, *Recruiting Social* [Online] https://recruitingsocial.com/2016/06/neuroscience-of-hiring/

de Swaan Arons, M, van den Driest, F and Weed, K (2014) The ultimate marketing machine, *Harvard Business Review*, July/August, pp 55–63

Denning, S (2014) [accessed 18 June 2018] Making Sense of Zappos and Holacracy, *Forbes* [Online] https://www.forbes.com/sites/stevedenning/2014/01/15/making-sense-of-zappos-and-holacracy/#18f3820c3207

Dimitriadis, N (2017) [accessed 18 June 2018] Purpose Fuels Success. Intentionality Fuels Leadership!, *LinkedIn* [Online] https://www.linkedin.com/pulse/purpose-fuels-success-intentionality-leadership-nikolaos-dimitriadis/

Dimitriadis, N and Psychogios, A (2016) *Neuroscience for Leaders: A brain adaptive leadership approach*, Kogan Page, London

Doyle, P (2003) *Marketing Management and Strategy*, 3rd edn, FT Prentice Hall, Harlow

EIU (2015) [accessed 18 June 2018] How Marketers Will Win: Six Marketing Visionaries Describe How In Five Years Marketing Will Be Transformed, *The Economist Intelligence Unit* [Online] http://futureofmarketing.eiu.com/

Feloni, R (2017) [accessed 18 June 2018] Consumer-Goods Giant Unilever Has Been Hiring Employees Using Brain Games and Artificial Intelligence – and It's a Huge Success, *Business Insider* [Online] http://www.businessinsider.com/unilever-artificial-intelligence-hiring-process-2017-6

Field, P (2010) [accessed 18 June 2018] Short-Termism: The Single Greatest Threat Facing Marketing, *WARC* [Online] https://www.warc.com/NewsAndOpinion/Opinion/1176

Fortune (2017) [accessed 18 June 2018] 100 Best Companies to Work For 2017, *Fortune* [Online] http://fortune.com/best-companies/

Hemsley, S (2017) [accessed 18 June 2018] Build the Marketing Team of the Future, *Marketing Week* [Online] https://www.marketingweek.com/2017/01/13/how-to-build-marketing-team-future/

Hollensen, S (2003) *Marketing Management: A relationship approach*, FT Prentice Hall, Harlow

Kahneman, D (2012) *Thinking, Fast and Slow*, Penguin Random House, London

Kaipia, R and Turkulainen, V (2017) Managing integration in outsourcing relationships – the influence of cost and quality priorities, *Industrial Marketing Management*, **61**, pp 114–29

Kotler, P (2000) *Marketing Management*, 10th edn, Prentice Hall International, London

Kotter, P J (2014) *XLR8* (Accelerate), Harvard Business Review Press, Boston

Laloux, F (2014) *Reinventing Organizations: A guide to creating organizations inspired by the next stage of human consciousness*, Nelson Parker, Brussels

Laloux, F (2015) [accessed 18 June 2018] The Future of Management is Teal, *Strategy + Business* [Online] https://www.strategy-business.com/article/00344?gko=10921

Magpili, N C and Pazos, P (2017) Self-managing team performance: a systematic review of multilevel input factors, *Small Group Research*, **49** (1), pp 3–33

Marrs, M (2015) [accessed 18 June 2018] 14 Marketing Skills to Add to Your Resume This Year, *Wordstream* [Online] https://www.wordstream.com/blog/ws/2015/04/07/marketing-skills

McKinsey (2017) [accessed 18 June 2018] 2017 Marketing Hiring Trends: An In-Depth Report on Factors Shaping Demand for Marketing and Creative Talent, *McKinsey Marketing Partners* [Online] http://pages.mckinleymarketingpartners.com/BD_WC-2017FEB22-ALL-WP-HiringTrends_ContentRequestPage.html?utm_source=marketingprofs&utm_medium=third-party-content&utm_campaign=2017-hiring-trends

Miller, J (2017) [accessed 18 June 2018] Are You Ready For the Rise of the Hybrid Marketer?, *LinkedIn Sales and Marketing Solutions EMEA Blog* [Online] https://business.linkedin.com/en-uk/marketing-solutions/blog/posts/content-marketing/2017/Are-you-ready-for-the-rise-of-the-hybrid-marketer

Moorman, C (2017) [accessed 18 June 2018] Hiring a Marketer? Join the Crowd!, *Forbes* [Online] https://www.forbes.com/sites/christinemoorman/2017/09/22/hiring-a-marketer-join-the-crowd/#65a5c8603422

Musi, G (2017) [accessed 18 June 2018] The Downside of Digital's Explosive Growth? Too Many Marketers Are Failing to Think Long-Term: Plan (and Measure) Like an Investor, *ADWEEK* [Online] http://www.adweek.com/brand-marketing/the-downside-of-digitals-explosive-growth-too-many-marketers-are-failing-to-think-long-term/

Nanji, A (2017) [accessed 18 June 2018] The Most In-Demand Marketing Skills in 2017, *MarketingProfs* [Online] https://www.marketingprofs.com/charts/2017/31918/the-most-in-demand-marketing-skills

Osorio, B R (2015) [accessed 18 June 2018] Think Feel Do, *Business Mirror* [Online] https://businessmirror.com.ph/think-feel-do/

Phys.org (2017) [accessed 18 June 2018] 'Some' job cuts confirmed by Microsoft, *Phys.org* [Online] https://phys.org/news/2017-07-microsoft-job.html

Przybylski, A K, Murayama, K, DeHaan, C R and Gladwell, V (2013) Motivational, emotional, and behavioral correlates of fear of missing out, *Computers in Human Behavior*, **29**, pp 1841–48

Pulizzi, J (2017) [accessed 18 June 2018] One Thing Is Killing Content Marketing and Everyone Is Ignoring It, *Content Marketing Institute* [Online] https://contentmarketinginstitute.com/2017/02/killing-content-marketing-ignoring/

Robertson, B J (2007) [accessed 18 June 2018] Organization at the Leading Edge: Introducing Holacracy™ [Online] http://www.integralesleben.org/fileadmin/user_upload/images/DIA/Flyer/Organization_at_the_Leading_Edge_2007-06_01.pdf

Rogers, C (2017) [accessed 18 June 2018] How to Mastermind a Career Rebrand, *Marketing Week* [Online] https://www.marketingweek.com/2017/06/19/mastermind-career-rebrand/

Rooney, J (2013) [accessed 18 June 2018] Here's What the Marketing Organization of the Future Should Look Like, *Forbes* [Online] https://www.forbes.com/sites/jenniferrooney/2013/10/04/heres-what-the-marketing-organization-of-the-future-should-look-like/#10c259ae49da

Scott, S (2015) [accessed 18 June 2018] The Marketing Department of the Future, *MOZ* [Online] https://moz.com/blog/the-marketing-department-of-the-future

Sinclair, L (2016) [accessed 18 June 2018] 9 Modern Marketing Organizational Charts, *Simple* [Online] https://simplehq.co/blog/marketing-organizational-charts-infographic/

Slefo, G (2017) [accessed 18 June 2018] Desktop and Mobile Ad Revenue Surpasses TV for the First Time, *Adage* [Online] http://adage.com/article/digital/digital-ad-revenue-surpasses-tv-desktop-iab/308808/

State of Inbound (2017) [accessed 18 June 2018] State of Inbound 2017 Report [Online] http://www.stateofinbound.com/?__hstc=20629287.c8d28d4e6cc2a09ab690f9a7465755f1.1503751357676.1507831647190.1514971895316.4&__hssc=20629287.1.1514971895316&__hsfp=2859026245

Suggett, P (2017) [accessed 18 June 2018] The Structure of an Advertising Agency: Get to Know the Typical Make-Up of an Ad Agency, *The Balance* [Online] https://www.thebalance.com/the-structure-of-an-advertising-agency-38911

Sweetwood, A (2014) [accessed 18 June 2018] How to Find, Assess, and Hire the Modern Marketer, *Harvard Business Review* [Online] https://hbr.org/2014/01/how-to-find-assess-and-hire-the-modern-marketer

Trefler, A (2014) *Build for Change: Revolutionizing customer engagement through continuous digital innovation*, Wiley, New Jersey

Turner, G (2016) [accessed 18 June 2018] Banks Turn to Mind Reading to Source Top Tech Graduates, *Bloomberg* [Online] https://www.bloomberg.com/news/articles/2016-12-15/banks-turn-to-mind-reading-to-source-top-tech-graduates

Vakratsas, D and Ambler, T (1999) How advertising works: what do we really know?, *The Journal of Marketing*, 63 (1), pp 26–43

Vanian, J (2016) [accessed 18 June 2018] The Human Cost of a 'Digital Transformation', *Fortune* [Online] http://fortune.com/2016/08/19/human-cost-layoff-digital-transformation/

Vesser, J, Field, D and Sheerin, A (2015) [accessed 18 June 2018] The Agile Marketing Organization, *BCG* [Online] https://www.bcg.com/publications/2015/marketing-brand-strategy-agile-marketing-organization.aspx

Whitler, K A (2017) [accessed 18 June 2018] The Biggest Challenges Facing Marketing Leaders, *Forbes* [Online] https://www.forbes.com/sites/kimberlywhitler/2017/08/05/the-biggest-challenges-facing-marketing-leaders/#33a385616560

Zak, P J (2013) [accessed 18 June 2018] Can Neuroscience Improve the Selection and Hiring Process?, *Psychology Today*, Blog [Online] https://www.psychologytoday.com/blog/the-moral-molecule/201311/can-neuroscience-improve-the-selection-and-hiring-process

Marketers: the new transformational leaders

09

CHAPTER LEARNING OBJECTIVES

After studying this chapter, you will be able to:

- Appreciate the holistic approach in this book for upgrading marketers in order to become full business partners, and true leaders, in their companies.

- Support the key takeaways from previous chapters even further with fresh insights provided in this one.

- Understand the importance of combining the four strategic skills for advanced marketers provided in this book.

- Scrutinize the monopoly of competition as the dominating business mindset and argue for the necessity of a more collaborative mindset.

- Take a last deep breath before your new journey as an advanced marketing manager!

Advanced practice

The challenge of the new marketer

Where is marketing going? Although this book offers numerous glimpses, within all chapters, into the present and future of marketing, it deliberately focuses more on the person than on the function; more on the marketer than on marketing itself. We profoundly believe that marketers need to take into their own hands the future of their profession and lead the way forward, instead of being followers or mere adaptors of market and organizational trends. The era of marketers as functional leaders is coming to an end. The era of marketers as corporate, and even whole industry, leaders is approaching fast! We wholeheartedly believe that this book can help considerably marketing students and young marketers, but also seasoned marketing professionals, to prepare appropriately for their new role. It is their destiny!

Four steps to the new marketer

Our approach, in this book, for tackling the challenge of creating the new marketer, included four major steps. These are now summarized, with a fresh view and new insights, below.

Step 1: The Marketing Paradox

Any change needs a strong wake-up call and a new purpose. Concerning the wake-up call, a strong feeling of urgency is necessary in changing attitudes and creating a behavioural momentum towards a new vision (Kotter, 2012). At the same time, a very strong and as clear as possible picture of the destination is equally important for both motivational and implementation issues (Kotter International, 2011). An exciting change vision can move people faster and with more determination towards the new goal but also can play the significant role of a feasibility compass for aligning different functions and different levels of execution towards this goal. Our approach to what we call The Marketing Paradox, which as explained in Chapter 1 is the increasing importance of marketing and the parallel questionable position of marketers in modern organizations, provides both the urgency and the vision for marketing change. If marketers do not answer convincingly to the call of our times for strategic, holistic and organization-wide leadership in customer focus, this call will be answered by others. This is already happening. For example, although marketers still command most of the decisions for marketing tech spending, chief information officers (CIOs) have an increasing role despite their potential conflicting motives (Glynn, 2017). There is no doubt that marketers, as will be explained in detail in this chapter, will need to upgrade their game concerning collaboration with other professionals inside and outside the company. Nevertheless, if they are to perform in a strong leadership role they have to become more scientific, more reliable and more total business-oriented.

Step 2: top or strategic skills

In order for marketers to achieve the above they need a new set of strategic, or top, skills. These skills have very little to do with the main skills that marketers have been traditionally educated in. They are less about the usual marketing expert areas that all in marketing should be aware of – such as segmentation, positioning, campaign management, social media marketing and marketing research, as found in most marketing textbooks – and more about a new way of looking at every aspect of the marketing profession, including those areas just mentioned here. The four skills we are suggesting are neuroscience, analytics, creative thinking and adaptable decision making. All four have their own significance *in and by* themselves but become really powerful when combined. The first skill, neuroscience, is explained in Chapter 2. In 2015's World Economic Forum in Davos, Switzerland, brain-related talks were amongst the most popular ones as reported by *Financial Times* contributor Andrew Hill (2015), with far-reaching implications discussed in both economics and management. Hill titled his FT report with the emphatic title 'Heads of business need neuroscience'. If there is one business function that needs neuroscience above any other, it is marketing, the obvious areas being consumer behaviour and marketing research. As highlighted by a neuromarketing pioneer, Christophe Morin (2011), in his paper 'Neuromarketing: The new science of consumer behaviour', 'conventional methods for testing and predicting the effectiveness of those investments [in advertising] have generally failed because they depend on consumers' willingness and competency to describe how they feel... Neuromarketing offers cutting edge methods for directly probing minds without requiring demanding cognitive or conscious participation.' Understanding better the unconscious reactions of customers' brains to marketing stimuli is of paramount importance to marketing since the vast majority of decisions humans make are subconscious. The second skill, analytics, is explained in Chapter 3. This is where most attention has been given in the last decade concerning the new versus traditional marketing. Analytical skills are absolutely necessary for the modern marketer.

Analytics, analytics, analytics...

… is the new location, location, location! Analytics is becoming almost synonymous with marketing and top marketers around the world are fully embracing the trend. A study of 200 senior marketers worldwide in 2017, conducted by Spencer Stuart and titled 'Whole brain marketing: data, creativity and the leadership challenge', found that the majority of respondents, two-thirds of them, valued analytical skills above traditional marketing skills (Duncan and d'Anglade, 2017). The report quoted marketers from various brands, such as Bas Verheijen, the CMO at online supermarket Picnic, saying that 'affinity with data and analysis is now an unconditional requirement', and Marco Sansavini, CMO at airline Iberia, arguing that 'analytical capabilities and big data skills are becoming increasingly important' (Duncan and d'Anglade, 2017). In a world engulfed with digital fever, analytical skills are the preferred option.

Many traditional marketing skills though, such as strategy and planning, copywriting, customer service and event management, are still quite important and need to be cultivated alongside digital skills, as supported by no other than the Digital Marketing Institute (Smith, 2016)! The third skill, creative problem solving, is explained in Chapter 4. Innovation is the name of the modern business game. There is very little doubt, if any, about that. But are marketers trained and educated to think creatively about various problems and challenges they encounter? Are they equipped with skills related to nurturing innovative mindsets and approaching their business with fresh ideas and solutions? Or are they afraid and defensive to tackling challenges boldly and head-on? Tim Kopp, an experienced brand marketer who worked in major brands such as Coca-Cola and P&G, and then became a venture capitalist, proves the answer to such questions in this way: 'I think a lot of what schools are teaching about marketing has nothing to do with how to be a marketer today' (Hunckler, 2017). His conclusion comes as he recounts the story of how he and his team took advantage of a potentially dangerous situation while working in Coca-Cola back in 2006. The Diet Coke and Mentos fountain online craze seemed to many top leaders in the company as a serious threat to the brand, while Kopp saw it as an opportunity. He contacted those behind the videos and collaboratively created the biggest and most impressive fountain of them all (Hunckler, 2017). Creative problem solving and innovation do not happen accidentally. They need specific approaches, roles and attitudes to become commonplace within the marketing team. We envision a marketing function that is an explosive fountain of innovations within companies, like when mixing Diet Coke with Mentos, and not the department called in at late stages just to 'monetize' innovations that happened elsewhere! The fourth skill, adaptive decision making, is explained in Chapter 5. Complex market situations require new approaches to decision making. Traditionally, marketing textbooks did not include decision-making science. They usually focused on marketing expertise. But if marketers are to lead their functions and companies into a brighter future they need to upgrade their decision approaches. Top-down, rigidly rational and linear models are less effective today and need to be replaced by more dynamic and intuitive models. Mindset is the keyword here and it precedes strategy. As entrepreneurial adviser Marla Tabaka (2011) points out: 'I believe it is important to evaluate your own belief system… But if your current marketing mindset is fearful and limiting, it is time to step into a new mindset and bring success to your door.' Successful mindsets for marketers are flexible, entrepreneurial, collaborative, learning-based, gentle to mistakes and failures, passionate, inspired and inclusive. The new marketing mindset is also ethics-oriented, and this cannot be overstated enough in the increasingly transparent world we live in.

The power of combining the four skills

Neuroscience, analytics, creative problem solving and adaptive decision making form together a powerful grid of skills for every transformational marketer. This is not a pick-and-mix list. All those four skills need to be developed and practised by marketing leaders in order for marketing teams to get the recognition, trust and role they deserve, and for brands to materialize their full potential. The main barrier is the simple fact that, traditionally, marketers could get away without deep knowledge and advanced practice of such diverse skills. But marketers cannot succeed today doing the same things, and employing the same ways, like they did yesterday. Tough times require tough solutions. Adaptive and visionary marketers will not be afraid of what is asked from them and will embrace the challenge willingly. Otherwise, their future will be even more uncertain than it is today.

Step 3: the new marketing mix

The marketing mix model of the 4Ps has proven resilient during the last few decades, regardless of the extensive criticism that it constantly attracts from both academic and consulting circles. Although many attempted to extend it or change it altogether, we opted for an upgrade. Transformational marketers need to use the 4Ps in an updated and modern way, without losing its timeless advantages. Our upgraded marketing toolbox, described in Chapters 6 and 7, is the 4EPs: the empathic product, the experiential price, the ever-present place and the engaging promotion. The addition of an E-word in front of every P is not a cosmetic one. The change is more qualitative in nature than quantitative. Product, service or customer experiences, the first EP, cannot be one-way any more. As communications stopped being one-way two decades ago, the same needs to happen with the first P nowadays. A two-way product is one that utilizes its unique nature to touch customers deeply and improve their wellbeing in a characteristically human and emotionally warm manner. Empathy is not only about understanding each other. It is also about connecting with each other and ultimately helping each other. An empathic product is built *in association* with customers, not just *for* customers, always reflecting upon its purpose, role, meaning and function to the target group(s). The second P, price, is experiential because of the amounting scientific evidence of what value means for humans and how price-relevant decision making is executed in our brains. Price is not a mere accounting process, responsibility or outcome. It is key in how customers approach a purchase and vital in how they evaluate their whole experience with a company or brand. But perceptions of price are mostly intuitive, subconscious and highly contextual. Marketers need to understand, accept and utilize the fact that pricing is far more exciting than ever before believed, requiring many times an experimental approach. Especially in the era of online price comparisons and dynamic pricing, marketers need to embrace price fully and unconditionally as a major marketing asset. The third P, place, is becoming ever-present in our upgrading model because of the fact that customers now have access to products, services, experiences, recommendations and comparisons everywhere they are. Instead of highlighting the differences between offline and online distribution models, we argue for integration and a holistic and seamless approach to the customer journey. Traditional retail is changing, not dying, and digital selling will require targeted human presence to create meaningful connections alongside convenience and speed. The last P, promotion, is becoming engaging. This is the normal evolution from two-way communications. Engaging is not just having the ability as a customer to respond. It is more about driving the conversation and interacting with brands, other stakeholders and fellow customers in continuous, natural and dynamic interactions. Modern marketing departments can now tap into this engaged communication and achieve growth faster than ever before in the history of business. But this requires a set of specific skills, processes and strategies. As mentioned throughout the book, the 4EPs are not intended for replacing the mainstream model. They are an addition to the existing model. Think of the 4Ps as the core that every marketer should be aware of and the 4EPs as the extension that upgrades the model for complex and contemporary business environments. The two are not mutually exclusive but complementary.

Step 4: the new marketing function

The fourth and last step concerns reapproaching the whole marketing function: operating skills, positions and structure. Restructuring, and especially marketing restructuring, should not be taken lightly. However, some companies fail to give strategic importance to transforming their marketing function in crisis situations and thus fail to achieve full turnaround (Dubrovski, 2014). Furthermore, many companies seem to still organize their marketing activities around functions such as research, promotions, advertising, digital, etc, while it is a shared belief nowadays that more customer-centric marketing systems are moving away from such a purely functional approach (Patterson, 2017). Although there is no magic solution that fits all cases, the transition from 'boxes and lines' organizational structures to ones that are more network-like and circle-like is evident, as explained in Chapter 8. Many companies have undertaken programmes to simplify and centralize marketing in order to become faster, tighter and more customer focused. Tesco, the retail giant, started such a reorganization in 2014 in order to create more simplicity, bring various teams together and help the whole organization come closer to its customers (Vizard, 2014). New functions need also new roles. We have separated marketing roles into three levels: transformational marketers at the strategic level; hybrid marketers at the tactical level; and expert marketers at the operational level. These three levels of marketers, organized in a new, more inclusive, dynamic and networked structure, can boost marketing within modern companies and deliver tangible business results in chaotic markets. Marketers need to be clever and critical towards structure and not to fall easily for trendy ideas that can be illusive and even dangerous for organizational stability and growth. The marketing structure is definitely taking a new form. But this form is more fluid than ever, requiring close attention, personal involvement and the existence of the strategic skills discussed in Chapters 2 to 5. Only then will marketers be able to construct and reconstruct their departments on demand and make sure the new structure fits the market conditions it needs to serve.

Marketing is collaboration

One of the elements that stands out in many of the conversations about the nature of modern marketing, both in academic and marketing practice outlets, is collaboration. For example, Glynn (2017) in his article on the roles of CMOs and of CIOs in controlling marketing tech in companies, cited earlier, highlights the fact that ultimately 'the future is collaboration' and enterprises should be '[w]orking towards a better partnership between marketing and IT'. The keyword is *relations*. Similarly, Justin Dunham (2017) of MarTech Today suggests that, instead of technology itself, 'better collaboration is the best MarTech investment you can make' since different experiences, skills, strong and weak points, and styles make it hard sometimes for people in marketing and IT to work together. Partnerships, inside and outside the company, are what Advanced Marketing Management is all about!

In Chapter 8 we presented the new marketing structure as circular and networked, with the transformational marketing leader at the very centre of the whole system. Being at the very centre of action is not the same as being at the top of a hierarchical pyramid. The circle's centre portrays less in terms of power and authority and more about direction, integration and support. New marketers are primarily connectors. As one of us explained in a LinkedIn article (Dimitriadis, 2016), new marketing leaders constantly connect different data points, but also:

> Teams, partners, technologies, customers and methods into one single, ever-changing entity. They know they cannot achieve anything meaningful alone so they draw their strength from synergies. No marketing budget in the world can help you ensure long-lasting, life-changing brand results. You need everyone. Go get them on your side.

Are marketers, though, trained and educated to collaborate and form strategic synergies? Is their knee-jerk, automatic and habitual response to challenges one of bridging gaps, bringing diverse people and resources together, and partnering? Or do they usually respond competitively, ego-centrically and in isolation? Looking at many traditional textbooks it becomes clear that usually competition takes a bigger part than collaboration; from competitive forces analysis to forming competitive advantages and from brand-positioning mapping to guerrilla-marketing techniques, the literature focuses more often on what sets us apart than on what brings us together. But those two should not be mutually exclusive: partnerships are a fantastic way to compete and win in the marketplace. A great example of this is Diet Coke and Mentos, mentioned earlier in this chapter. Knopp, Coke's brand manager at the time, reached out to the people demonstrating the Coke and Mentos fountains instead of attacking them (Hunckler, 2017). He created a synergy, utilizing the momentum and scoring points for the brand. This kind of response requires an open mind, fast reflexes and a partnering attitude.

This is not an entirely new attitude; it is one though that asks for urgent attention and implementation in all levels of marketing action. In Chapter 1, we discussed Grönroos's influential paper on relationship marketing as a paradigm shift. Grönroos was not alone, nor even the first, to emphasize relations as *the* focal point for marketers. Academics Martin Christopher, Adrian Payne and David Ballantyne published the book *Relationship Marketing* in 1991, at the time the first two at Cranfield School of Management in the UK and the third at Syme School of Marketing, Monash University in Australia. In that book, which reads like a manifesto for a new way of thinking and doing marketing, they claim that traditionally marketing was about acquiring customers while relationship marketing is about acquiring *and* maintaining customers. But their view of relationships in marketing went beyond the dyadic interaction between brand and customer. They include three issues in their model (Christopher, Payne and Ballantyne, 1991):

- A relationship marketing approach goes beyond customers, including other external entities such as suppliers and influencers.

- This approach also recognizes the strategic role of employees in marketing success. Internal marketing is thus a prerequisite of external marketing.

- Ultimately, a better marketing performance is achieved through a major shift in how activities are managed internally and externally (by aligning the competing interests of various groups like customers and shareholders).

A few years later, the network marketing approach emerged, with one of its main advocates, Dawn Iacobucci (1996) explaining the logic of this newest marketing field as follows: 'much of marketing is relational; networks are an excellent means of studying relational phenomena; networks are an excellent means of studying much of marketing'. In this, marketers were not alone. Business strategists and industry analysts also joined forces in changing the leading business mindset: from extreme competition to a more collaborative one. The pinnacle of the new business mindset was the book *Co-opetition*, by Adam Brandenburger and Barry Nalebuff (1996), who set out to challenge ultra-competitive business understanding and analytical models, and suggest one that featured cooperation as key to successful corporate strategy. The 1990s were becoming the collaboration decade in business and marketing. But this did not continue in the noughties. Why? Our understanding is that the dot.com bubble burst at the end of the 1990s and, mainly, the disruptive power of many newcomers in various industries, that killed off tradition-ally successful businesses, shifted again attention to individual corporate strategies and storytelling instead of collaboration, networks and synergies. Transformational marketing leaders need to shift their attention back to part-nerships in a more aggressive way and with a wider scope than ever before.

This is easier said than done. Years of a strong competition-inspired narrative and the more recent glorification of successful individuals in the Digital Era are making the adoption of a collaborative mindset challeng-ing. But as Margaret Heffernan (2014), international businesswoman and author, stresses – this needs to change because such a competitive thinking is 'constrained by benchmarks, scorecards, and comparisons' and 'cannot wander and explore new territory but stays fettered to old ideas and models'. Especially in very important situations, with high risks and unpredictable outcomes, Heffernan (2014) believes that extreme competitiveness 'backfires spectacularly, undermining exactly what it hopes to build'. There is no one, single model of collaboration though, as she admits, making plurality the key characteristic of systems based on cooperative mindsets.

Heffernan's approach is very similar to that of the renowned British busi-nessperson and former CEO of energy corporation British Petroleum, John Brownie. Brownie (2015), in his book *Connect: How companies succeed by engaging radically with society*, emphasizes that:

> [Connectivity] is only possible if business people are willing to adopt an entirely
> new attitude... to engage radically. This means being brave enough to embrace
> genuine openness, farsighted enough to make friends before they need them and
> to communicate in a language that exudes authenticity rather than propaganda.

Transformational marketers, in leading the marketing function, their brands and even the corporation as a whole, need to apply such a *radical engagement* attitude. Brownie (2015) recommends a four-step approach in making this happen, adapted here for new marketers:

1 **Map your world**. A wide view of the market, and of the company itself, is necessary to make sure that as many as possible stakeholders are captured on the marketing radar. Different actors might have different weights in different moments but none of them should be excluded a priori. New actors should be added constantly, based on market and organizational dynamics.

2 **Set your contribution**. Marketers should be always aware of the value they bring, or they can potentially bring, to different actors, internally and externally. By never forgetting their own purpose and brand vision, they should offer powerful solutions to separate actors based on momentary interrelations and market conditions.

3 **Do your best**. Relations are not a by-product of doing business, nor a mere tool/technique. They form the very core of marketing success and should be given utmost attention. Cutting-edge technology, relentless personal involvement and strategic resources should be dedicated to creating and nurturing relations inside and outside the company.

4 **Commit long term**. As continuation of the previous point, relations are not one-off, nor are they a trendy approach that will come and go. It is a life-long attitude with the power to transform teams, brands and even industries. Radical engagement asks for mental flexibility, transparency, proactiveness and a strong will for positive impact.

Competition will always be a big part of marketers' work, if not the biggest one. Brands from all around the world will always compete fiercely for our attention, our time, our hearts and our wallet. However, cooperation and relationship building emerge as the most credible and long-lasting strategy to compete more effectively and efficiently in the marketplace. It is not about choosing the one over the other. It is more about blending the two. As Galinsky and Schweitzer (2015) concluded in their book *Friend & Foe: When to cooperate, when to compete, and how to succeed at both*:

> What comes next will not take the shape of cooperation or competition, but rather a shifting dynamic between the two. As we compete for scarce resources in our unstable social world, it is not enough to be prepared to cooperate or compete. We must be prepared to do both.

Paul Zak's trust model applied in marketing leadership

Dr Paul Zak, the well-known neuroscientist specializing in human relations, trust and the moral molecule of oxytocin, has devised a model for explaining and boosting collaboration within organizations. He has named this model OXYTOCIN and we believe that it can be equally applied to both internal and external business relations. Transformational marketers, please take notice (Zak, 2017, adapted for the purposes of this book):

- **Ovation.** Marketing leaders should encourage and motivate internal and external partners by actively and openly appreciating their achievements and acknowledging their contribution. Paying an external vendor the agreed fee for a job well done is simply not enough. Celebrating together and promoting further their successful efforts is nowadays a necessity.

- **eXpectation.** Great teams perform exceptionally well in challenging situations. Advanced marketers should engage their functions in such situations by believing in the team, supporting it and steering it firmly whenever needed. This includes both internal and external members of the team.

- **Yield.** Micro-management kills trust and collaboration. Marketing leaders should actively engage internal and external partners for latest ideas and ways of allocating resources. Team members should be given a high degree of freedom in project management.

- **Transfer.** Similarly, when it comes to implementing the project, marketing teams consisting of people from inside and outside the company should also be empowered to perform the tasks as they seem fit. High degrees of self-management, self-evaluation and self-determination contribute directly to more trust.

- **Openness.** Transparency and authenticity create trust while secrecy and trickery destroy it. Marketing leaders should be as open and clear as possible concerning information.

- **Caring.** Human connectivity is based on a shared feeling of warmth intentionality and a support system that includes all. Advanced marketers should allow team members to express their own personalities and should care for their wellbeing, tangibly and continuously.

- **Invest.** All relationships, business or otherwise, require personal investment in time, effort and even financial resources. Modern marketers should be ready and willing to demonstrate their commitment to nurturing a mutually beneficial relation by investing actively in the personal and professional growth of all partners.

- **Natural.** Trust cannot be forced or manufactured. It should come naturally and convincingly by being present, listening and asking the right questions.

What comes next?

We sincerely hope you enjoyed reading this book. We do not expect all its points to resonate in the same way with every reader and we also do not expect everyone to agree unconditionally with all our arguments. We do expect, though, marketers to fortify their vision, fuel their passion and reaffirm their purpose in the chaotic business universe we live in.

Marketing has been, is currently and will always be changing in order to be able to answer better to contemporary market challenges. But to do so as effectively as possible, marketers should not hold back. Marketers need to lead, to transform and to create value in everything they do. In a fluid world of disruptive technologies and emerging business models, customers are becoming more demanding and more important than ever. Serving them is not easy. Understanding them is not as straightforward as before. Engaging them is getting harder and harder. As a true leader, now is the time to act. This book has given you enough concepts, methods and tools to respond successfully to the call of our times. This is just the beginning. Enjoy the journey.

Last thought

You made it. You now know more about the current state and future of the marketing profession. Reading has just finished… and implementing is about to commence. Make no mistake, though – marketers will become true business leaders only through assertive and powerful decision making and behaviour. Lead by example. Lead by empathy. But above all, do not hesitate to lead your teams, brands and companies into a better future for all of us. We count on you!

SUMMARY CHECKLIST

- Fully embrace the urgency and value of applying a more advanced approach to marketing.
- Apply a collaborative mindset to increase your competitiveness by considering every market development as an opportunity for cooperation with the right partners.
- Use Paul Zak's OXYTOCIN model for building trustful relationships inside and outside the company.
- Become the transformational marketing leader the world needs you to be!

Resources to inspire you

- Kotter on change vision: https://www.youtube.com/watch?v=yA1a0khcuKo
- Dr Nikolaos Dimitriadis's speech on the new transformational marketer: https://www.youtube.com/watch?v=_vvDqxjVPBg

Revision questions

1 Provide the summary of the four steps necessary for developing the new marketer.

2 Why is collaboration considered such a critical element of Advanced Marketing Management?

3 Critically discuss the OXYTOCIN model for developing trust in the marketing function.

4 What would be your first personal step in becoming a positive change agent for marketing? Explain why.

References

Brandenburger, A and Nalebuff, B (1996) *Co-opetition*, HarperCollinsBusiness, London

Brownie, J (2015) *Connect: How companies succeed by engaging radically with society*, W H Allen, London

Christopher, M, Payne, A and Ballantyne, D (1991) *Relationship Marketing: Bringing quality, customer service and marketing together*, Butterworth-Heinemann, Oxford

Dimitriadis, N (2016) [accessed 18 June 2018] Marketing Success Re-Positioned: From Luck to Leadership, *LinkedIn* [Online] https://www.linkedin.com/pulse/marketing-success-re-positioned-from-luck-leadership-dimitriadis/

Dubrovski, D (2014) The role of marketing restructuring in a company crisis, *International Journal of Economic Practices and Theories*, 4 (5), pp 658–67

Duncan, G and d'Anglade, A (2017) [accessed 18 June 2018] Marketing Leaders Favour Digital Over More Traditional Skills, *Campaign* [Online] https://www.campaignlive.co.uk/article/marketing-leaders-favour-digital-traditional-skills/1435048

Dunham, J (2017) [accessed 18 June 2018] Better Collaboration is the Best MarTech Investment You Can Make, *MarTech Today* [Online] https://martechtoday.com/better-collaboration-best-martech-investment-can-make-195420

Galinsky, A and Schweitzer, M (2015) *Friend & Foe: When to cooperate, when to compete, and how to succeed at both*, Penguin Random House, London

Glynn, F (2017) [accessed 18 June 2018] CIO vs. CMO: Who Owns What?, *Business.com* [Online] https://www.business.com/articles/cio-vs-cmo-who-owns-what/

Grönroos, C (1994) Quo Vadis, marketing? Toward a relationship marketing paradigm, *Journal of Marketing Management*, 10 (5), pp 347–60

Heffernan, M (2014) *A Bigger Prize: Why competition isn't everything and how we do better*, Simon & Schuster, London

Hill, A (2015) [accessed 18 June 2018] Heads of Business Need Neuroscience, *Financial Times* [Online] https://www.ft.com/content/11812676-d79a-11e4-94b1-00144feab7de

Hunckler, (2017) [accessed 18 June 2018] 3 Strategies for Marketing Innovation from Former Marketing Exec at P&G and Coca-Cola Turned VC, *Forbes* [Online] https://www.forbes.com/sites/matthunckler/2017/08/04/3-strategies-for-marketing-innovation-from-former-marketing-exec-at-pg-and-coca-cola-turned-vc/#460c7b5e7e00

Iacobucci, D (1996) Introduction, in *Networks in Marketing*, ed D Iacobucci, Sage, Thousand Oaks

Kotter International (2011) [accessed 18 June 2018] How to Create a Powerful Vision for Change, *Forbes* [Online] https://www.forbes.com/sites/johnkotter/2011/06/07/how-to-create-a-powerful-vision-for-change/#3c0741a451fc

Kotter, J P (2012) [accessed 18 June 2018] Accelerate, *Harvard Business Review* [Online] https://hbr.org/2012/11/accelerate

Morin, C (2011) Neuromarketing: The new science of consumer behavior, *Society*, 48 (2), pp 131–35

Patterson, L (2017) [accessed 18 June 2018] Want Higher Growth? Revisit Your Marketing Structure First, *The Marketing Scope* [Online] https://www.themarketingscope.com/want-higher-growth-revisit-marketing-structure-first/

Smith, S E (2016) [accessed 18 June 2018] The Traditional Marketing Skills You Should Still Be Using, *Digital Marketing Institute* [Online] https://digitalmarketinginstitute.com/blog/2016-12-21-the-traditional-marketing-skills-you-should-still-be-using

Tabaka, M (2011) [accessed 18 June 2018] Discover Your Marketing Mindset, *INC.COM* [Online] https://www.inc.com/marla-tabaka/discover-your-marketing-mindset.html

Vizard, S (2014) [accessed 18 June 2018] Tesco Simplifies Marketing Structure in Focus on the Customer, *Marketing Week* [Online] https://www.marketingweek.com/2014/09/10/tesco-simplifies-marketing-structure-in-focus-on-the-customer/

Zak, P J (2017) *Trust Factor: The science of creating high-performance companies*, AMACOM, New York

GLOSSARY

4EPs model By adding an 'E' in front of every 'P' (empathic product, experiential price, ever-present place, engaging promotion), the traditional 4Ps marketing mix model is updated to a more relevant one in the contemporary marketing environment.

AARRR system The principles created by Dave McClure that help move the customer from one stage of a purchase funnel to another. These stages include acquisition, activation, retention, referral and revenue.

adblocking Software used for blocking invading ads in online content.

advanced business ecosystem The business environment nowadays characterized by huge amounts of data available even in real time, the substantial and at times conflicting academic and market research, the large number of actors that influence marketing decisions and outcomes, and the general higher complexity of the current business reality.

advanced marketer Modern marketers that in addition to the traditional skills also possess the new set of skills (neuroscience, predictive, innovation and adaptability skills) and utilize new tools (the 4EPs and marketing reorganization), which are necessary to thrive in the contemporary business environment and lead business transformation.

Advanced Marketing Management model The model presented in this book, which points out necessary new skills (neuroscience, predictive, innovation, adaptability) and new tools (the 4EPs and marketing reorganization) required for the advanced marketers of the 21st century and their role as transformational leaders.

assembly line marketing function Opposite of the trading room marketing function concept (see relevant term in glossary), assembly line is an outdated approach marketing function because of its time-consuming, flexibility-decreasing and authority-protecting nature.

behavioural data analysis The ability to analyse data holistically and through a human-centred view to understand why people have behaved in a particular manner.

big data Data sets that are too large and complex for traditional data processing because they require increased processing power.

big number fallacy The tendency to use large numbers to measure the success of marketing activity. The big number fallacy is closely linked to vanity metrics (see relevant term in glossary).

biometrics Measures the nonconscious responses of the body such as heart rate, respiratory rate and skin conductance, which can indicate intensity of reaction to marketing stimuli (arousal) as well as primal emotional reactions such as transfixion, fight or flight responses, fear, nervousness, stress and relief.

black box of consumer behaviour The model of consumer behaviour that recognizes that between the inputs (various marketing and environmental stimuli) for consumer decision making and the outputs (actual customer decisions and behaviour) there are big unknowns – regarding how the customer decision was really taken – that marketers could not comprehend in depth. With the advancements in neuromarketing, it is finally possible to 'open' the consumer black box.

Black Swan theory A theory by Nassim Nicholas Taleb explaining that people tend to be overconfident and very comfortable about the status quo before a significant and unexpected event with major consequences (dubbed the Black Swan) happens. After such a cataclysmic event occurs, people also tend to rationalize it and become oversensitive to new ones, until they settle into a new comfort zone with a renewed belief in the stability of the new situation.

boardroom war A concept based on the book by Ries and Ries, *War in the Boardroom: Why left-brain management and right-brain marketing don't see eye-to-eye and what to do about it*. The concept points to the differences between the left-brain (analytical, verbal, certainty-driven) management of the company, represented by CEOs and CFOs, and the right-brain (holistic, visual, creativity-driven) marketers.

Capilano Suspension Bridge Experiment An experiment conducted by psychologists Dutton and Aaron in the 1970s, which showed that there is gap between brain reactions, in other words real emotions, and perception/interpretation of those emotions.

Censydiam Framework for Social The proprietary framework developed by research company Ipsos to understand deep-seated consumer emotions and needs. The framework has been adapted to analyse social data. There are eight Censydiam motivations that leverage personal and social dimensions of consumer behaviour – enjoyment, conviviality, belonging, security, control, recognition, power and vitality.

circular and networked marketing structure The proposed marketing structure, different than traditional boxes-and-lines structures, where every unit is open to its immediate surroundings, creating multidisciplinary, multipurpose teams with members from both inside and outside the company. The CMO is at the very centre, overviewing and orchestrating teams of experts.

consumer power sources A framework created by Labrecque and associates that documents the consumer power sources that have risen as a result of the internet and social media. These sources include demand, information, network and crowd.

content shock The increasing volume of content about specific topics and subjects that leads to reader fatigue due to limited human capacity to process the information.

creative thinking model This model for advanced marketers points to the specifics that should be taken into account at each of the four levels (personal, team, organizational and market level) in order to achieve a holistic approach to creative thinking and innovation.

customer advocacy The tendency for customers to advocate or promote brands, products and services voluntarily and without compensation.

customer-centricity The fundamental idea at the heart of the marketing philosophy that everything that a company offers should be seen from the eyes of the customer.

data complexity The consequential outcome of big data, since the increased volume, variety, velocity and veracity of data require more effort to prepare and analyse the data.

design thinking The concept of applying empathy in product and service development in order to achieve innovative solutions.

disruptive innovation The launch of a new innovation that is designed to create a new market and can lead to the displacement of market-leading organizations. Disruptive innovation seeks to solve an unmet customer need through technological and/or other developments.

dual organizational system An approach to organizational structure developed by John P Kotter that suggests a dual system of two structures that run in parallel with the stable, predictable, operational system that takes care of everyday business and helps the company survive today; and the passionate, creative, flexible and engaging system that leads to drastic innovations that can help the company stay competitive and to thrive in the future.

EEG (electroencephalography) A device that measures the electrical activity of the brain through electrodes placed on the scalp of the subject in the form of a cap or band.

emotion economy The emerging and fast-developing industry of technology enabling us to decode the emotional and mental states of our customers.

emotion voice recognition The technology used to detect changes in people's uttered speech when they talk about a marketing activity or element in order to reveal emotions and attitudes.

emotional facial recognition Based on interpretation of involuntary and voluntary facial muscles movement, different emotions can be observed as a reaction to marketing stimuli. This interpretation is nowadays typically performed by sophisticated computer software.

emotional needs continuum A concept defined by Dr Mark Ingwer that includes six core, universal and deeply motivating human emotional needs: control, self-expression, growth, recognition, belonging and care – placed on a continuum with individuality at one end and connectedness at the other. Looking closely into these needs can help marketers to develop emphatic products and services.

empathic product A component of the updated 4EPs marketing mix model, the empathic product is developed through design thinking, an advanced understanding of empathy, and it strategically considers customers' emotional needs.

empathy deficit The drop in overall empathy levels in society observed in the last 30 years, which is attributed to a more egoistic and self-indulging culture.

engaging promotion A component of the updated 4EPs marketing mix model, the engaging promotion is developed through contemporary concepts such as growth hacking. It is based on the premise that modern marketing communications are not about simply informing people but actively engaging them in the whole marketing process.

ever-present place A component of the updated 4EPs marketing mix model. It involves utilizing new technologies and data available to create a unique, integrated and powerful experience for customers, whenever and wherever they are.

experiential price A component of the updated 4EPs marketing mix model. Price should not be a rigid number, controlled solely by the company, as was traditionally the case – it should be experienced within its emotional context, taking into account the psychological forces that shape customers' interaction with prices.

eye tracking The technology that allows for measuring involuntary eye activity such as eye fixation, pattern of eye movement, blinking rate and pupil dilations.

five customer behaviour environments The five different environments (societal, general commerce, specific product industry, direct competitors, brand) that can shape and influence consumers' needs and expectations. The five customer behaviour environments can be used to identify disruptive innovation opportunities.

fMRI (functional magnetic resonance imaging) A device that measures the change in the blood flow in the brain, which indicates the activity taking place in certain areas of the brain.

FOMO and marketers FOMO (an acronym for fear of missing out) in the marketing function relates to marketers trying to keep up with or outperform competition in the digital arena by focusing too much on technical skills. This can lead to two main negative implications for marketing, namely *narrowness* and *short termism.*

Four Horsemen of the Apocalypse In the business context this phrase refers to four everyday elements that hinder creativity and innovation, namely meetings, presentations, e-mails and spreadsheets.

four Vs of big data A concept developed by Hopkins and Evelson that highlights the four challenges posed by big data. These four challenges are data volume (the amount of data available), data variety (the number of different types of data available), data velocity (the speed of data processing), data veracity (the biases, noise or abnormality in the data).

foxes versus hedgehogs Two broad styles in forecasting as identified by Professor Philip E Tetlock. While *hedgehogs* tend to specialize, focus on one solution, blame others, strive for simplistic solutions and are less accurate forecasters, *foxes* use diverse ideas from multiple disciplines, pursue several solutions at the same time, happily recognize mistakes, embrace complexity and are more accurate forecasters.

global economic meltdown The financial crisis that started with the crisis in the subprime mortgage market in 2007 in the United States, triggering a global economic downturn that peaked in 2008.

growth hacking Creating a marketing system that is driven by peer-to-peer sharing and influence that eventually becomes self-perpetuating.

growth versus fixed mindset Two key mindsets, as identified by Carol Dweck, relating to opposite aptitudes for learning and personal development. At the epicentre of her approach is the revolutionary insight that improving performance is based not on personality traits but on people's own perception of their abilities.

Heath and Heath's decision framework The framework, developed by Heath and Heath, specifying the process, the obstacles and solutions for improving the decision-making process. It includes the following key phases: choice, options, decision, impact.

herd marketing The seven marketing principles created by Mark Earls that use the nature of human behaviour to influence mass consumer-behaviour change. The principles include interaction, influence, us-talk, just believe, (re)lighting the fire, co-creating, letting go.

Holacracy The concept proposed by the tech entrepreneur Brian Robertson, describing an organizational structure with self-organizing teams, called circles, with specific roles assigned to appropriate members to achieve the goals of the circle as best as possible.

Homo economicus The theoretical model of human behaviour, dominating the world since the 18th century, which focuses on a completely individualistic, rational, calculative view of human behaviour. This model is finally subsiding and is being replaced by other models such as *Homo reciprocans*, *Homo sociologicus* and *Homo socioeconomicus*.

Hype Cycle A tool created by Gartner, the information technology research and consultancy company. The tool is a representation of the life-cycle stages a technology flows through from conception to maturity and widespread adoption.

illusion of control The perceived illusion or belief that marketers (and brands) had full control or autonomy over brand messages and brand perception.

implicit response tests Typically computer tests that provide measures of unconscious impact of a marketing output (eg ad, brand). The more the participants have been primed for a certain concept, the faster they will react to something they implicitly associate with that concept when they are exposed to it on a screen.

instantly changeable product Products are not as rigid as before and are becoming instantly, constantly and collaboratively changeable, much like services.

interruptive marketing An approach to marketing where individuals have to stop what they are doing in order to pay attention to a marketing message. Interruptive marketing is believed to be the traditional mode of product promotion.

key dilemmas in organizing marketing Within the many structural decisions that marketers have to take, the two key dilemmas concerning the organization of modern marketing departments are: in-house versus eternal expertise; machines versus human resources.

machine learning The use of statistical techniques that allows a computer to learn with data without being explicitly programmed.

The Marketing Paradox While marketing is becoming more important than ever, marketers themselves are not so highly perceived by CEOs, other top management professionals and industry influencers.

marketing profession's problem The absence of reliability and predictability associated with the marketing profession that has led to the misguided notion that marketing is half science and half art.

marketing's mid-life crisis A state of confusion that the marketing profession has found itself in, due to the major changes and increased complexity occurring in the marketing landscape during the last two decades.

marking their own homework The tendency for marketers to run evaluation exercises on their own marketing activities that can lead to biased results and the use of the big number fallacy.

motivational systems The two fundamental motivational systems in the human brain, namely the *approach mechanism* and the *avoidance mechanism*. Those who activate more the approach mechanism engage more with daily challenges to devise solutions and solve problems, thriving more in life than those who do not.

neuromarketing The application of neuroscience and bio-feedback technologies to understand better and reveal the emotional and subconscious drivers of customer behaviour.

new types of marketers In order to address effectively the marketing challenges facing companies today, three new types of marketers are needed: transformational marketers at the strategic level; hybrid marketers at the tactical level; and specialized marketers at the operational level.

omnipresent versus ever-present strategy While omnipresence is about the immersive brand experience that removes barriers between channels, ever-present place strategy emphasizes the EVER component (wherever, whenever and whatever customers prefer and are doing in their lives) rather than ALL and allows for distinction and prioritization.

OXYTOCIN trust model The model developed by the neuroscientist Dr Paul Zak for explaining and boosting collaboration within organizations. OXYTOCIN stands for ovation, eXpectation, yield, transfer, openness, caring, invest, natural.

passive and active attention In passive attention the focus is split between multiple tasks, resulting in lower levels of attention, while in active attention the focus is on one particular task, resulting in actively processing communication.

peak data complexity The complexity of using a hybrid of old and new systems, and the data created through them.

peer-to-peer influence The direct influence of other people (peers) on an individual's attitudes, values or behaviours.

permission-based marketing An approach to marketing where individuals explicitly agree in advance to receive marketing information.

predictive analytics The ability to identify patterns in data that can predict future outcomes and trends.

progression model The model presented in this book that shows how innovation capacity and loyal customers lead to higher performance of a company's stock in the market and eventually to a happy CEO and a successful CMO.

psychological pricing principles Principles based on research from psychology and other brain-related sciences for contemporary pricing that aim to achieve a deeper connection with, and reaction from, customers. These include the relativity principle, the mental accounting principle, the pain avoidance principle, the anchoring principle, the ownership principle, the fairness principle, the framing principle, the rituals principle, the expectations principle, the willpower principle and the money principle.

psychological targeting Communication that is tailored to the psychological profiles of a person or group of similar people in an attempt to influence their behaviour.

put the customer to work Marketing and product design initiatives that use the theories of behavioural science to influence customers to share the brand/product with friends, family and wider networks. It is a form of customer advocacy that is intentionally designed into campaigns, activations and products.

relationship marketing An approach to marketing that emphasizes maintaining customers as opposed to simply acquiring them. This view of marketing was followed by *network marketing* that focuses on collaboration within complex industry relations.

research fallacy The behavioural bias of marketers and other business people to use data to validate or back up an existing idea rather than to generate the idea.

right- versus left-brain perceptual systems While the right-brain perceptual system is in direct contact with reality, connects us with the world and to other people, has a more holistic view of a situation, is conceptual rather than procedural concerning language, applies metaphors, and emotionally is mellower, the left-brain perceptual system develops abstract models of reality, it does not prioritize connectivity with people, it uses only sequential logic, it is very skilful with language, it is literal not metaphorical, it is attracted by novelty, and emotionally is more joyful.

social data The data created through online participation in social networks and other interactive online features.

social listening tools The software solutions that are designed to gather social media conversations that provide the user with the ability to manipulate, mine and analyse the data to generate marketing and business insights.

social media analytics The quantitative analysis of social media data in an attempt to understand behaviour around content, a topic or trend.

STEPPS method The six principles of content and messages that have a tendency to go viral online, created by Jonah Berger. These principles include social currency, triggers, emotion, public, practical value, and stories.

Teal organization The new stage in organizational evolution, as proposed by Frederic Laloux, where organizations are much like living organisms, using self-managed teams to achieve their true evolutionary purpose through a shared feeling of wholeness.

technicalization of the marketing profession The contemporary tendency to equate the marketing profession with digital skills exclusively.

think–feel–do model While the think–feel–do model usually refers to the basic hierarchy of effects theory in marketing communications, some authors also use this model to suggest reorganizing the marketing function in companies around the three main capabilities, namely think (data and analytics), feel (consumer engagement) and do (content and production).

trading room marketing function As opposed to the assembly line marketing function (see relevant term in glossary), this approach emphasizes the need for faster marketing responses in today's dynamic, unpredictable and interactive business environment.

traditional marketing process The simple model of marketing that includes the following five steps in a linear logic that marketers need to go through in order to execute marketing appropriately in companies:

- Understanding customers and the wider context the company operates in.

- Designing a marketing strategy with customers at its very core.

- Constructing marketing programmes to create value for customers.

- Building relations and making customers happy.

- Capturing value from clients to generate profitability.

traditional marketing research steps Typically five steps that create the traditional marketing research process: problem definition, research design developed, data collection, data analysis, report presentation.

traditional marketing structures Marketing function typically tends to be organized in some of the following pyramid-shaped structures: functional structure, product or brand structure, geographical structure, and customer or market structure. The most widespread structure, especially in larger corporations, is the complicated structure, which is a combination of two or more of the above approaches.

triune brain theory Theory developed by the neuroscientist Paul MacLean that views the evolution of the human brain as a linear progression of three distinct structures, each of which has a separate function: the old or reptilian brain (behavioural function), the mammalian or limbic system (emotional function) and the primate or neocortex (cognitive function).

user-generated content Content created by users of a social networking site or other online platform that allows any person to post content to the internet.

vanity metrics The metrics used by marketers that have a tendency to show big numbers, and that do not focus on the things that matter to business growth. They tend to be nice-to-know rather than actionable.

viral loops The initiatives or design features where consumers inadvertently drive their friends, family and wider networks to become customers through their online engagement.

VUCA The acronym standing for volatility, uncertainty, complexity and ambiguity, which has become a standard term in business for describing a world that is full of surprises. VUCA asks for adaptable and flexible approaches to decision making.

warmth and competence model According to the model developed by Fiske, Cuddy and Glick, warmth and competence are the two variables that people's brains use automatically when evaluating other people they come in contact with. These variables are also important factors in explaining concepts such as brand loyalty, purchase intention and attitude towards brands.

WOW moments The intentional design of experiences into product design that provide customers with an unexpected act of courtesy, kindness or beneficial surprise.

INDEX

Note: Numbers within main headings and 'Mc' are filed as spelt out. Acronyms and other series of letters are filed as presented. Page locators in *italics* denote information contained within a Figure or Table; those in roman numerals denote information within the preliminary pages. The prefix 'el' is ignored for filing purposes.